AF580843

Also from Information Publications, Inc.

State & Municipal Profiles Series™

Almanac of the 50 States

California Cities, Towns & Counties

Connecticut Municipal Profiles

Massachusetts Municipal Profiles

The New Jersey Municipal Data Book

Florida Municipal Profiles

American Profiles Series™

Asian Americans: A Statistical Sourcebook

Black Americans: A Statistical Sourcebook

Hispanic Americans: A Statistical Sourcebook

Printed in the United States of America

ISBN 0-929960-38-6

Black Americans: A Statistical Sourcebook, 2005

Information Publications, Inc.
3790 El Camino Real #162
Palo Alto, CA 94306

(877)544-INFO (4636) • (650)851-4250

www.informationpublications.com • www.statebooks.us

Black Americans:

A Statistical Sourcebook

Chapter 3 - Education 89

Introduction

Black Americans: A Statistical Sourcebook 2005 Edition is the sixteenth annual publication as part of the American Profiles Series – a series of statistical sourcebooks covering significant topics in American life. Black Americans resulted from the view that, despite the fact that there is coverage of Black Americans in an assortment of reference sources, there is a need for a single volume statistical reference devoted entirely to this important segment of the population.

Black Americans provides an extensive collection of tables that display information on a wide variety of topics. With a few exceptions, each table presents information about the Black population, the White population, and a total for Americans of all races and ethnic groups. The purpose in doing so is not to advance a specific perspective about Black Americans but to provide a context within which the tabular data can be more fully understood and evaluated.

Presenting data by race and ethnicity always puts one at risk of being labeled racist. Although undoubtedly there will be persons on both sides - those who see Black Americans as a propagandistic derogation of the Black community and those who feel that the book eloquently proves the inherent prejudice of our culture - the intent here is to serve neither cause. In fact, Black Americans is not intended to serve any cause or advance any point of view but to serve as a reportorial resource, providing access to federal government information. By researching and presenting this sometimes difficult to find, hard to understand information, Black Americans can serve students, business persons, social scientists, researchers, and others who need basic data about Black Americans.

The use of the term 'Black' itself can also be a cause for controversy. A number of terms have been used by Black Americans to name themselves, and in fact, as this is written there seems to be some evidence that 'African-American' is coming to replace the term Black. Black is used here solely because it is the word currently used by the federal government in gathering data. Federal usage has changed over the years, and as it continues to change, those changes will be reflected here.

The next sensitive question is, just who is Black? For federal data collection purposes, Black persons are those who say they are Black (or, in some surveys, Negro, or Afro-American). For statistical reporting purposes, being Black is based solely on self-identification.

The federal government considers Black to be a racial group, like White, Asian, etc. However, being of Hispanic origin, or identifying as Spanish is not counted as a racial group. For almost all federal data collection programs, persons may be of any race and also of Hispanic origin. The major exception concerns some U.S. Department of Education data that counts Hispanics separately from non-Hispanic Blacks, and non-Hispanic Whites. As a general guideline, it is believed that the overwhelming majority of persons identifying themselves as Hispanic for federal data collection purposes also are counted as White, although there are persons who are both Black and Hispanic.

Organization

The main portion of this book has been divided into eight chapters of tables:

Chapter 1: Demographics & Characteristics of the Population

Chapter 2: Vital Statistics & Health

Chapter 3: Education

Chapter 4: Government, Elections, & Public Opinion

Chapter 5: Crime, Law Enforcement, & Corrections

Chapter 6: The Labor Force, Employment & Unemployment

Chapter 7: Earnings, Income, Poverty, & Wealth

Chapter 8: Special Topics

The tables in each chapter represent results of a comprehensive review of all available federal government statistical information on the Black population. This material was edited and organized into chapters and arranged in a sequence roughly following the pattern found in publications of the U.S. Bureau of the Census.

Each table presents pertinent information from the source or sources in a clear, comprehensible fashion. As users of this book will likely be a diverse group ranging from librarians to business planners, from social scientists to marketers, all with different uses for the same data, the information selected for presentation was chosen for its broad scope and general appeal.

The Sources

All of the information in Black Americans comes from U.S. Government sources either originally or by way of republication by the federal government. In turn, most of the federal information is from the U.S. Bureau of the Census. Without question, the Bureau is the largest data gathering organization in the nation. It collects information on an exceptionally broad range of topics, not only for its own use and for the use of Congress and the Executive, but also for other federal agencies and departments. The reach of the Bureau is wider than most people realize. It encompasses the decennial Census of Population, the Current Population Survey, and the Annual Housing Survey. In cooperation with other agencies, the Bureau extends to the Consumer Expenditure Survey, the National Crime Survey, the National Family Growth Survey, and many others. The fact that the Bureau is responsible for so much of the federal government's data collection adds uniformity to the statistical information published by different agencies. Although the uniformity is not complete, there is enough to make the work of data users a lot easier.

The influence of the Bureau of the Census extends beyond federal government data collection. Because of the sheer volume of data it collects, many private data collectors have adopted some of its procedures and terminology. This has the added value for researchers of making private and public data more compatible.

Observant readers will note that the source of many tables is a Census publication, Statistical Abstract of the United States. There are a number of reasons for this. First, due to federal budget cuts, a growing quantity of information used in Statistical Abstract has never been published elsewhere before or it has never been published in such a detailed way. Second, as the preeminent federal data publisher, the Census Bureau has access to a wealth of raw data in machine readable form. It is able to aggregate data geographically on regional lines and break out other detail such as age, sex, race, etc., using its own parameters for publication. Thus, even when information is published elsewhere, the manner of presentation in Statistical Abstract is likely to be unique. Data from this source is presented in a more general way so as to be useful to many different types of data users.

On all tables where Statistical Abstract is cited as the source, the original source also has been checked for additional information. To make more detailed research easier, Statistical Abstract's own source (if it is not the Bureau itself), is listed as well.

Types of Information

Regardless of its source, there are basically two types of data presented in the tables of this book.

The first is complete count data. For example, the five questions asked of all Americans by the Bureau of the Census in its decennial census was an attempt at a complete count of a given universe.

The second type of data is survey information. Here a fairly large, specifically chosen segment of a population is studied. This sample is drawn to be statistically representative of the entire population or universe. Information about housing units and money income are some of the items in this book based on this type of survey information. Of course, survey information is only as good as the survey itself; therefore, the reader should always be the judge of the significance and accuracy of the material presented as it applies to his or her own research. Although specific survey methodology is not discussed here, a full reference to each source is made on every table. Interested readers may consult the original source materials, which in most cases contain a detailed explanation of survey methodology.

The Tables

This section details how the tables have been prepared and presented. Table titles are the first source of valuable information:

Table 2.01 Births and Birth Rates, by Age of the Mother, 2000 and 2003

The table number contains the chapter number to the left of the decimal and the location of the table within the chapter to the right of the decimal. Thus Table 2.01 is the first table of Chapter 2. With a few exceptions, tables have been arranged within a chapter to present the oldest, most general information first, followed by newer, more specific information. This pattern is mirrored in the tables themselves, which present the oldest, most general information at the beginning.

In a table title, the word or words before the first comma identify the general topic of the table. Following the first comma is descriptive wording which identifies the detail presented about the general topic; i.e., the data is presented by age, sex, marital status, etc., in this case, by age. After the description of the presentation of the data, the years for which data is presented are shown.

It should be noted that both the table titles and the tables themselves retain the original terms of the source material. This has the advantage of making the book compatible with the original sources.

To further facilitate use, every table in the book presents data in two, three, five, or six columns. The left-most column or columns are for the Black population; the center column or columns are for the White population; and the right-hand column or columns present data for all races.

Along the left margin of each table appears a column of line descriptors. Here, after a general heading, subgroups of the heading (usually indented) are shown. Two principles cover arranging and presenting the line descriptors: the oldest, most general information appears first, progressing to the newer, more specific; and quantities appear first, followed by percentages, medians, means, and per capita amounts.

Wherever available and appropriate, a time span of data is presented, usually going back five to ten years. This provides readers with a historical context for the information. However, readers should be cautioned that the years selected have been chosen from no special knowledge of the subject, nor to make any specific point. The fact that there has been a decrease or increase in a given indicator for the period displayed does not mean that the same trend will continue, or that it represents the continuation of a historical trend, or even that which appears to be a trend within this period actually is one. The time span and specific dates have been chosen largely to create a congruity of data, and a basis of comparison between different categories of information.

Table Notes

At the bottom of each table three key paragraphs appear: Source, Notes, and Units. The **Source** paragraph lists the source of the data presented in the table. When more than one source was used, the sources are listed in the same order in which the data itself appears in the table. As all sources are government publications, the issuing agency is listed as the author. All citations provide both the page and table number in the source from which the material was taken. An increasing number of sources are now available on the internet, and in many cases, only on the internet. For tables pulled exclusively from on-line sources, the Universal Resource Locator (URL) is listed as the source.

This bibliographic detail on each table makes a separate bibliography at the end of the book unnecessary. A Superintendent of Documents Classification Number is also provided. This number is used as a locator number in most government depository libraries, and documents are shelved or filed according to it, just the way books in some public libraries are organized by the Dewey Decimal System.

The paragraph of **Notes** includes pertinent facts about the data, the time of year covered by the survey, and the scope of the survey universe. One general note can be made here at the outset about all tabular data: detail (subgroups) may not add to the total shown, due to either rounding or the fact that only selected subgroups are displayed.

The final paragraph of a table, **Units,** identifies the units used, specifically stating that the quantity is millions of persons, thousands of workers, dollars per capita, etc. Readers are urged to pay special attention to this especially when a median, mean, percent, rate, or a per capita amount is provided.

The Glossary

It is important to be clear about terminology in a work such as this. Not only does the government have overtly specialized terms that clearly require a definition or explanation, but many government agencies use ordinary words in specialized ways. There are real differences between: a household and a family; a family and a married couple; the resident population and the civilian non-institutional population; a service industry and a service occupation; an urban area and a metropolitan area; to name just a few. All specialized terms are defined either in the table or in the glossary. Needless to say, it is absolutely vital to understand the meaning of all terms used in a table before drawing any conclusions from the data. When in doubt, consult the glossary.

For many tables, it is not possible to fully define a term or concept in the table notes, so the glossary serves as an important tool in using the tables. All terms that appear in either the title or text of a table that may be unclear or are used in a special way are defined in the glossary. Wherever possible, the definition is adapted (and in many cases taken verbatim) from the definition provided in the source publication. Not all source materials provide definitions, so sometimes a definition has been constructed by reviewing and summarizing explanatory and supplementary material from the source.

In compiling the glossary the intention was to provide short clear definitions, including only as much background material as necessary to make a term understandable. However, in practice this resulted in compromises. For certain terms (such as metropolitan area concepts), some methodological background is essential in order to achieve an understanding. Where such background is vital it has been included. Readers requiring additional technical or methodological detail are referred to the sources for more complete explanations.

The Index

Every key term from the tables has been indexed. Readers should note that the index provides table numbers as opposed to page numbers.

A Suggestion on How to Use This Book

One way to use this book is by locating the subject of general interest in the Table of Contents, and turning to that chapter. While the Table of Contents is detailed enough to narrow a search and the index can speed access to specific items, sometimes paging through the dozen or so tables in a given field uncovers unanticipated information of genuine importance. It is just this type of serendipity that has lead to the inclusion of information in this book, and sometimes such an unexpected find can greatly enhance a research project.

A Final Word

As this book is updated on an annual basis, questions, comments, and criticisms from users are vital to making informed editorial choices about succeeding editions. If you have a suggestion or comment, be assured that it will be both appreciated and carefully considered. If you should find an error here, please let us know so that it may be corrected. Our goal is to provide accurate, easy to use, statistical compendiums that serve our readers' needs. Your help enables us to do our job better.

Chapter 1: Demographics & Characteristics of the Population

Table 1.01 Resident Population and Median Age, 1790 – 2002

	Black		White		All Races	
	total	median age	total	median age	total	median age
1790 (August 2)	757	na	3,172	na	3,930	na
1800 (August 4)	1,002	na	4,306	16.0	5,308	na
1820 (August 7)	1,772	17.2	7,867	16.5	9,638	16.7
1840 (June 1)	2,874	17.3	14,196	17.9	17,069	17.8
1860 (June 1)	4,442	17.7	26,923	19.7	31,443	19.4
1880 (June 1)	6,581	18.0	43,403	21.4	50,156	20.9
1900 (June 1)	8,834	19.4	66,809	23.4	75,995	22.9
1920 (January 1)	10,463	22.3	94,821	25.6	105,711	25.3
1940 (April 1)	12,866	25.3	118,215	29.5	131,669	29.0
1960 (April 1)	18,872	23.5	158,832	30.3	179,323	29.5
1980 (April 1)	26,683	24.9	194,713	30.9	226,546	30.0
1990 (April 1)	29,986	na	199,686	na	248,710	32.8
1995 (July 1)	33,141	29.2	218,085	35.3	262,755	34.3
2000 (April)	35,704	30.0	228,104	36.6	281,422	35.3
2001 (July 1)	36,247	30.3	230,290	36.9	284,797	35.6
2002 (July 1)	36,746	30.5	232,647	37.1	288,369	35.7

SOURCE: U.S. Bureau of the Census, Statistical Abstract of the United States, 1989; p. 17, table 21; 1990; p. 17, table 19; 1991; p. 12, table 12; p. 22, table 27; 1995, pp. 22-23, table 22; 2000, pp. 20-21, table 19; 2002; p. 18, table 15; 2003; p. 15, table 13. C 3 134 (year)
U.S. Bureau of the Census, Current Population Reports: Population Profile of the United States 1989, P23-159; p. 31. C 3 186/8.989

NOTES: 'All Races' includes other races not shown separately.

UNITS: Population in thousands of persons; median age in years.

Table 1.02 Population Projections, by Age, 2005 and 2010

	Black	White	All Races
2005			
total	38,056	236,924	295,507
under 5 years	3,113	15,503	20,495
5 to 9 years	2,941	14,862	19,467
10 to 14 years	3,332	15,881	20,838
15 to 19 years	3,306	16,281	21,272
20 to 24 years	3,078	16,153	20,823
25 to 29 years	2,807	15,377	19,753
30 to 34 years	2,678	15,466	19,847
35 to 39 years	2,732	16,538	20,869
40 to 44 years	2,892	18,318	22,735
45 to 49 years	2,736	18,312	22,453
50 to 54 years	2,276	16,499	19,983
55 to 59 years	1,788	14,582	17,359
60 to 64 years	1,250	11,075	13,017
65 to 69 years	972	8,629	10,123
70 to 74 years	767	7,348	8,500
75 to 79 years	591	6,506	7,376
80 to 84 years	407	4,993	5,576
85 to 89 years	231	2,890	3,206
90 to 94 years	112	1,286	1,431
95 to 99 years	37	366	412
100 years old and over	9	60	71

continued on the next page

Table 1.02 continued

	Black	White	All Races
2010			
total	40,454	244,995	308,936
under 5 years	3,332	15,995	21,426
5 to 9 years	3,127	15,639	20,706
10 to 14 years	2,976	15,049	19,767
15 to 19 years	3,396	16,203	21,336
20 to 24 years	3,357	16,591	21,676
25 to 29 years	3,130	16,495	21,375
30 to 34 years	2,856	15,654	20,271
35 to 39 years	2,701	15,597	20,137
40 to 44 years	2,724	16,566	20,984
45 to 49 years	2,844	18,213	22,654
50 to 54 years	2,657	18,066	22,173
55 to 59 years	2,176	16,102	19,507
60 to 64 years	1,674	14,004	16,679
65 to 69 years	1,127	10,357	12,172
70 to 74 years	838	7,767	9,097
75 to 79 years	622	6,226	7,186
80 to 84 years	440	5,005	5,665
85 to 89 years	274	3,321	3,713
90 to 94 years	136	1,546	1,727
95 to 99 years	53	503	569
100 years old and over	14	98	114

SOURCE: U.S. Bureau of the Census, Statistical Abstract of the United States, 2003, p. 19, table 16; 2004; page 18, table 16 (data from US. Bureau of the Census, *Current Population Reports*, Series P-25,). C 3 134 (year)

NOTES: 'All Races' includes other races not shown separately. Population projections as of July 1, of the year shown.

UNITS: Estimates of the total population in thousands of persons, includes armed forces overseas.

Table 1.03 Resident Population, by Age and Sex, 1980 - 2003

	Black	White	All Races
1980			
Both sexes			
total	26,683	194,713	226,546
under 5 years old	2,459	13,414	16,348
16 years old and older	18,425	149,121	171,196
65 years old and older	2,092	23,162	25,549
male			
total	12,612	94,924	110,053
under 5 years old	1,240	6,882	8,362
16 years old and older	8,454	71,559	81,766
65 years old and older	849	9,316	10,305
female			
total	14,071	99,788	116,493
under 5 years old	1,220	6,532	7,986
16 years old and older	9,971	77,562	89,429
65 years old and older	1,243	13,846	15,245
1985			
Both sexes			
total	28,887	202,768	238,740
under 5 years old	2,706	14,636	18,037
16 years old and older	20,380	157,584	183,010
65 years old and older	2,343	25,743	28,530
male			
total	13,683	99,006	116,161
under 5 years old	1,370	7,509	9,230
16 years old and older	9,374	75,820	87,631
65 years old and older	940	10,390	11,529
female			
total	15,204	103,762	122,579
under 5 years old	1,335	7,127	8,806
16 years old and older	11,006	81,764	95,379
65 years old and older	1,403	15,353	17,002

continued on the next page

Table 1.03 continued

	Black	White	All Races
2000			
Both sexes			
total	35,704	228,104	281,422
under 5 years old	2,925	14,656	19,176
5-13 years old	5,923	28,381	37,025
14-17 years old	2,426	12,522	16,093
85 years old and older	316	3,827	4,240
2001			
Both sexes			
total	36,247	230,290	284,797
under 5 years old	2,932	14,784	19,369
5-13 years old	5,907	28,316	37,002
14-17 years old	2,463	12,560	16,181
85 years old and older	322	3,974	4,404
2003			
Both sexes			
Total	37,099	234,196	290,810
under 5 years old	2,998	15,119	19,769
5-13 years old	5,792	28,057	36,752
14-17 years old	2,565	12,745	16,522
85 years old and older	338	4,244	4,713

SOURCE: U.S. Bureau of the Census, Statistical Abstract of the United States, 1985; p. 28, table 30; 1987; p. 18, table 20; 1996; p. 21, table 21; 2000; p. 13, table 12; p. 18, table 17; 2002; p. 18, table 15; 2004; p. 15, table 14 (data from US. Bureau of the Census, *Current Population Reports*, Series P-25). C 3 134 (year)

NOTES: 'All races' includes other races not shown separately.

UNITS: Resident population in thousands of persons.

Table 1.04 Components of Population Change, 1985 - 2003

	Black	White	All Races
1985			
population on January 1	28,802	202,464	238,207
+ births during year	609	2,983	3,750
- deaths during year	244	1,816	2,083
+ net civilian immigration	58	352	648
net population increase	**422**	**1,521**	**2,316**
July, 2000 – July, 2001			
population on July 1, 2000	na	na	282,178
+ births during period	na	na	4,047
- deaths during period	na	na	2,419
+ net international migration	na	na	1,288
net population increase	**na**	**na**	**2,916**
July, 2001 – July, 2002			
population on July 1, 2000	na	na	285,094
+ births during period	na	na	4,023
- deaths during period	na	na	2,432
+ net international migration	na	na	1,290
net population increase	**na**	**na**	**2,880**
July, 2002 – July, 2003			
population on July 1, 2003	na	na	287,974
+ births during period	na	na	4,027
- deaths during period	na	na	2,477
+ net international migration	na	na	1,286
net population increase	**na**	**na**	**2,836**

SOURCE: U.S. Bureau of the Census, Statistical Abstract of the United States, 1991, p. 14, table 14; p. 15, table 16; 1994; p. 19, table 19; 1999; p. 9, table 4; p. 20, table 20; 2004; p. 8, table 4. C 3 134 (year)

NOTES: 'All races' includes other races not shown separately.

UNITS: Population in thousands of persons.

Table 1.05 Population Projections, 2000 - 2100 (revised)

	Black	White	All Races
2000*	35,818	228,548	282,125
2005	37,619	234,221	287,715
2010*	40,454	244,995	308,936
2015	42,385	249,467	312,268
2020*	45,365	260,629	335,805
2025	47,089	265,305	337,814
2030*	50,442	275,731	363,584
2035	52,019	280,555	364,319
2040*	55,876	289,690	391,946
2045	56,862	295,019	390,397
2050*	61,361	302,626	419,854
2055	61,627	310,300	417,477
2060	64,055	318,752	432,010
2065	66,544	327,907	447,415
2070	69,096	337,719	463,639
2075	71,705	348,027	480,504
2080	74,367	358,664	497,829
2085	77,082	369,547	515,528
2090	79,852	380,674	533,605
2095	82,684	392,063	552,085
2100	85,579	403,696	570,954

SOURCE: U.S. Bureau of the Census, Projections of the Resident Population by Race, Hispanic Origin, and Nativity: Middle Series, 1999 to 2100 Tables NP-T5-A - NP-T5-H
<www.census gov/population/www/projections/natproj html> accessed 1 February 2000
*U.S. Bureau of the Census, Projected Population of the United States by Race, and Hispanic Origin: 2000 to 2050, Table 1a (data from "U.S. Interim Projections by Age, Sex, Race, and Hispanic Origin," <http://www.census.gov/ipc/www/usinterimproj/>, Internet release date: 18 March, 2004).

NOTES: 'All Races' includes other races not shown separately. Population projections as of July 1, of the year shown.

UNITS: Estimates of the total population in thousands of persons, includes armed forces overseas.

Table 1.06 Resident Population, by State, 1970 and 1980

	1970			1980		
	Black	White	All Races	Black	White	All Races
Alabama	903	2,534	3,444	996	2,873	3,894
Alaska	9	237	300	14	310	402
Arizona	53	1,605	1,771	75	2,241	2,718
Arkansas	352	1,566	1,923	374	1,890	2,286
California	1,400	17,761	19,953	1,819	18,031	23,668
Colorado	66	2,112	2,207	102	2,571	2,890
Connecticut	181	2,835	3,032	217	2,799	3,108
Delaware	78	466	548	96	488	594
District of Columbia	538	209	757	449	172	638
Florida	1,042	5,719	6,789	1,343	8,185	9,746
Georgia	1,187	3,391	4,590	1,465	3,947	5,463
Hawaii	8	298	769	17	319	965
Idaho	2	699	713	3	902	944
Illinois	1,426	9,600	11,114	1,675	9,233	11,427
Indiana	357	4,820	5,194	415	5,004	5,490
Iowa	33	2,783	2,824	42	2,839	2,914
Kansas	107	2,122	2,247	126	2,168	2,364
Kentucky	231	2,982	3,219	259	3,379	3,661
Louisiana	1,087	2,541	3,641	1,238	2,912	4,206
Maine	3	985	992	3	1,110	1,125
Maryland	699	3,195	3,922	958	3,159	4,217
Massachusetts	176	5,478	5,689	221	5,363	5,737
Michigan	991	7,833	8,875	1,199	7,872	9,262
Minnesota	35	3,736	3,805	53	3,936	4,076
Mississippi	816	1,393	2,217	887	1,615	2,521
Missouri	480	4,177	4,677	514	4,345	4,917
Montana	2	663	694	2	740	787
Nebraska	40	1,433	1,483	48	1,490	1,570
Nevada	28	448	489	51	700	800
New Hampshire	3	733	738	4	910	921
New Jersey	770	6,350	7,168	925	6,127	7,365
New Mexico	20	916	1,016	24	978	1,303
New York	2,169	15,834	18,237	2,402	13,961	17,558

continued on the next page

Table 1.06 continued

	1970			1980		
	Black	White	All Races	Black	White	All Races
North Carolina	1,126	3,902	5,082	1,319	4,458	5,882
North Dakota	2	599	618	3	626	653
Ohio	970	9,647	10,652	1,077	9,597	10,798
Oklahoma	172	2,280	2,559	205	2,598	3,025
Oregon	26	2,032	2,091	37	2,491	2,633
Pennsylvania	1,017	10,738	11,794	1,047	10,652	11,864
Rhode Island	25	915	947	28	897	947
South Carolina	789	1,794	2,591	949	2,147	3,122
South Dakota	2	630	666	2	640	691
Tennessee	621	3,294	3,924	726	3,835	4,591
Texas	1,399	9,717	11,197	1,710	11,198	14,229
Utah	7	1,032	1,059	9	1,383	1,461
Vermont	1	443	444	1	507	511
Virginia	861	3,762	4,648	1,009	4,230	5,347
Washington	71	3,251	3,409	106	3,779	4,132
West Virginia	67	1,673	1,744	65	1,875	1,950
Wisconsin	128	4,259	4,418	183	4,443	4,706
Wyoming	3	323	332	3	446	470

SOURCE: U.S. Bureau of the Census, Statistical Abstract of the United States, 1972; p. 12, table 12; p. 28, table 30. C 3 134.972
U.S. Bureau of the Census, Census of Population: General Population Characteristics: United States Summary PC80-1-B1; p. 1-125, table 62. C 3 223/6.980/B1

NOTES: 'All Races' includes other races not shown separately.

UNITS: Population in thousands of persons.

Table 1.07 Resident Population, by State, 1990 and Projections for 2020

	1990			2020		
	Black	White	All Races	Black	White	All Races
Alabama	1,021	2,976	4,041	26.0%	72.0%	5,231
Alaska	22	415	550	3.6	65.2	866
Arizona	111	2,963	3,665	2.7	85.0	5,713
Arkansas	374	1,945	2,351	14.4	83.1	3,005
California	2,209	20,524	29,760	8.0	71.0	47,953
Colorado	133	2,905	3,294	4.6	90.1	4,871
Connecticut	274	2,859	3,287	11.1	85.2	3,617
Delaware	112	535	666	24.7	70.7	871
District of Columbia	400	180	607	63.5	33.0	636
Florida	1,760	10,749	12,938	17.9	78.9	19,449
Georgia	1,747	4,600	6,478	30.2	66.9	9,426
Hawaii	27	370	1,108	3.2	47.9	1,815
Idaho	3	950	1,007	0.6	95.3	1,600
Illinois	1,694	8,953	11,431	18.4	75.2	13,218
Indiana	432	5,021	5,544	10.0	87.7	6,488
Iowa	48	2,683	2,777	3.0	94.6	3,038
Kansas	143	2,232	2,478	7.1	87.4	3,130
Kentucky	263	3,392	3,685	9.0	89.7	4,313
Louisiana	1,299	2,839	4,220	32.5	63.9	5,193
Maine	5	1,208	1,228	0.4	97.7	1,400
Maryland	1,190	3,394	4,781	32.6	59.6	6,289
Massachusetts	300	5,405	6,016	6.9	86.5	6,363
Michigan	1,292	7,756	9,295	19.2	77.0	10,377
Minnesota	95	4,130	4,375	2.4	90.1	5,426
Mississippi	915	1,633	2,573	35.2	63.1	3,100
Missouri	548	4,486	5,117	11.9	85.5	6,123
Montana	2	741	799	0.3	90.4	1,071
Nebraska	57	1,481	1,578	4.5	92.5	1,885
Nevada	79	1,013	1,202	7.7	81.3	2,145
New Hampshire	7	1,087	1,109	0.9	95.6	1,399
New Jersey	1,037	6,130	7,730	18.2	73.5	9,058
New Mexico	30	1,146	1,515	1.7	82.7	2,338

continued on the next page

Table 1.07 continued

	1990			2020		
	Black	White	All Races	Black	White	All Races
New York	2,859	13,385	17,990	21.1%	70.6%	19,111
North Carolina	1,456	5,008	6,629	23.5	72.3	9,014
North Dakota	4	604	639	0.8	90.8	719
Ohio	1,155	9,522	10,847	13.8	83.8	11,870
Oklahoma	234	2,584	3,146	7.3	80.0	4,020
Oregon	46	2,637	2,842	1.9	89.1	4,367
Pennsylvania	1,090	10,520	11,882	11.4	85.4	12,656
Rhode Island	39	917	1,003	5.2	88.6	1,090
South Carolina	1,040	2,407	3,487	31.7	66.5	4,685
South Dakota	3	638	696	0.6	83.7	863
Tennessee	778	4,048	4,877	17.5	80.6	6,434
Texas	2,022	12,775	16,987	12.6	82.9	25,592
Utah	12	1,616	1,723	0.7	90.9	2,749
Vermont	2	555	563	0.6	97.1	658
Virginia	1,163	4,792	6,187	21.6	72.5	8,388
Washington	150	4,309	4,867	2.6	84.8	7,960
West Virginia	54	1,792	1,856	2.7	95.6	1,852
Wisconsin	245	4,513	4,892	8.0	87.8	5,846
Wyoming	4	427	454	0.9	93.9	658

SOURCE: U.S. Bureau of the Census, Statistical Abstract of the United States, 1991; p. 22, table 27 (data from U.S. Bureau of the Census, *Current Population Reports*, Series P-25 and Census Press Release CB91-100). C 3 134 (year)
U.S. Bureau of the Census, Population Projections for States, by Age, Sex, Race, and Hispanic Origin: 1993 to 2020, tables 1 and 4. From *Current Population Reports*, P25-1111, downloaded from Census Bureau Bulletin Board. Telnet cenbbs.census.gov.

NOTES: 'All Races' includes other races not shown separately. 1990 data from the 1990 Census, 2000 data from projections by the US Bureau of the Census.

UNITS: Population in thousands of persons.

Table 1.08 Population of Cities with 250,000 or More Inhabitants, 2000

	Black	White	All Races
Albuquerque, NM	13.9	321.2	448.6
Anaheim, CA	8.7	179.6	328.0
Anchorage, AK	15.2	188.0	260.3
Arlington, TX	45.7	225.4	333.0
Atlanta, GA	255.7	138.4	416.5
Aurora, CO	37.1	190.3	276.4
Austin, TX	66.0	429.1	656.6
Baltimore, MD	419.0	206.0	651.2
Boston, MA	149.2	320.9	589.1
Buffalo, NY	109.0	159.3	292.6
Charlotte, NC	177.0	315.1	540.8
Chicago, IL	1,065.0	1,215.3	2,896.0
Cincinnati, OH	142.2	175.5	331.3
Cleveland, OH	243.9	198.5	478.4
Colorado Springs, CO	23.7	291.1	360.9
Columbus, OH	174.1	483.3	711.5
Corpus Christi, TX	13.0	198.7	277.5
Dallas, TX	308.0	604.2	1,188.6
Denver, CO	61.6	362.2	554.6
Detroit, MI	775.8	116.6	951.3
El Paso, TX	17.6	413.1	563.7
Fort Worth, TX	108.3	319.2	534.7
Fresno, CA	35.8	214.6	427.7
Honolulu, HI	6.0	73.1	371.7
Houston, TX	494.5	962.6	1,953.6
Indianapolis, IN	199.4	540.2	781.9
Jacksonville, FL	213.5	474.3	735.6
Kansas City, MO	137.9	267.9	441.5
Las Vegas, NV	49.6	334.2	478.4
Lexington-Fayette, KY	35.1	211.1	260.5
Long Beach, CA	68.6	208.4	461.5
Los Angeles, CA	415.2	1,734.0	3,694.8
Louisville, KY	84.6	161.3	256.2
Memphis, TN	399.2	223.7	650.1
Mesa, AZ	10.0	323.7	396.4
Miami, FL	80.9	241.5	362.5
Milwaukee, WI	222.9	298.4	597.0

continued on the next page

Table 1.08 continued

	Black	White	All Races
Minneapolis, MN	68.8	249.2	382.6
Nashville-Davidson, TN	146.2	359.6	545.5
New Orleans, LA	325.9	136.0	484.7
New York, NY	2,129.8	3,576.4	8,008.3
Newark, NJ	146.3	72.5	273.5
Oakland, CA	142.5	125.0	399.5
Oklahoma City, OK	77.8	346.2	506.1
Omaha, NE	51.9	305.7	390.0
Philadelphia, PA	655.8	683.3	1,517.6
Phoenix, AZ	67.4	938.9	1,321.0
Pittsburgh, PA	90.8	226.3	334.6
Portland, OR	35.1	412.2	529.1
Raleigh, NC	76.8	174.8	276.1
Riverside, CA	18.9	151.4	255.2
Sacramento, CA	63.0	196.5	407.0
San Antonio, TX	78.1	774.7	1,144.6
San Diego, CA	96.2	736.2	1,223.4
San Francisco, CA	60.5	385.7	776.7
San Jose, CA	31.3	425.0	894.9
Santa Ana, CA	5.7	144.4	338.0
Seattle, WA	47.5	394.9	563.4
St. Louis, MO	178.3	152.7	348.2
St. Paul, MN	33.6	192.4	287.2
Tampa, FL	79.1	194.9	303.4
Toledo, OH	73.9	220.3	313.6
Tucson, AZ	21.1	341.4	486.7
Tulsa, OK	60.8	275.5	393.0
Virginia Beach, VA	80.6	303.7	425.3
Washington, DC	343.3	176.1	572.1
Wichita, KS	39.3	258.9	344.3

SOURCE: U.S. Bureau of the Census, Statistical Abstract of the United States, 2003; p. 38, table 32. C 3 134-003

NOTES: As of April. Data refer to boundaries in effect on January 1, 2000.

UNITS: Population in thousands of persons.

Table 1.09 Marital Status, Persons 15 Years Old and Older, 1990 - 2003

	Black		White		All Races	
	number	percent	number	percent	number	percent
1990						
All marital statuses	21,914	100.0%	163,417	100.0%	191,793	100.0%
single, never married	8,735	39.9	39,516	24.2	50,223	26.2
married, spouse present	7,619	34.8	95,337	58.3	106,513	55.3
married, spouse absent	1,683	7.7	4,191	2.6	6,118	3.2
widowed	1,730	7.9	11,731	7.2	13,810	7.2
divorced	2,146	9.8	12,643	7.7	15,128	7.9
2000						
All marital statuses	25,855	100.0%	177,581	100.0%	213,773	100.0%
married, spouse present	8,391	32.5	99,258	55.9	113,002	52.9
married, spouse absent	430	1.7	1,971	1.1	2,730	1.3
widowed	1,695	6.6	11,532	6.5	13,665	6.4
divorced	2,778	10.7	16,547	9.3	19,881	9.3
separated	1,307	5.1	2,976	1.7	4,479	2.1
never married	11,253	43.5	45,297	25.5	60,016	28.1
2003						
All marital statuses	26,249	100.0%	184,361	100.0%	225,057	100.0%
married, spouse present	8,527	32.5	101,412	55.0	117,172	52.1
married, spouse absent	511	1.9	2,246	1.2	3,139	1.4
widowed	1,697	6.5	11,662	6.3	13,995	6.2
divorced	2,882	11.0	17,835	9.7	21,649	9.6
separated	1,250	4.8	3,158	1.7	4,723	2.1
never married	11,383	43.4	48,048	26.1	64,380	28.6

SOURCE: U.S. Bureau of the Census, Current Population Reports: Marital Status and Living Arrangements, March, 1985, Series P-20, #410; p. 17, table 1; March, 1990, #450; p. 17, table 1 C3.186/6 (year).
U.S. Bureau of the Census, Current Population Reports: America's Families and Living Arrangements: 2000; Series P-20, #537, table A1, issued June 2001; 2003; "Table A1. Marital Status of People 15 Years and Over, by Age, Sex, Personal Earnings, Race, and Hispanic Origin: March 2003", issued June 2004. <www census gov>

NOTES: 'All Races' includes other races not shown separately.

UNITS: Number in thousands of persons 15 years old and older; percent as a percent of total (percents **not** standardized for age).

Table 1.10 Marital Status, Men 15 Years Old and Older, 1990 - 2003

	Black		White		All Races	
	number	percent	number	percent	number	percent
Men:						
1990						
All marital statuses	9,948	100.0%	78,908	100.0%	91,033	100.0%
single, never married	4,319	43.4	22,078	28.0	27,422	30.1
married, spouse present	3,862	38.8	47,700	60.4	52,924	58.1
married, spouse absent	627	6.3	1,842	2.3	2,360	2.6
widowed	338	3.4	1,930	2.4	2,282	2.5
divorced	802	8.1	5,359	6.8	6,045	6.6
2000						
All marital statuses	11,687	100.0%	86,443	100.0%	103,114	100.0%
married, spouse present	4,294	36.7	49,672	57.5	56,501	54.8
married, spouse absent	207	1.8	979	1.1	1,365	1.3
widowed	328	2.8	2,196	2.5	2,604	2.5
divorced	1,108	9.5	7,246	8.4	8,572	8.3
separated	504	4.3	1,237	1.4	1,818	1.8
never married	5,246	44.9	25,113	29.1	32,253	31.3
2003						
All marital statuses	11,791	100.0%	89,998	100.%	108,696	100.0%
married, spouse present	4,360	37.0	50,822	56.5	58,586	53.9
married, spouse absent	205	1.7	1,228	1.4	1,651	1.5
widowed	323	2.7	2,257	2.5	2,697	2.5
divorced	1,029	8.7	7,587	8.4	8,976	8.3
separated	457	3.9	1,332	1.5	1,905	1.8
never married	5,417	45.9	26,772	29.7	34,881	32.1

SOURCE: U.S. Bureau of the Census, Current Population Reports: Marital Status and Living Arrangements, March, 1985, Series P-20, #410; p. 17, table 1; March, 1990, #450; p. 17, table 1 C3 186/6.(year).
U.S. Bureau of the Census, Current Population Reports: America's Families and Living Arrangements: 2000; Series P-20, #537, table A1, issued June 2001; 2003; "Table A1. Marital Status of People 15 Years and Over, by Age, Sex, Personal Earnings, Race, and Hispanic Origin: March 2003". <www.census gov>

NOTES: 'All Races' includes other races not shown separately.

UNITS: Number in thousands of men 15 years old and older; percent as a percent of total (percents **not** standardized for age).

Table 1.11 Marital Status, Women 15 Years Old and Older, 1990 - 2003

	Black		White		All Races	
	number	percent	number	percent	number	percent
Women:						
1990						
All marital statuses	11,966	100.0%	84,508	100.0%	99,838	100.0%
single, never married	4,416	36.9	17,438	20.6	22,718	22.8
married, spouse present	3,757	31.4	47,637	56.4	53,256	53.3
married, spouse absent	1,056	8.8	2,349	2.8	3,541	3.5
widowed	1,392	11.6	9,800	11.6	11,477	11.5
divorced	1,344	11.2	7,284	8.6	8,845	8.9
2000						
All marital statuses	14,167	100.0%	91,138	100.0%	110,660	100.0%
married, spouse present	4,097	28.9	49,586	54.4	56,501	51.1
married, spouse absent	223	1.6	992	1.1	1,365	1.2
widowed	1,367	9.6	9,336	10.2	11,061	10.0
divorced	1,670	11.8	9,301	10.2	11,309	10.2
separated	803	5.7	1,739	1.9	2,661	2.4
never married	6,008	42.4	20,184	22.1	27,763	25.1
2003						
All marital statuses	14,458	100.0%	94,363	100.0%	116,361	100.0%
married, spouse present	4,167	28.8	50,590	53.6	58,586	50.3
married, spouse absent	306	2.1	1,017	1.1	1,488	1.3
widowed	1,374	9.5	9,405	10.0	11,297	9.7
divorced	1,853	12.8	10,248	10.9	12,673	10.9
separated	792	5.5	1,826	1.9	2,817	2.4
never married	5,966	41.3	21,276	22.5	29,499	25.4

SOURCE: U.S. Bureau of the Census, Current Population Reports: Marital Status and Living Arrangements, March, 1985, Series P-20, #410; p. 17, table 1; March, 1990, #450; p. 17, table 1 C3 186/6 (year).
U.S. Bureau of the Census, Current Population Reports: America's Families and Living Arrangements: 2000; Series P-20, #537, table A1, issued June 2001; 2003; "Table A1. Marital Status of People 15 Years and Over, by Age, Sex, Personal Earnings, Race, and Hispanic Origin: March 2003". <www census gov>

NOTES: 'All Races' includes other races not shown separately.

UNITS: Number in thousands of women 15 years old and older; percent as a percent of total (percents **not** standardized for age).

Table 1.12 Characteristics of Unmarried and Married Male-Female Couples: March 2000

	Unmarried couples	Married Couples
Same race couples	3,614	55,029
both White	3,040	48,917
both Black	480	3,989
Interracial couples	165	1,047
Black/White	88	363

SOURCE: U.S. Bureau of the Census, Current Population Reports: America's Families and Living Arrangements, June 2001 Series P20, #537; p. 15, table 8.

UNITS: Thousands of couples.

Table 1.13 Age, Educational Attainment, and Residence, 1985

	Black	White	All Races
Age			
Persons of all ages	28,151	199,117	234,066
persons:			
under 5 years old	2,699	14,610	17,958
5-14 years old	5,218	27,417	33,792
15-44 years old	13,590	93,852	110,948
45-64 years old	4,406	39,033	44,549
65 years old and over	2,238	24,205	26,818
Years of school completed			
All persons 25 years old and over	14,820	124,905	143,524
persons completing:			
0-8 years of school	3,113	16,224	19,893
1-3 years high school	2,851	14,365	17,553
4 years high school	5,027	48,728	54,866
1-3 years college	2,188	20,652	23,405
4 or more years college	1,640	24,935	27,808
Residence			
Northeast	5,296	43,185	49,276
Midwest	5,549	52,280	58,587
South	14,920	63,155	79,165
West	2,290	40,394	46,489
nonfarm	na	na	na
farm	na	na	na
inside metro areas	na	na	na
outside metro areas	na	na	na

SOURCE: U.S. Bureau of the Census, Statistical Abstract of the United States, 1987; p. 35, table 39, (data from U.S. Bureau of the Census, *Current Population Reports*, Series P-25). C 3 134.987
U.S. Bureau of the Census, Current Population Reports: Money Income of Households, Families and Persons in the United States, 1984, Series P-60 (#151), pp. 10-15, table 4. C3 186/22 984

NOTES: 'All Races' includes other races not shown separately.

UNITS: Population in thousands of persons.

Table 1.14 Age, Educational Attainment, and Residence, 1990

	Black	White	All Races
Age			
Persons of all ages			
persons:	30,332	206,853	245,992
under 18 years old	10,012	51,400	64,144
18-24 years old	3,568	20,767	25,311
25-44 years old	9,498	67,925	80,435
45-64 years old	4,766	40,281	46,536
65 years old and over	2,487	26,479	29,566
Years of school completed			
All persons 25 years old and over	16,751	134,687	156,537
persons completing:			
0-8 years of school	2,701	14,131	17,590
1-3 years high school	2,968	14,080	17,462
4 years high school	6,239	52,449	60,119
1-3 years college	2,952	24,349	28,075
4 or more years college	1,891	29,676	33,291
Residence			
Northeast	5,282	43,650	50,520
Midwest	5,991	52,399	59,428
South	16,499	66,004	84,044
West	2,561	44,800	52,000
nonfarm	30,276	202,339	241,374
farm	56	4,515	4,618
inside metro areas	25,402	158,087	191,169
outside metro areas	4,930	48,766	54,824

SOURCE: U.S. Bureau of the Census, Statistical Abstract of the United States, 1990; p. 38, table 43 (data from U.S. Bureau of the Census, *Current Population Reports*, Series P-25). C 3.134.990
U.S. Bureau of the Census, Current Population Reports: Poverty in the United States: 1988 and 1989, Series P-60, #171; p. 19, table 4; table 20; p. 149. C3 186/11.989
U.S. Bureau of the Census, Current Population Reports: Money Income of Households, Families, and Persons in the United States: 1988 and 1989, Series P-60, #172, pp. 124-145, table 29. C3 186/2 989

NOTES: 'All Races' includes other races not shown separately.

UNITS: Population in thousands of persons.

Table 1.15 Age and Residence, 2003

	Black	White	All Races
Age			
Persons of all ages			
persons:	35,989	231,866	287,699
under 18 years old	11,367	55,779	72,999
18-24 years old	3,809	21,936	27,824
25-34 years old	5,041	30,799	39,201
35-44 years old	5,402	35,095	43,573
45-54 years old	4,715	33,873	41,068
55-59 years old	1,544	13,725	16,158
60-64 years old	1,235	10,354	12,217
65 years old and over	2,876	30,303	34,659
Residence			
Northeast	6,591	44,036	53,608
Midwest	6,561	55,322	64,655
South	19,576	79,023	103,347
West	3,261	53,485	66,089
inside metro areas	31,612	185,582	234,908
outside metro areas	4,376	46,284	52,791

SOURCE: U.S. Bureau of the Census, Current Population Reports: Poverty in the United States: 2003; "Table POV01: Age and Sex of All People, Family Members and Unrelated Individuals Iterated by Income-to-Poverty Ratio and Race: 2003, Below 100% of Poverty"; "Table POV41: Region, Division and Type of Residence – Poverty Status for All People, Family Members and Unrelated Individuals by Family Structure: 2003, Below 100% of Poverty".

NOTES: 'All Races' includes other races not shown separately. 'White' and 'Black' as shown are respectively equivalent to 'White Alone' and 'Black Alone' that refer to people who reported 'White' or 'Black' and did not report any other race category.

UNITS: Population in thousands of persons.

Table 1.16 Selected Characteristics of Households, 1985

	Black	White	All Races
Marital status and sex of the householder			
All households, both sexes	9,480	75,328	86,789
male householder	4,665	53,868	60,025
married, wife present	3,077	43,444	47,683
married, wife absent	349	1,013	1,416
widowed	211	1,386	1,620
divorced	415	3,078	3,535
single, never married	623	4,947	5,772
female householder	4,815	21,461	26,763
married, husband present	392	2,199	2,667
married, husband absent	777	1,668	2,497
widowed	1,271	8,304	9,728
divorced	950	5,203	6,265
single, never married	1,425	4,087	5,606
Age of the householder			
All ages	9,480	75,328	86,789
15-24 years old	669	4,626	5,438
25-34 years old	2,470	17,010	20,013
35-44 years old	1,947	15,024	17,481
45-54 years old	1,488	10,792	12,628
55-64 years old	1,350	11,471	13,073
65 years old and over	1,556	16,406	18,155
Housing tenure			
All tenures	9,480	75,328	86,789
own housing unit	4,185	50,611	55,845
rent housing unit	5,295	24,667	30,943

continued on the next page

Table 1.16 continued

	Black	White	All Races
Size of the household			
All household sizes	9,480	75,328	86,789
one person	2,367	17,876	20,602
two persons	2,391	24,558	27,289
three persons	1,795	13,336	15,465
four persons	1,441	11,795	13,631
five persons	800	5,061	6,108
six persons	370	1,819	2,299
seven or more persons	317	882	1,296
persons per household	2.96	2.64	2.69
Residence			
All residences	9,480	75,328	86,789
Northeast	1,860	16,244	18,348
Midwest	1,863	19,599	21,697
South	4,924	24,283	29,581
West	834	15,202	17,163
inside metropolitan areas	na	na	na
outside metropolitan areas	na	na	na
nonfarm	na	na	na
farm	na	na	na

SOURCE: U.S. Bureau of the Census, Current Population Reports: Money Income of Households Families and Persons in the United States; March 1984, Series P-60, #151, pp. 10-14, table 4. C3.186/2:984
U.S. Bureau of the Census, Current Population Reports: Household & Family Characteristics, March 1985, Series P-20, #411, pp. 107-112, table 22. C3 186/17·985

NOTES: All Races' includes other races not shown separately.

UNITS: Number of households in thousands of households; persons per household, average.

Table 1.17 Selected Characteristics of Households, 1990

	Black	White	All Races
Marital status and type of householder			
All households	10,486	80,163	93,347
family households	7,470	56,590	66,090
married couple families	3,750	46,981	52,317
male householder, no wife present	446	2,303	2,884
female householder, no husband present	3,275	7,306	10,890
non-family households	3,015	23,573	27,257
male householder	1,313	9,951	11,606
-living alone	1,084	7,718	9,049
female householder	1,702	13,622	15,651
-living alone	1,525	12,161	13,950
Age of the householder			
All ages	10,486	80,163	93,347
15-24 years old	709	4,222	5,121
25-34 years old	2,625	17,137	20,472
35-44 years old	2,456	17,395	20,554
45-54 years old	1,606	12,404	14,514
55-64 years old	1,395	10,862	12,529
65 years old and over	1,695	18,144	20,156
Housing tenure			
All tenures	10,486	80,163	93,347
own housing unit	4,445	54,094	59,846
rent housing unit	5,862	24,685	31,895

continued on the next page

Table 1.17 continued

	Black	White	All Races
Size of the household			
All household sizes	10,486	80,163	93,347
one person	2,610	19,879	22,999
two persons	2,721	26,714	30,114
three persons	2,043	13,585	16,128
four persons	1,550	12,399	14,456
five persons	858	5,104	6,213
six persons	412	1,615	2,143
seven or more persons	293	877	1,295
persons per household	2.89	2.58	2.63
Residence			
All residences	10,486	80,163	93,347
Northeast	1,866	16,773	19,127
Midwest	2,092	20,339	22,760
South	5,622	26,155	32,262
West	906	16,896	19,197
inside metropolitan areas	8,816	61,155	72,331
outside metropolitan areas	1,670	19,009	21,016
nonfarm	10,464	78,556	91,710
farm	21	1,608	1,637

SOURCE: U.S. Bureau of the Census, Current Population Reports: Money Income of Households Families and Persons in the United States: 1988 and 1989, Series P-60, #172, pp. 9-11, table 1. C3 186/2 989

NOTES: All Races' includes other races not shown separately.

UNITS: Number of households in thousands of households; persons per household, average.

Table 1.18 Selected Characteristics of Households, 2003

	Black	White	All Races
Marital status and type of householder			
All households, both sexes	13,629	91,962	112,000
family households	8,912	62,609	76,217
married couple families	4,146	50,021	57,719
male householder, no spouse present	782	3,537	4,717
female householder, no spouse present	3,984	9,051	13,781
non-family households	4,716	29,353	35,783
male householder	2,024	13,283	16,136
-living alone	1,698	10,233	12,562
female householder	2,692	16,070	19,647
-living alone	2,439	13,860	17,024
Age of the householder			
All ages	13,629	91,962	112,000
15-24 years old	1,092	5,039	6,610
25-34 years old	2,728	14,919	19,159
35-44 years old	3,075	18,638	23,222
45-54 years old	2,889	18,974	23,137
55-64 years old	1,797	14,196	16,824
65 years old and over	2,047	20,196	23,048

continued on the next page

Table 1.18 continued

	Black	White	All Races
Size of the household			
All household sizes	13,629	91,962	112,000
one person	4,137	24,094	29,586
two persons	3,684	31,960	37,366
three persons	2,452	14,257	17,968
four persons	1,897	13,025	16,065
five persons	874	5,719	7,150
six persons	349	1,904	2,476
seven or more persons	236	1,002	1,388
Residence			
All residences	13,629	91,962	112,000
Northeast	2,402	17,613	21,017
Midwest	2,550	22,218	25,643
South	7,452	31,729	40,742
West	1,225	20,402	24,598
inside metropolitan areas	11,965	72,930	90,613
outside metropolitan areas	1,664	19,031	21,387

SOURCE: U.S. Bureau of the Census, Current Population Reports: Income 2003, "(Table) HINC-01. Selected Characteristics of Households, by Total Money Income in 2003".

NOTES: 'All Races' includes other races not shown separately. 'White' as shown is equivalent to 'White alone' that refers to people who reported White and did not report any other race category.

UNITS: Number of households in thousands of households.

Table 1.19 Selected Characteristics of Family Households, 1985

	Black	White	All Races
Type of family			
All families	6,778	54,400	62,706
married couple families	3,469	45,643	50,350
male householder, no wife present	344	1,816	2,228
female householder, no husband present	2,964	6,941	10,129
Size of family			
All family sizes	6,778	54,400	62,706
two persons	2,261	22,711	25,349
three persons	1,730	12,743	14,804
four persons	1,358	11,517	13,259
five persons	762	4,894	5,894
six persons	366	1,704	2,175
seven or more persons	300	831	1,225
average per family	3.60	3.16	3.23
Number of related children under 18 years old			
All families	6,778	54,400	62,706
no children	2,887	28,169	31,594
one child	1,579	11,174	13,108
two children	1,330	9,937	11,645
three children	612	3,695	4,486
four children	223	1,049	1,329
five children	97	261	373
six or more children	50	115	171
average per family	1.14	0.88	0.92
average per family with children	1.99	1.83	1.85

continued on the next page

Table 1.19 continued

	Black	White	All Races
Number of earners			
All families	6,671	53,777	61,930
no earner	1,376	7,674	9,221
one earner	2,312	15,219	17,949
two earners	2,237	23,303	26,160
three earners	527	5,317	6,029
four earners or more	218	2,263	2,570
Housing tenure			
All tenures	6,778	54,400	62,706
own housing unit	3,271	40,865	45,015
rent housing unit	3,508	13,535	17,691
Residence			
All residences	6,778	54,400	62,706
Northeast	1,322	11,631	13,149
Midwest	1,345	14,309	15,839
South	3,561	17,953	21,781
West	550	10,507	11,938
nonfarm	na	na	na
farm	na	na	na
inside metropolitan areas	na	na	na
outside metropolitan areas	na	na	na

SOURCE: U.S. Bureau of the Census, Current Population Reports: Money Income of Households, Families, and Persons in the United States, 1984, Series P-60, #151, pp. 76-77, table 21. C3 186/2 984
U.S. Bureau of the Census, Current Population Reports: Household & Family Characteristics, March 1985, Series P-20, #437, pp. 13-45, table 1; pp. 107-111, table 22. C3 186/17 985

NOTES: 'All Races' includes other races not shown separately. 'Number of earners' excludes families with members in the armed forces.

UNITS: Number of households in thousands of family households.

Table 1.20 Selected Characteristics of Family Households, 1990

	Black	White	All Races
Type of family			
All families	7,470	56,590	66,090
married couple families	3,750	46,981	52,317
male householder, no wife present	446	2,303	2,884
female householder, no husband present	3,275	7,306	10,890
Size of family			
All family sizes	7,470	56,590	66,090
two persons	2,574	24,438	27,606
three persons	1,951	12,937	15,353
four persons	1,478	12,048	14,036
five persons	819	4,882	5,938
six persons	371	1,505	1,997
seven or more persons	276	781	1,170
average per family	3.46	3.11	3.17
Number of related children under 18 years old			
All families	7,470	56,590	66,090
no children	3,093	29,872	33,801
one child	1,894	11,186	13,530
two children	1,433	10,342	12,263
three children	635	3,853	4,650
four children	256	970	1,279
five children	107	247	379
six or more children	51	121	188
average per family	1.09	0.86	0.89
average per family with children	1.86	1.82	1.83

continued on the next page

Table 1.20 continued

	Black	White	All Races
Number of earners			
All families	7,470	56,590	66,090
no earner	1,396	7,816	9,439
one earner	2,601	14,970	18,146
two earners	2,609	25,737	29,235
three earners	659	5,832	6,724
four earners or more	259	2,236	2,546
Housing tenure			
All tenures	7,470	56,590	66,090
own housing unit	3,448	42,588	47,142
rent housing unit	4,023	14,003	18,948
Residence			
All residences	7,470	56,590	66,090
Northeast	1,279	11,837	13,494
Midwest	1,446	14,370	16,059
South	4,147	18,746	23,244
West	598	11,638	13,293
nonfarm	7,453	55,225	64,701
farm	17	1,365	1,390
inside metropolitan areas	6,256	42,592	50,619
outside metropolitan areas	1,215	13,999	15,471

SOURCE: U.S. Bureau of the Census, Current Population Reports: Money Income of Households, Families, and Persons in the United States: 1988 and 1989, Series P-60, #172, pp. 9-11, table 1; pp. 48-50, table 13; pp. 76-80, table 18. C3 186/2 989

U.S. Bureau of the Census, Current Population Reports: Household & Family Characteristics: March 1990 and 1989, Series P-20, #447, pp. 13-16, table 1; pp. 18-20, table 2. C3 186/17 989

NOTES: 'All Races' includes other races not shown separately. 'Number of earners' excludes families with members in the armed forces.

UNITS: Number of households in thousands of family households.

Table 1.21 Selected Characteristics of Family Households, 2003

	Black	White	All Races
Marital status and type of householder			
Type of family			
All families	8,914	62,620	76,232
married couple families	4,146	50,025	57,725
male householder, no wife present	782	3,537	4,717
female householder, no husband present	3,986	9,058	13,791
Size of family			
All family sizes	8,914	62,620	76,232
two persons	3,437	29,092	34,096
three persons	2,414	13,166	16,749
four persons	1,740	12,409	15,245
five persons	795	5,345	6,662
six persons	329	1,761	2,305
seven or more persons	199	846	1,175

continued on the next page

Table 1.21 continued

	Black	White	All Races
Number of earners			
All families	8,914	62,620	76,232
no earner	1,435	9,005	10,929
one earner	3,695	18,861	24,168
two earners	3,113	27,846	32,981
three earners	562	5,137	6,102
four earners or more	109	1,770	2,053
Residence			
All residences	8,914	62,620	76,232
Northeast	1,543	11,695	13,994
Midwest	1,645	15,100	17,378
South	4,916	21,958	28,000
West	809	13,867	16,860
inside metropolitan areas	7,792	49,408	61,403
outside metropolitan areas	1,122	13,212	14,829

SOURCE: U.S. Bureau of the Census, Current Population Reports: Income 2003, "(Table) FINC-01. Selected Characteristics of Families by Total Money Income in 2003".

NOTES: 'All Races' includes other races not shown separately. Number of families as of March of the following year. 'White' and 'Black' as shown are respectively equivalent to 'White Alone' and 'Black Alone' that refer to people who reported 'White' or 'Black' and did not report any other race category. 'Number of earners' excludes families with members in the armed forces.

UNITS: Number of households in thousands of family households.

Table 1.22 Single Parents Living With Own Children Under 18 Years Old, 2000 and 2003

	Black	White	All Races
2000			
Single Fathers			
with own children under 18	335	1,622	2,044
with own children under 12	225	1,145	1,441
with own children under 6	138	647	819
with own children under 3	95	393	511
with own children under 1	38	152	196
Single Mothers			
with own children under 18	3,060	6,216	9,681
with own children under 12	2,484	4,558	7,337
with own children under 6	1,459	2,519	4,115
with own children under 3	846	1,396	2,319
with own children under 1	307	499	824
2003			
Single Fathers			
with own children under 18	353	1,758	2,260
with own children under 12	254	1,187	1,547
with own children under 6	139	668	878
with own children under 3	84	404	530
with own children under 1	27	162	203
Single Mothers			
with own children under 18	3,124	6,471	10,142
with own children under 12	2,391	4,624	7,417
with own children under 6	1,395	2,575	4,234
with own children under 3	789	1,364	2,287
with own children under 1	241	446	734

SOURCE: U.S. Bureau of the Census, Current Population Reports: America's Families and Living Arrangements: 2000; Series P-20, #537, p. 8, table 4, issued June 2001; 2003;"Table FG5. One-Parent Family Groups with Own Children Under 18, by Labor Force Status, Race, and Hispanic Origin of the Reference Person: March 2003". <www census gov>

NOTES: 'All races' includes other races not shown separately.

UNITS: Thousands of fathers or mothers.

Table 1.23 Living Arrangements of Children Under 18 Years of Age, 2000 and 2003

	Black children	White children	All children
2000			
Living with both parents	4,286	42,497	49,795
Living with mother only	5,596	9,765	16,162
Living with father only	484	2,427	3,058
Living with neither parent	1,046	1,752	2,981
2003			
Living with both parents	4,094	41,805	49,903
Living with mother only	5,762	9,799	16,770
Living with father only	517	2,535	3,323
Living with neither parent	967	1,781	3,004

SOURCE: U.S. Bureau of the Census, Current Population Reports: America's Families and Living Arrangements: 2000; Series P-20, #537, pp. 1, 25, 37, and 60, table C2, issued June 2001; 2003; "Table C2. Household Relationship and Living Arrangements of Children Under 18 Years, by Age, Sex, Race, Hispanic Origin, and Metropolitan Residence: March 2003". <www census.gov>

NOTES: 'All children' includes children of other races not shown separately.

UNITS: Thousands of children.

Table 1.24 Primary Child Care Arrangements Used for Preschoolers by Families With Employed Mothers, Spring 1997 and Spring 1999

	Black children	White children	All children
Spring 1997			
All preschoolers with employed mothers	1,525	8,154	10,116
Mother while working	1.1	6.0	5.1%
Father	16.8	32.8	30.6
Grandparent	32.2	28.8	29.6
Sibling	20.3	13.7	14.8
Daycare center	21.1	18.6	18.9
Nursery/preschool	6.0	7.2	7.0
Head start	8.7	3.4	4.2
Family day care	7.3	13.9	13.0
Other non-relative	7.1	10.1	9.8
Spring 1999			
All preschoolers with employed mothers	1,735	8,411	10,587
Designated parent	1.9	3.4%	3.2%
Other parent	13.9	20.4	19.3
Grandparent	26.5	19.4	21.7
Other relative or sibling	11.3	7.8	8.4
Daycare center	24.8	18.0	18.7
Nursery/preschool	3.1	4.1	4.0
Head start	1.2	0.2	0.4
Family day care	5.2	13.2	11.4
Other non-relative	8.2	10.2	9.7

SOURCE: U.S. Bureau of the Census, Current Population Reports: Who's Minding the Kids? Child Care Arrangements: Spring 1997 Series P70-86, table 2. C3 186/P70-86
U.S. Bureau of the Census, Current Population Reports: Who's Minding the Kids? Child Care Arrangements: Spring 1999 Series PPL-168, table 2B.

NOTES: 'All children' includes children of other races not shown separately. Because of multiple arrangements, numbers and percentages may exceed the total number of children. 'Designated parent' is selected in households where both parents are present to report child care arrangements for each child.

UNITS: Thousands of children living in family households.

Chapter 2: Vital Statistics & Health

Table 2.01 Births and Birth Rates, by Age of the Mother, 2000 and 2003

	Black	White	All Races
2000 (Preliminary)			
Live births	619,970	3,202,932	4,064,948
Fertility rate	71.4	66.7	67.6
Birth rate per 1,000 women, by age group			
10-14 years old	2.5	0.6	0.9
15-19 years old	79.2	43.9	48.7
20-24 years old	143.7	108.3	112.5
25-29 years old	104.8	124.9	121.7
30-34 years old	67.0	97.6	94.2
35-39 years old	32.0	40.7	40.3
40-44 years old	7.1	7.7	7.9
45-49 years old	0.4	0.4	0.5
2003			
Live births	599,414	3,227,755	4,091,063
Fertility rate	66.2	66.2	66.1
Birth rate per 1,000 women, by age group			
10-14 years old	1.6	0.5	0.6
15-19 years old	63.7	38.3	41.7
20-24 years old	126.0	100.6	102.6
25-29 years old	100.3	119.6	115.7
30-34 years old	66.5	99.4	95.2
35-39 years old	33.1	44.8	43.8
40-44 years old	7.7	8.7	8.7
45-49 years old	0.5	0.5	0.5

SOURCE: U.S. Department of Health and Human Services, National Vital Statistics Report: Births: Preliminary Data for 2000, Volume 49, No. 5, July 24, 2001; p. 9, table 2; p. 10, table 3; Births: Final Data for 2003, Volume 52, No. 10, December 17, 2004; p. 10, table 2; p. 11, table 3.

NOTES: 'All Races' includes other races not shown separately. Data based on race of the mother. Fertility rate is the total number of births, regardless of age of mother, per 1,000 women aged 15-44 years.

UNITS: Live births in number of births; rates as shown.

Table 2.02 Birth Rates for Women 15-44 Years of Age, by Live Birth Order, 2000 and 2003

	Black mothers	White mothers	mothers of All Races
2000 (Preliminary)			
All live births	71.4	66.7	67.6
first child	26.7	26.9	27.1
second child	21.2	22.0	22.0
third child	12.8	11.2	11.3
fourth child and over	10.7	6.6	7.2
2002			
All live births	65.8	64.8	64.8
first child	24.8	25.7	25.8
second child	19.2	21.5	21.1
third child	11.7	11.0	10.9
fourth child and over	10.0	6.5	7.0
2003			
All live births	66.2	66.2	66.1
first child	25.4	26.7	26.7
second child	19.5	21.9	21.5
third child	11.7	11.1	11.0
fourth child and over	9.6	6.5	6.8

SOURCE: U.S. Department of Health and Human Services, National Vital Statistics Report: Births: Preliminary Data for 2000, Volume 49, No. 5, July 24, 2001; p. 10, table 3; Births: Final Data for 2002, Volume 52, No. 10, December 17, 2003; p. 32, table 3; 2003, Volume 52, No. 10, November 23, 2004; p. 11, table 3.

NOTES: Data based on race of the mother.

UNITS: Live births per 1,000 women 15-44 years of age.

Table 2.03 Selected Characteristics of Live Births, 1980 - 2002

	Black births	White births	births of All Races
1980			
birth weight under 2,500 grams	12.49%	5.70%	6.84%
birth weight under 1,500 grams	2.44	0.90	1.15
mother under 18 years old	12.2	4.5	5.8
mother 18-19 years old	14.3	9.0	9.8
births to unmarried mothers	55.2	11.0	18.4
mother with less than 12 years of school	36.2	20.7	23.7
mother with 16 years or more of school	6.3	15.6	14.0
prenatal care began in 1st trimester	62.7	79.3	76.3
prenatal care began in 3rd trimester or no prenatal care	8.8	4.3	5.1
1990			
birth weight under 2,500 grams	13.25%	5.70%	6.97%
birth weight under 1,500 grams	2.92	0.95	1.27
mother under 18 years old	10.1	3.6	4.7
mother 18-19 years old	13.0	7.3	8.1
births to unmarried mothers	66.5	20.4	28.0
mother with less than 12 years of school	39.2	22.4	23.8
mother with 16 years or more of school	7.2	19.3	17.5
prenatal care began in 1st trimester	60.6	79.2	75.8
prenatal care began in 3rd trimester or no prenatal care	11.3	4.9	6.1

continued on the next page

Table 2.03 continued

	Black births	White births	births of All Races
2000			
birth weight under 2,500 grams	12.99%	6.55%	7.57%
birth weight under 1,500 grams	3.07	1.14	1.43
mother under 18 years old	7.8	3.5	4.1
mother 18-19 years old	11.9	7.1	7.7
births to unmarried mothers	68.5	27.1	33.2
mother with less than 12 years of school	25.5	21.4	21.7
mother with 16 years or more of school	11.7	26.3	24.7
prenatal care began in 1st trimester	74.3	85.0	83.2
prenatal care began in 3rd trimester or no prenatal care	6.7	3.3	3.9
2002			
birth weight under 2,500 grams	13.29%	6.80%	7.82%
birth weight under 1,500 grams	3.13	1.17	1.46
mother under 18 years old	6.9	3.1	3.6
mother 18-19 years old	11.1	6.6	7.1
births to unmarried mothers	68.2	28.5	34.0
mother with less than 12 years of school	24.4	21.6	21.5
mother with 16 years or more of school	12.7	27.3	25.9
prenatal care began in 1st trimester	75.2	85.4	83.7
prenatal care began in 3rd trimester or no prenatal care	6.2	3.1	3.6

SOURCE: U.S. Department of Health and Human Services, Health United States, 2004; p. 113, table 6; p. 116, table 8; p. 117, table 9; p. 118, table 10; p. 120, table 12. (Centers for Disease Control and Prevention, National Center for Health Statistics) HE 20 6223· (year)

NOTES: Data based on race of the mother.

UNITS: Percent, as a percent of all live births, 100.0%.

Table 2.04 Fertility Rates and Birth Rates by Age of Mother, 1990 - 2002

	Black women	White women	women of All Races
1990			
fertility rate	86.8	68.3	70.9
women 15-19 years old	112.8	50.8	59.9
women 20-24 years old	160.2	109.8	116.5
women 25-29 years old	115.5	120.7	120.2
women 30-34 years old	68.7	81.7	80.8
women 35-39 years old	28.1	31.5	31.7
women 40-44 years old	5.5	5.2	5.5
2000			
fertility rate	70.0	65.3	65.9
women 15-19 years old	77.4	43.2	47.7
women 20-24 years old	141.3	106.6	109.7
women 25-29 years old	100.3	116.7	113.5
women 30-34 years old	65.4	94.6	91.2
women 35-39 years old	31.5	40.2	39.7
women 40-44 years old	7.2	7.9	8.0
2002			
fertility rate	65.8	64.8	64.8
women 15-19 years old	66.6	39.4	43.0
women 20-24 years old	127.1	101.6	103.6
women 25-29 years old	99.0	117.4	113.6
women 30-34 years old	64.4	95.5	91.5
women 35-39 years old	31.5	42.4	41.1
women 40-44 years old	7.4	8.2	8.3

SOURCE: U.S. Department of Health and Human Services, Health United States, 2004; pp. 109-110, table 3 (data from U.S. Bureau of the Census, *Current Population Reports*, series P-20). HE 20 6223: (year)

NOTES: 'Women of All Races' includes women of other races not shown separately. 'Fertility Rate' is total number of live births regardless of age of mother per 1,000 women, 15-44 years of age.

UNITS: Live births per 1,000 women

Table 2.05 Nonmarital Childbearing, 1980 - 2002

	Black women	White women	women of All Races
Percent of live births to unmarried mothers			
1980	56.1%	11.2%	18.4%
1985	61.2	14.7	22.0
1990	66.5	20.4	28.0
1995	69.9	25.3	32.2
2000	68.5	27.1	33.2
2001	68.4	27.7	33.5
2002	66.2	38.9	43.7
Live births per 1,000 unmarried mothers*			
1980	81.1	18.1	29.4
1985	77.0	22.5	32.8
1990	90.5	32.9	43.8
1995	75.9	37.5	45.1
2000	72.5	38.9	45.2
2001	70.1	39.2	45.0
2002	68.2	28.5	34.0

SOURCE: U.S. Department of Health and Human Services, Health United States, 2004; p. 117, table 9 (data from U.S. Bureau of the Census, *Current Population Reports*, series P-20). HE 20 6223 (year)

NOTES: 'Women of All Races' includes women of other races not shown separately.

UNITS: *Live births per 1,000 unmarried women 15-44 years of age.

Table 2.06 Projected Fertility Rates, Women 10-49 Years Old, 2000 and 2010

	Black women	White women	women of All Races
2000			
Total fertility rate	2,193	2,114	2,130
birth rates			
10-14 years old	2.4	0.6	0.9
15-19 years old	79.4	43.6	48.5
20-24 years old	144.2	107.9	112.3
25-29 years old	105.3	124.3	121.4
30-34 years old	67.5	97.4	94.1
35-39 years old	32.2	40.7	40.4
40-44 years old	7.2	7.8	7.9
45-49 years old	0.4	0.4	0.5
2010			
Total fertility rate	2,140	2,098	2,123
birth rates			
10-14 years old	3.5	0.9	1.3
15-19 years old	95.6	54.3	43.6
20-24 years old	137.1	112.6	107.9
25-29 years old	95.5	118.5	124.3
30-34 years old	63.4	90.0	97.4
35-39 years old	28.9	36.6	40.7
40-44 years old	6.0	7.1	7.8
45-49 years old	0.3	0.3	0.4

SOURCE: U.S. Bureau of the Census, Statistical Abstract of the United States, 2002; p. 62, table 72; 2003; p. 75, table 89; 2004; p. 63, table 76. C 3 134 (year)

NOTES: 'All Races' includes women of other races not shown separately. The total fertility rate is the number of births that 1,000 women would have in their lifetime if, at each year of age they experienced the birth rates occurring in the specified year. Projections are based on middle fertility assumptions.

UNITS: Total fertility rate and birth rate in births per 1,000 women.

Table 2.07 Abortions, 1973 - 2001

	Black	White	All Races
1973	42.0	32.6	19.6
1975	47.6	27.7	27.2
1980	54.3	33.2	35.9
1985	47.2	27.7	35.4
1987	50.0	26.7	35.6
1988	48.9	25.9	35.2
1989	49.6	25.2	34.6
1990	52.1	25.8	34.5
1991	50.2	24.6	33.9
1992	51.8	23.6	33.5
1993	55.2	23.1	33.4
1994	53.8	21.7	32.1
1995	53.4	20.4	31.1
1996	55.5	20.2	31.4
1997	54.3	19.4	30.6
1998*	51.2	18.9	26.4
1999*	52.9	17.7	25.6
2000*	50.3	16.7	24.5
2001*	49.1	16.5	24.6

SOURCE: U.S. Department of Health and Human Services, Health, United States, 2004 (data from Centers for Disease Control and Prevention, National Center for Health Statistics); p. 126, table 16. HE 20 6223· (year)

NOTES: 'All Races' includes women of other races not shown separately. 1989 and later, "White" includes women of Hispanic ethnicity. CA, AK, NH, OK did not report abortion data in 1998*.

UNITS: Abortions per 100 live births.

Table 2.08 Contraceptive Usage for Women 15-44 Years of Age, by Method of Contraception, 1982 and 1995

	Black women	White women	women of All Races
1982			
all methods	51.6%	57.3%	55.7%
female sterilization	21.9	23.0	23.2
male sterilization	13.0	*	10.9
birth control pill	26.8	30.2	28.0
intrauterine device	5.8	19.2	7.1
diaphragm	9.2	*	8.1
condom	13.1	6.9*	12.0
1995			
all methods	62.1%	66.1%	64.2%
female sterilization	40.1	24.6	27.8
male sterilization	1.7*	13.6	10.9
birth control pill	23.8	28.5	26.9
intrauterine device	*	0.7	0.8
diaphragm	*	2.3	1.9
condom	20.2	19.7	20.4

SOURCE: U.S. Department of Health and Human Services, Health United States, 2003; pp. 117-119, table 17 (data from the National Survey of Family Growth). HE 20.6223. (year)

NOTES: 'Women of All Races' includes women of other races not shown separately. Data are based on household interviews of samples of women in the childbearing ages. * Relative standard error is greater than 30%.

UNITS: 'All methods' in percent of women using contraception; individual methods in percent, as a percent of all women using some form of contraception.

Table 2.09 Life Expectancy at Birth, by Sex, 1970 - 2000; Projections, 2005 - 2010

	Black		White		All Races	
	male	female	male	female	male	female
1970	60.0	68.3	68.0	75.6	67.1	74.7
1975	62.4	71.3	69.5	77.3	68.8	76.6
1980	63.8	72.5	70.7	78.1	70.0	77.4
1985	65.0	73.4	71.8	78.7	71.1	78.2
1990	64.5	73.6	72.7	79.4	71.8	78.8
1995	65.2	73.9	73.4	79.6	72.5	78.9
1996	66.1	74.2	73.8	79.6	73.0	79.0
1997	67.2	74.7	74.3	79.9	73.6	79.4
1998	67.6	74.8	74.5	80.0	73.8	79.5
1999	67.8	74.7	74.6	79.9	73.9	79.4
2000	68.2	74.9	74.8	80.0	74.1	79.5
2005	69.9	76.8	75.4	81.1	74.9	80.7
2010	70.9	77.8	76.1	81.8	75.6	81.4

SOURCE: U.S. Bureau of the Census, Statistical Abstract of the United States, 2002; p. 71, table 91; 2004; p. 83, table 105.

NOTES: 'All Races' includes other races not shown separately. Projections based on middle mortality assumptions.

UNITS: Life expectancy in years.

Table 2.10 Life Expectancy, by Sex, by Age, 1999 and 2001

	Black		White		All Races
	male	female	male	female	both sexes
1999					
at birth	67.8	74.7	74.6	79.9	76.7
age 10	59.2	66.0	65.3	70.5	67.4
age 20	49.6	56.2	55.6	60.7	57.7
age 30	40.7	46.6	46.2	50.9	48.2
age 40	31.9	37.4	36.9	41.3	38.8
age 50	24.0	28.7	28.0	32.0	29.8
age 60	17.2	20.9	19.8	23.2	21.5
age 70	11.6	14.0	12.9	15.5	14.3
age 80	7.3	8.6	7.5	9.1	8.5
2001					
at birth	68.6	75.5	75.0	80.2	77.2
age 10	59.8	66.6	65.6	70.8	67.9
age 20	50.3	56.8	56.0	60.9	58.1
age 30	41.4	47.2	46.6	51.2	48.6
age 40	32.5	38.0	37.3	41.6	39.2
age 50	24.4	29.3	28.4	32.3	30.3
age 60	17.5	21.5	20.2	23.5	21.9
age 70	11.7	14.7	13.2	15.7	14.6
age 80	7.3	9.2	7.7	9.3	8.8

SOURCE: U.S. Bureau of the Census, Statistical Abstract of the United States, 2002; p. 73, table 93; 2004; p. 73, table 94. C 3 134:(year)

NOTES: 'All Races' includes other races not shown separately.

UNITS: Life expectancy in years.

Table 2.11 Infant Mortality, Fetal Deaths, and Perinatal Mortality Rates, 1990 - 2002

	Black	White	All Races
1990			
infant mortality rate	18.0	7.6	9.2
neonatal mortality rates:			
- under 28 days	11.6	4.8	5.8
- under 7 days	9.7	3.9	4.8
post neonatal mortality rate	6.4	2.8	3.4
fetal death rate	13.3	6.4	7.5
late fetal death rate	6.7	3.8	4.3
perinatal mortality rate	16.4	7.7	9.1
2000			
infant mortality rate	14.1	5.7	6.9
neonatal mortality rates:			
- under 28 days	9.4	3.8	4.6
- under 7 days	7.6	3.0	3.7
post neonatal mortality rate	4.7	1.9	2.3
fetal death rate	12.4	5.6	6.6
late fetal death rate	5.4	2.9	3.3
perinatal mortality rate	13.0	5.9	7.0
2002			
infant mortality rate	14.4	5.8	7.0
neonatal mortality rates:			
- under 28 days	9.5	3.9	4.7
- under 7 days	7.8	3.1	3.7
post neonatal mortality rate	4.8	1.9	2.3
fetal death rate	11.9	5.5	6.4
late fetal death rate	5.2	2.8	3.2
perinatal mortality rate	12.8	5.9	6.9

SOURCE: U.S. Department of Health and Human Services, Health United States, 2004; p. 135, table 22. HE 20 6223: (year)

NOTES: 'All Races' includes other races not shown separately. Data based on race of the mother. Infant mortality rate is the number of deaths of infants under one year; neonatal deaths occur within 28 days of birth; post-neonatal deaths occur 28-365 days after birth; deaths within 7 days of birth are early neonatal deaths; fetal deaths are deaths of fetuses of more than 20 weeks gestation; late fetal deaths are deaths of fetuses of more than 28 weeks of gestation; perinatal mortality is the sum of late fetal deaths and infant deaths within the first 7 days of life.

UNITS: All rates per 1,000 live births, as shown.

Table 2.12 Death Rates, by Age and Sex, 1980 - 2002

	Black		White		All Races	
	male	female	male	female	male	female
1980						
All ages	1,034	733	983	806	977	785
under 1 year old	2,587	2,124	1,230	963	1,429	1,142
1-4 years old	111	84	66	49	73	55
5-14 years old	47	31	35	23	37	24
15-24 years old	209	71	167	56	172	58
25-34 years old	407	150	171	65	196	76
35-44 years old	690	324	257	138	299	159
45-54 years old	1,480	768	699	373	767	413
55-64 years old	2,873	1,561	1,729	876	1,815	934
65-74 years old	5,131	3,057	4,036	2,067	4,105	2,145
75-84 years old	9,232	6,212	8,830	5,402	8,817	5,440
85 years old and over	16,099	12,367	19,097	14,980	18,801	14,747
1990						
All ages	1,008	748	931	847	918	812
under 1 year old	2,112	1,736	896	690	1,083	856
1-4 years old	86	68	46	36	52	41
5-14 years old	41	28	26	18	29	19
15-24 years old	252	69	131	46	147	49
25-34 years old	431	160	176	62	204	74
35-44 years old	700	299	268	117	310	138
45-54 years old	1,261	639	549	309	610	343
55-64 years old	2,618	1,453	1,467	823	1,553	879
65-74 years old	4,946	2,866	3,398	1,924	3,492	1,991
75-84 years old	9,130	5,688	7,845	4,839	7,889	4,883
85 years old and over	16,955	13,310	18,268	14,401	18,057	14,274

continued on the next page

Table 2.12 continued

	Black		White		All Races	
	male	female	male	female	male	female
2000						
All ages	834	733	888	912	853	855
under 1 year old	1,568	1,280	668	551	807	663
1-4 years old	55	45	33	26	36	29
5-14 years old	28	20	20	14	21	15
15-24 years old	181	58	106	41	115	43
25-34 years old	261	122	124	55	139	64
35-44 years old	453	272	237	126	255	143
45-54 years old	1,018	588	497	281	543	313
55-64 years old	2,080	1,227	1,163	731	1,231	772
65-74 years old	4,254	2,690	2,906	1,868	2,980	1,921
75-84 years old	8,486	5,697	6,933	4,785	6,973	4,815
85 years old and over	16,791	13,941	17,716	14,891	17,501	14,719
2002 (preliminary)						
All ages	814.6	723.3	885.9	909.5	847.8	849.9
under 1 year old	1,334.9	1,165.7	651.6	520.1	758.7	652.3
1-4 years old	54.3	39.3	31.6	24.5	35.3	27.0
5-14 years old	29.1	20.1	18.4	13.8	20.0	14.8
15-24 years old	172.5	54.3	109.9	42.5	117.3	43.7
25-34 years old	263.3	116.5	128.5	56.9	142.3	64.0
35-44 years old	433.1	272.3	238.8	133.4	256.8	148.8
45-54 years old	979.9	577.8	505.0	286.8	546.8	316.7
55-64 years old	2,036.6	1,181.4	1,120.6	700.5	1,185.6	739.3
65-74 years old	4,011.4	2,544.1	2,804.4	1,826.4	2,862.2	1,870.2
75-84 years old	8,154.7	5,580.3	6,756.0	4,757.2	6,774.3	4,770.9
85 years old and over	15,622.6	13,693.5	16,519.4	14,420.6	16,295.3	14,240.5

SOURCE: U.S. Bureau of the Census, Statistical Abstract of the United States, 2003; p. 87, table 105; 2004; p. 75, table 96. C 3.134 9 (year)

NOTES: 'All Races' includes other races not shown separately. 'All Ages' includes ages not stated.

UNITS: Rates per 100,000 of population in specified age groups, as shown.

Table 2.13 Deaths, by Selected Cause of Death, 1999 and 2000

	Black	White	Total
1999			
cerebrovascular diseases			
men	87.4	60.1	62.4
women	78.1	58.8	60.5
heart disease			
men	na	na	328.1
women	na	na	220.9
suicide			
men	10.4	19.4	na
women	1.6	4.4	na
HIV (human immunodeficiency virus)			
men	37.1	5.0	8.4
women	13.4	1.0	2.6
malignant neoplasms			
men	340.5	246.4	251.6
women	200.0	168.6	169.9
2000			
cerebrovascular diseases			
men	87.1	58.6	61.1
women	78.1	57.8	59.7
heart disease			
men	na	na	315.0
women	na	na	213.0
suicide			
men	10.0	19.1	na
women	1.8	4.3	na
HIV (human immunodeficiency virus)			
men	35.1	4.6	8.0
women	13.2	1.0	2.6
malignant neoplasms			
men	333.2	242.5	247.4
women	196.6	168.7	205.9

SOURCE: U.S. Bureau of the Census, Statistical Abstract of the United States, 2003; p. 96, table 120 and 121; p. 98, table 123 and 124; p. 97, table 122.
C 3 134 003

NOTES: 'All Races' includes other races not shown separately.

UNITS: Deaths per 100,000 population.

Table 2.14 Maternal Mortality Rates, by Age of the Mother, 1970 – 2002

	Black mothers	White mothers	mothers of All Races
1970			
All persons	342	445	803
All ages, age adjusted rate	65.5	14.5	21.5
women under 20 years old	32.3	13.8	18.9
women 20-24 years old	41.9	8.4	13.0
women 25-29 years old	65.2	11.1	17.0
women 30-34 years old	117.8	18.7	31.6
women 35 years old and over	207.5	59.3	81.9
1980			
All persons	127	193	334
All ages, age adjusted rate	24.9	6.7	9.6
women under 20 years old	13.1	5.8	7.6
women 20-24 years old	13.9	4.2	5.8
women 25-29 years old	22.4	5.4	7.7
women 30-34 years old	44.0	9.3	13.6
women 35 years old and over	100.6	25.5	36.3
1990			
All persons	153	177	343
All ages, age adjusted rate	21.7	5.1	7.6
women under 20 years old	12.0	5.3	7.5
women 20-24 years old	14.7	3.9	6.1
women 25-29 years old	14.9	4.8	6.0
women 30-34 years old	44.2	5.0	9.5
women 35 years old and over	79.7	12.6	20.7

continued on the next page

Table 2.14 continued

	Black mothers	White mothers	mothers of All Races
2000			
All persons	137	240	396
All ages, age adjusted rate	20.1	6.2	8.2
women under 20 years old	*	*	*
women 20-24 years old	15.3	5.6	7.4
women 25-29 years old	21.8	5.9	7.9
women 30-34 years old	34.8	7.1	10.0
women 35 years old and over	62.8	18.0	22.7
2001			
All persons	150	228	399
All ages, age adjusted rate	22.4	6.5	8.8
women under 20 years old	*	7.4	8.8
women 20-24 years old	14.6	5.3	6.9
women 25-29 years old	24.7	5.8	8.5
women 30-34 years old	30.6	8.1	10.1
women 35 years old and over	71.0	11.4	18.9
2002			
All persons	148	190	357
All ages, age adjusted rate	22.9	4.8	7.6
women under 20 years old	*	*	6.7
women 20-24 years old	14.9	3.4	5.8
women 25-29 years old	27.1	4.6	7.5
women 30-34 years old	28.4	6.7	9.3
women 35 years old and over	62.9	13.3	18.4

SOURCE: U.S. Department of Health and Human Services, Health United States, 2003; p. 179, table 43, 2004, p. 189, table 43. HE 20 6223 (year)

NOTES: 'Mothers of All Races' include mothers of other races not show separately. Data for maternal mortality for complications of pregnancy, childbirth and the puerperium. Rates for women 35 years old and over computed by relating deaths to live births to women in this age group. *Indicates data based on fewer than 20 deaths.

UNITS: Rate is the number of deaths of mothers per 100,000 live births.

Table 2.15 Death Rates for Malignant Neoplasms of the Breast, for Females, by Age, 1980 – 2002

	Black women	White women	women of All Races
1980			
All ages, age adjusted rate	31.7	32.1	31.9
All ages, crude rate	22.9	32.3	30.6
35-44 years old	24.1	17.3	17.9
45-54 years old	52.7	48.1	48.1
55-64 years old	79.9	81.3	80.5
65-74 years old	84.3	103.7	101.1
75-84 years old	114.1	128.4	126.4
85 years old and over	149.9	171.7	169.3
1990			
All ages, age adjusted rate	38.1	33.2	33.3
All ages, crude rate	29.0	35.9	34.0
35-44 years old	25.8	17.1	17.8
45-54 years old	60.5	44.3	45.4
55-64 years old	93.1	78.5	78.6
65-74 years old	112.2	113.3	111.7
75-84 years old	140.5	148.2	146.3
85 years old and over	201.5	198.0	196.8

continued on the next page

Table 2.15 continued

	Black women	White women	women of All Races
2000			
All ages, age adjusted rate	34.5	26.3	26.8
All ages, crude rate	27.9	30.7	29.2
35-44 years old	20.9	11.3	12.4
45-54 years old	51.5	31.2	33.0
55-64 years old	80.9	57.9	59.3
65-74 years old	98.6	89.3	88.3
75-84 years old	139.8	130.2	128.9
85 years old and over	238.7	205.5	205.7
2002			
All ages, age adjusted rate	34.0	25.0	25.6
All ages, crude rate	28.2	29.5	28.3
35-44 years old	22.0	10.7	12.0
45-54 years old	49.8	29.4	31.4
55-64 years old	76.6	55.0	56.2
65-74 years old	101.1	84.6	84.4
75-84 years old	145.0	126.5	125.9
85 years old and over	209.1	192.6	191.5

SOURCE: U.S. Department of Health and Human Services, Health United States, 2004, (Centers for Disease Control and Prevention, National Center for Health Statistics); pp. 182-183, table 40. HE 20 6223 (year)

NOTES: 'Women of All Races' includes women of other races not shown separately. Data excludes deaths of nonresidents of the United States. Age-adjusted rates for all years differ from those shown in previous editions of Health, United States. Age-adjusted rates are calculated using the year 2000 standard population starting with Health, United States, 2001.

UNITS: Rate is the number of deaths per 100,000 resident female population, by age group.

Table 2.16 Death Rates for Motor Vehicle Accidents, by Sex and Age, 2000 and 2002

	Black		White		All Races	
	male	female	male	female	male	female
2000						
All ages, age adjusted	24.4	8.4	21.8	9.8	21.7	9.5
All ages, crude	22.5	8.2	21.6	10.0	21.3	9.7
under 1 year	6.7	*	4.2	3.5	4.6	4.2
1-14 years old	5.5	3.9	4.8	3.7	4.9	3.7
15-24 years old	30.2	11.7	39.6	17.1	37.4	15.9
25-34 years old	32.6	9.4	25.1	8.9	25.5	8.8
35-44 years old	27.2	8.2	21.8	8.9	22.0	8.8
45-64 years old	27.1	9.0	19.7	8.7	20.2	8.7
65 years old and over	32.1	10.4	29.4	16.2	29.5	15.8
2002						
All ages, age adjusted	23.2	8.2	22.4	9.8	22.1	9.6
All ages, crude	21.5	8.0	22.4	10.1	21.9	9.8
under 1 year	*	*	2.9	2.2	3.3	2.8
1-14 years old	5.3	3.5	4.5	3.2	4.6	3.3
15-24 years old	29.6	11.6	41.9	17.9	39.3	16.6
25-34 years old	31.7	8.8	26.6	9.0	26.5	8.8
35-44 years old	25.3	9.4	22.3	9.4	22.3	9.3
45-64 years old	24.8	8.4	20.6	8.7	20.7	8.7
65 years old and over	30.4	9.5	29.8	16.3	29.8	15.7

SOURCE: U.S. Department of Health and Human Services, Health United States, 2004, (Centers for Disease Control and Prevention, National Center for Health Statistics) pp. 190-193, table 44. HE 20 6223 (year)

NOTES: 'All Races' includes other races not shown separately. Excludes deaths of nonresidents of the United States. *Indicates data based on fewer than 20 deaths. Age-adjusted rates for all years differ from those shown in previous editions of Health, United States. Age-adjusted rates are calculated using the year 2000 standard population starting with Health, United States, 2001.

UNITS: Rate is the number of deaths per 100,000 resident population.

Table 2.17 Death Rates for Assault (Homicide), by Sex and Age, 2000 and 2002

	Black		White		All Races	
	male	female	male	female	male	female
2000						
All ages, age adjusted	35.4	7.1	5.2	2.1	9.0	2.8
All ages, crude	37.2	7.2	5.2	2.1	9.3	2.8
under 1 year	23.3	22.2	8.2	5.0	10.4	7.9
1-14 years old	3.1	2.7	1.2	0.8	1.5	1.1
15-24 years old	85.3	10.7	9.9	2.7	20.9	3.9
25-44 years old	55.8	11.0	7.4	2.9	13.3	4.0
45-64 years old	21.9	4.5	4.1	1.8	6.0	2.1
65 years old and over	12.8	3.5	2.5	1.6	3.3	1.8
2002						
All ages, age adjusted	36.4	6.9	5.3	2.0	9.4	2.8
All ages, crude	38.4	7.0	5.4	2.0	9.6	2.7
under 1 year	16.3	18.5	6.2	4.6	7.9	7.1
1-14 years old	3.8	2.6	1.0	0.9	1.5	1.3
15-24 years old	83.1	10.3	10.6	2.5	21.5	3.8
25-44 years old	60.0	11.1	7.7	2.8	14.2	4.0
45-64 years old	22.9	4.5	4.2	1.9	6.2	2.2
65 years old and over	11.2	3.1	2.6	1.4	3.2	1.6

SOURCE: U.S. Department of Health and Human Services, Health United States, 2003, pp. 184-186, table 45; 2004, pp. 194-196, table 45. (Centers for Disease Control and Prevention, National Center for health Statistics) HE 20 6223 (year)

NOTES: 'All Races' includes other races not shown separately. Excludes deaths of nonresidents of the United States. Age-adjusted rates for all years differ from those shown in previous editions of Health, United States. Age-adjusted rates are calculated using the year 2000 standard population starting with Health, United States, 2001.

UNITS: Rate is the number of deaths per 100,000 resident population

Table 2.18 Death Rates for Suicide, by Sex and Age, 2000 and 2002

	Black		White		All Races	
	male	female	male	female	male	female
2000						
All ages, age adjusted	10.0	1.8	19.1	4.3	17.7	4.0
All ages, crude	9.4	1.7	18.8	4.4	17.1	4.0
15-24 years old	14.2	2.2	17.9	3.1	17.1	3.0
25-44 years old	14.3	2.6	22.9	6.0	21.3	5.4
45-64 years old	9.9	2.1	23.2	6.9	21.3	6.2
65 years old and over	11.5	1.3	33.3	4.3	31.1	4.0
2002						
All ages, age adjusted	9.8	1.6	20.0	4.7	18.4	4.2
All ages, crude	9.1	1.5	19.9	4.8	17.9	4.3
15-24 years old	11.3	1.7	17.7	3.1	16.5	2.9
25-44 years old	15.1	2.4	24.0	6.6	22.2	5.8
45-64 years old	9.6	2.1	25.9	7.5	23.5	6.7
65 years old and over	11.7	1.1	34.2	4.3	31.8	4.1

SOURCE: U.S. Department of Health and Human Services, Health United States, 2003, pp. 187-189, table 46; 2004; pp. 197-199, table 46. (Centers for Disease Control and Prevention, National Center for Health Statistics)
HE 20 6223 (year)

NOTES: 'All Races' includes other races not shown separately. Excludes deaths of nonresidents of the United States. Age-adjusted rates for all years differ from those shown in previous editions of Health, United States. Age-adjusted rates are calculated using the year 2000 standard population starting with Health, United States, 2001.

UNITS: Rate is the number of deaths per 100,000 resident population.

Table 2.19 AIDS (Acquired Immunodeficiency Syndrome) Cases, by Sex and Age, 1985 – 2003

	Black	White	All Races
All years*			
children under 13 years old	5,504	1,613	8,939
persons over 13 years old			
male	253,078	333,873	708,452
female	96,338	33,766	156,837
1985			
children under 13 years old	87	26	131
persons over 13 years old			
male	1,710	4,746	7,504
female	280	143	524
1990			
children under 13 years old	390	157	725
persons over 13 years old			
male	10,239	20,825	36,179
female	2,557	1,228	4,544
1995			
children under 13 years old	483	117	745
persons over 13 years old			
male	20,833	26,028	56,689
female	7,586	3,042	12,978

continued on the next page

Table 2.19 continued

	Black	White	All Races
2000			
children under 13 years old	122	32	189
persons over 13 years old			
male	13,082	11,314	30,135
female	6,489	1,859	9,958
2001			
children under 13 years old	111	30	170
persons over 13 years old			
male	13,764	11,054	30,663
female	6,963	1,993	10,617
2002			
children under 13 years old	99	23	150
persons over 13 years old			
male	14,310	11,221	31,644
female	7,339	1,930	10,951
2003			
children under 13 years old	93	23	153
persons over 13 years old			
male	13,820	11,831	32,781
female	7,373	1,923	11,297

SOURCE: U.S. Department of Health and Human Services, Health United States, 2004, (Centers for Disease Control and Prevention, National Center for Health Statistics) p. 208, table 52 (data from National Center for HIV, STD, and TB Prevention, Division of HIV/AIDS). HE 20 6223: (year)

NOTES: 'All Races' includes other races not shown separately. 'Black' excludes Black Hispanics, 'White' excludes white Hispanics. Data excludes residents of U.S. Territories. Historic data is revised continually on an ongoing basis. *'All years' includes cases prior to 1985. Data for all years have been updated through June 30, 2000, to include temporarily delayed case reports and may differ from previous editions of Health, United States.

UNITS: Number of cases known to the Centers for Disease Control, by year of report.

Table 2.20 Death rates for Human Immunodeficiency Virus (HIV) infection, 1987 – 2002

	Black		White		All Races	
	Male	female	male	female	male	female
1987	26.2	4.6	8.7	0.6	10.4	1.1
1990	46.3	10.1	15.7	1.1	18.5	2.2
1995	89.0	24.4	20.4	2.5	27.3	5.3
1997	40.9	13.7	5.9	1.0	9.6	2.6
1998	33.2	12.0	4.5	0.8	7.6	2.2
1999	36.1	13.1	4.9	1.0	8.2	2.5
2000	35.1	13.2	4.6	1.0	7.9	2.5
2001	33.8	13.4	4.4	0.9	7.5	2.5
2002	33.3	13.4	4.3	0.9	7.4	2.5

SOURCE: U.S. Department of Health and Human Services, Health United States, 2004, (Centers for Disease Control and Prevention, National Center for Health Statistics) pp. 187-188, table 42. HE 20 6223· (year)

NOTES: 'All Races' includes other races not shown separately. Data excludes residents of U.S. Territories. Age-adjusted rates for all years differ from those shown in previous editions of Health, United States. Age-adjusted rates are calculated using the year 2000 standard population starting with Health, United States, 2001.

UNITS: Number of deaths known to the Centers for Disease Control, by year of report.

Table 2.21 AIDS (Acquired Immunodeficiency Syndrome) Cases, by Transmission Category, 1990 – 2001

	Black	White	All Races
All years*			
all transmission categories	296,214	335,375	758,434
men who have sex with men	80,555	226,714	357,583
injecting drug use	104,468	40,591	184,247
men who have sex with men and injecting drug use	16,243	25,427	48,132
hemophilia/coagulation disorder	685	3,939	5,171
heterosexual contact	47,965	17,445	79,769
sex with injecting drug user	16,348	6,675	28,368
transfusion	2,436	5,034	8,698
undetermined	43,862	16,225	74,834
1990			
all transmission categories	12,796	22,062	40,740
men who have sex with men	4,453	16,474	23,658
injecting drug use	5,170	2,054	9,270
men who have sex with men and injecting drug use	941	1,646	2,943
hemophilia/coagulation disorder	34	279	347
heterosexual contact	1,216	650	2,253
sex with injecting drug user	851	349	1,484
transfusion	160	505	770
undetermined	822	454	1,499

continued on the next page

Table 2.21 continued

	Black	White	All Races
2000			
all transmission categories	19,608	13,242	40,230
men who have sex with men	4,067	7,239	13,648
injecting drug use	4,626	1,852	8,099
men who have sex with men and injecting drug use	585	765	1,587
hemophilia/coagulation disorder	14	73	98
heterosexual contact	4,329	1,121	6,562
sex with injecting drug user	910	354	1,490
transfusion	148	95	297
undetermined	5,839	2,097	9,939
2001, January – June			
all transmission categories	9,505	6,168	19,002
men who have sex with men	1,881	3,277	6,241
injecting drug use	1,835	799	3,169
men who have sex with men and injecting drug use	251	316	657
hemophilia/coagulation disorder	8	38	48
heterosexual contact	1,869	477	2,757
sex with injecting drug user	384	142	611
transfusion	46	38	96
undetermined	3,615	1,223	6,034

SOURCE: U.S. Department of Health and Human Services, Health United States, 2002, (Centers for Disease Control and Prevention, National Center for Health Statistics) p. 183, table 55 (data from National Center for HIV, STD, and TB Prevention, Division of HIV/AIDS). HE 20 6223 002

NOTES: 'All Races' includes other races not shown separately. 'Black' excludes Black Hispanics, 'White' excludes White Hispanics. Data excludes cases of residents of U.S. Territories. 'Heterosexual' includes persons who have had heterosexual contact with a person with HIV infection or at risk of HIV infection. * 'All years' includes cases prior to 1985. Data for all years have been updated through June 30, 2001, to include temporarily delayed case reports and may differ from previous editions of Health, United States.

UNITS: Number of cases for persons 13 years of age and over at diagnosis known to the Centers for Disease Control, by year of report.

Table 2.22 Vaccinations of children 19-35 Months of Age for Selected Diseases, 2000 and 2003

	Black	White	All Races
2000			
combined series (4:3:1:3)	71%	79%	76%
DTP (4 doses or more)	76	84	82
Polio (3 doses or more)	87	91	90
Measles-containing	88	92	91
Hib (3 doses or more)	93	95	93
Hepatitis B (3 doses or more)	89	91	90
Varicella	67	66	68
2003			
combined series (4:3:1:3)	75%	84%	81%
DTP (4 doses or more)	80	88	85
Polio (3 doses or more)	89	93	92
Measles-containing	92	93	93
Hib (3 doses or more)	92	95	94
Hepatitis B (3 doses or more)	92	93	92
Varicella	85	84	85

SOURCE: U.S. Department of Health and Human Services, Health United States, 2003; p. 261, table 73; 2004; pp. 250-251, table 72 (Data from the National Immunization Survey, Centers for Disease Control and Prevention, National Center for Health Statistics).

NOTES: 'All Races' includes other races not shown separately. 'Black' excludes Black Hispanics, 'White' excludes White Hispanics. Data excludes cases of residents of U.S. Territories. The 4:3:1:3 combined series consists of 4 doses of diphtheria-tetanus-pertussis (DTP) vaccine, 3 doses of polio vaccine, 1 dose of a measles-containing vaccine, and 3 doses of Haemophilus influenza type b (Hib) vaccine. DTP is the Diphtheria-tetanus-pertussis vaccine. Hib is the Haemophilus influenza type b (Hib) vaccine.

UNITS: Percent of children 19-35 months of age.

Table 2.23 Five Year Relative Cancer Survival Rates for Selected Cancer Sites, 1992 – 2000

	Black		White	
	male	female	male	female
1992 – 2000				
All cancer sites	55.8	51.8	64.8	64.9
oral cavity and pharynx	31.5	-	59.2	-
esophagus	9.5	-	15.4	-
stomach	20.0	-	20.0	-
colon	53.8	52.8	64.2	63.0
rectum	52.7	56.0	62.6	64.9
pancreas	3.4	4.2	4.3	4.6
lung and bronchus	11.3	14.8	13.5	17.5
prostrate gland	94.3	-	99.0	-
urinary bladder	68.4	-	84.6	-
non-Hodgkin's lymphoma	43.2	55.4	55.3	61.7
leukemia	38.7	-	49.2	-
melanoma of skin	-	71.9	-	92.2
breast	-	74.1	-	88.3
cervix uteri	-	62.6	-	73.3
corpus uteri	-	60.8	-	86.3
ovary	-	42.0	-	43.4

SOURCE: U.S. Department of Health and Human Services, Health United States, 2004, (Centers for Disease Control and Prevention, National Center for Health Statistics) p. 212, table 54; (data from National Cancer Institute, National Institutes of Health, Cancer Statistics Branch.) HE 20 6223· (year)

NOTES: 'All Races' includes other races not shown separately. Data are based on the Surveillance, Epidemiology, and End Results program's population-based registries in Atlanta, Detroit, Seattle-Puget Sound, San Francisco-Oakland, Connecticut, Iowa, New Mexico, Utah, and Hawaii. Rates are based on follow-up of patients through 1998.

UNITS: The five year cancer relative survival rate is the ratio of the observed survival rate for the patient group to the expected survival rate for persons in the general population similar to the patient group with respect to age, sex, race, and calendar year of observation. It estimates the chance of surviving cancer. Percent of patients surviving is shown.

Table 2.24 Current Cigarette Smoking by Persons 18 Years Old and Older, by Sex and Age, 2000 and 2002

	Black		White		All Races	
	male	female	male	female	male	female
2000						
18 years old and over, age adjusted	25.7%	20.7%	25.5%	22.0%	25.2%	21.1%
18 years old and over, crude	26.1	20.8	25.8	21.6	25.7	21.0
18-24 years old	20.8	14.2	30.9	28.7	28.5	25.1
25-34 years old	23.3	15.5	29.9	25.1	29.0	22.5
35-44 years old	30.8	30.2	30.6	26.6	30.2	26.2
45-64 years old	32.2	25.6	25.8	21.4	26.4	21.6
65 years old and over	14.2	10.2	9.8	9.1	10.2	9.3
2002						
18 years old and over, age adjusted	26.7%	18.3%	25.0%	21.1%	24.8%	20.1%
18 years old and over, crude	27.0	18.5	25.2	20.7	25.2	20.0
18-24 years old	22.8	17.1	34.5	26.9	32.4	24.6
25-34 years old	28.8	13.9	28.1	24.1	27.5	21.6
35-44 years old	28.3	24.0	29.7	24.5	29.7	23.7
45-64 years old	29.9	22.2	24.4	21.5	24.5	21.1
65 years old and over	19.4	9.4	9.3	8.5	10.1	8.6

SOURCE: U.S. Department of Health and Human Services, Health United States, 2002; p. 196, table 61; 2004; pp. 223-224, table 60 (data from National Health Interview Survey, Centers for Disease Control and Prevention, National Center for Health Statistics). HE 20 6223 (year)

NOTES: 'All Races' includes other races not shown separately.

UNITS: Percent as a percent of total U.S. civilian non-institutionalized population, 100.0%.

Table 2.25 Current Cigarette Smoking by Persons 25 Years Old and Older, by Sex and Education, 2000 and 2002

	Black	White	All Races
2000			
Males	26.5%	24.7%	24.8%
no high school diploma or GED	38.3	38.6	36.4
high school diploma or GED	29.1	32.5	32.1
some college, no bachelor's degree	20.0	23.6	23.3
bachelor's degree or higher	14.7	11.3	11.6
Females	21.6%	21.1%	20.6%
no high school diploma or GED	31.2	28.6	27.3
high school diploma or GED	25.4	27.9	26.7
some college, no bachelor's degree	20.4	21.1	20.4
bachelor's degree or higher	10.8	10.2	10.1
2002			
Males	27.2%	23.5%	23.6%
no high school diploma or GED	37.2	36.2	34.7
high school diploma or GED	31.3	31.2	31.1
some college, no bachelor's degree	25.6	23.4	23.4
bachelor's degree or higher	*10.8	11.1	11.0
Females	18.4	20.3	19.4
no high school diploma or GED	27.1	29.5	27.3
high school diploma or GED	19.5	26.9	25.4
some college, no bachelor's degree	20.7	20.6	20.1
bachelor's degree or higher	*7.7	9.7	9.0

SOURCE: U.S. Department of Health and Human Services, Health United States, 2004, (Centers for Disease Control and Prevention, National Center for Health Statistics) p. 225, table 61 (data from National Health Interview Survey). HE 20 6223· (year)

NOTES: 'All Races' includes other races not shown separately.
* Estimates are considered unreliable.

UNITS: Percent as a percent of total U.S. civilian non-institutionalized population, 100.0%.

Table 2.26 Use of Selected Substances by Persons 12 Years and Older, 2000 and 2003

	Black	White	All Races
2000			
any illicit drug	6.4%	6.4%	6.3%
marijuana	5.2	4.9	4.8
psychotherapeutic drug*	1.2	1.8	1.7
alcohol	33.7	50.7	46.6
binge alcohol	17.7	21.2	20.6
any tobacco	26.7	31.0	29.3
cigarettes	23.3	25.9	24.9
cigars	5.1	5.0	4.8
2003			
any illicit drug	8.7%	8.3%	8.2%
marijuana	6.7	6.4	6.2
psychotherapeutic drug*	1.8	2.8	2.7
alcohol	37.9	54.4	50.1
binge alcohol	19.0	23.6	22.6
any tobacco	41.8	30.0	29.8
cigarettes	36.1	25.9	25.4
cigars	8.3	7.2	5.4

SOURCE: U.S. Department of Health and Human Services, Health United States, 2003; pp. 217-218, table 62; 2004; pp. 228-229, table 63. HE 20 6223 (year)

NOTES: 'All Races' includes other races not shown separately. Both 'Black' and 'White' exclude Hispanic persons. Use of selected substances in the past month by person 12 years of age and over.

Any illicit drug includes marijuana/hashish, cocaine, heroin, hallucinogens, or any psychotherapeutic drug for nonmedical use.

*Psychotherapeutic drug for nonmedical use includes prescription-type pain relievers, tranquilizers, stimulants, or sedatives; does not include over-the-counter drugs.

Binge Alcohol: Five or more drinks on the same occasion at least once in the past month.

UNITS: Percent as a percent of population by selected substance.

Table 2.27 Limitation of Activity, 1998 and 2002

	Black	White	All Races
1998			
Total with any limitation of activity	31.5%	33.6%	31.9%
very difficult or unable to			
walk a quarter of a mile	9.1	7.1	7.0
stand or be one's feet for 2 hours	10.3	8.4	8.2
stoop, bend or kneel	8.8	8.1	7.8
climb up to 10 steps without resting	7.8	5.1	5.2
sit for 2 hours	3.7	2.8	2.9
reach over one's head	3.3	2.5	2.6
use fingers to grasp or handle small objects	1.9	1.6	1.6
lift or carry a heavy object*	6.4	4.3	4.5
push or pull large objects	9.2	7.5	7.4
2002			
Physical activities that are very difficult or cannot be done at all			
any physical difficulty	17.1%	13.6%	14.0%
walk a quarter of a mile	9.6	6.2	6.5
climb up to 10 steps without resting	8.6	4.5	4.9
stand or be one's feet for 2 hours	11.5	8.1	8.5
sit for 2 hours	4.1	3.0	3.1
stoop, bend or kneel	10.1	7.9	8.2
reach over one's head	3.1	2.3	2.4
use fingers to grasp or handle small objects	2.8	1.6	1.7
lift or carry a heavy object*	6.4	3.6	4.0
push or pull large objects	8.8	5.7	6.0

SOURCE: U.S. Department of Health and Human Services, Vital and Health Statistics, Series 10; #207 (1998); pp. 52-54, table 19; #222 (2002); pp. 53-54, table 19 (data from the National Health Interview Survey).

NOTES: 'All Races' includes other races not shown separately. *Heavy object is defined as something as heavy as 10 pounds (such as a full bag of groceries).

UNITS: Percent as a percent of the population of 18 years of age and over.

Table 2.28 Selected Characteristics of Persons With a Work Disability, 2003

	Black	White	All Races
Persons with a work disability by age			
Total	3,515	13,541	18,058
persons 16-24 years old	344	962	1,395
persons 25-34 years old	515	1,516	2,173
persons 35-44 years old	736	2,752	3,708
persons 45-54 years old	1,007	3,739	5,010
persons 55-64 years old	913	4,572	5,772
Work Disabled as a percent of total population, by age			
Total	na	na	na
persons 16-24 years old	6.7	3.4	3.9
persons 25-34 years old	10.4	4.9	5.6
persons 35-44 years old	13.7	7.8	8.5
persons 45-54 years old	22.0	11.3	12.5
persons 55-64 years old	34.8	19.6	21.1
Percent of work disabled:			
Receiving Social Security Income	30.3%	34.7%	33.4%
Receiving Food Stamps	26.1	14.5	17.1
covered by Medicaid	53.5	69.1	65.7
Residing in public housing	14.6	4.9	6.9
Residing in subsidized housing	6.6	3.1	3.9

SOURCE: U.S. Bureau of the Census, Statistical Abstract of the United States, 2004, p. 355, table 539 (data from the Current Population Survey). C 3 134· (year)

NOTES: 'All Races' includes other races not shown separately. Covers the civilian noninstitutional population and members of the armed forces living off post or with members of their families on post. Persons are classified as having a work disability if they (1) have a health problem or disability which prevents them from or which limits the kind or amount of work they can do; (2) have a service disability or ever retired or left a job for health reasons; (3) did not work in survey reference week or previous year because of long-term illness or disability; or, (4) are under age 65 and are covered by Medicare or receive Supplemental Security Income.

UNITS: Persons with a work disability in thousands of persons; work disabled as a percent of total population in percent; percent of the work disabled by characteristic as a percent of the work disabled.

Table 2.29 Work-Loss Days, 1998 and 2002

	Black	White	All Races
1998			
All persons	22,055	147,652	197,304
bed days in the past 12 months	134,759	678,508	928,891
Days per person	6.3	4.6	4.8
All employed persons	15,459	106,575	142,153
work-loss days in the past 12 months	91,673	480,483	647,934
Days per person	6.0	4.6	4.6
2002			
All persons	23,499	166,362	205,825
bed days in the past 12 months	140,457	735,923	947,246
Days per person	6.2	4.5	4.7
All employed persons	16,869	118,761	147,474
work-loss days in the past 12 months	85,599	500,148	638,545
Days per person	5.2	4.3	4.4

SOURCE: U.S. Department of Health and Human Services, Vital and Health Statistics, Series 10; #209 (1998); pp. 46-48, table 17; #222 (2002); pp. 48-49, table 17 (data from the National Health Interview Survey).

NOTES: 'All Races' includes other races not shown separately. Respondents were asked how many times in the last 12 months an injury or illness caused them to miss a day of work or had kept them in bed more than half a day.

UNITS: Number of work-loss days per 100 persons 18 years old and over, currently employed.

Table 2.30 Medical Injury and Poisoning Episodes, 1998 and 2003

	Black	White	All Races
1998			
all persons	32,877	193,384	269,007
all episodes	3,264	27,144	34,020
fall	1,019	8,433	10,523
struck by person or object	417	3,925	4,886
transportation	628	3,213	4,459
over exertion	315	4,046	4,679
cutting / piercing instrument	240	2,305	2,837
other causes	452	3,924	4,983
poisoning	193	1,298	1,654
2003			
all persons	35,337	233,582	286,010
all episodes	1,944	20,975	23,782
fall	631	7,056	8,002
struck by person or object	314	2,546	2,990
transportation	458	3,094	3,775
over exertion	214	3,071	3,369
cutting / piercing instrument	*144	1,729	1,881
other causes	138	2,809	3,043
poisoning	*45	670	722

SOURCE: U.S. Department of Health and Human Services, Vital and Health Statistics, Series 10; #207 (1998); pp. 32-34, table 9 and 10; #220 (2003); pp.25-27, table 8 and 9; #224 (2005); pp.25-27, table 8 and 9 (data from the National Health Interview Survey).

NOTES: 'All Races' includes other races not shown separately. Based on a question in survey that asked all respondents whether they had been poisoned and/or injured seriously enough in the past 3 months to seek medical advice or treatment. '*' represents estimates that do not meet standard of reliability or precision.

UNITS: Number of persons or incidents in thousands.

Table 2.31 Injuries, by Selected Characteristic, 2003

	Black	White	All Races
2003			
all persons	35,337	233,582	286,010
by activity engaged			
- driving	347	2,217	2,744
- working at paid job	393	2,835	3,335
- working around house or yard	*142	3,138	3,376
- attending school	*99	402	510
- sports	182	2,839	3,206
- leisure activities (non-sports)	433	4,634	5,182
by place of occurrence			
- at home inside	380	5,445	5,926
- at home outside	265	4,454	4,949
- at school/childcare center	*158	1,077	1,261
- at hospital	*72	320	392
- on a street or highway	460	3,135	3,832
- at a recreational center	178	2,711	3,039
- at an industrial place	*31	1,010	1,089
- at a service area	175	880	1,082

SOURCE: U.S. Department of Health and Human Services, Vital and Health Statistics, Series 10; #224 (2005); pp. 28-29,table 8, table 11; pp. 32-33, table 11 (data from the National Health Interview Survey).

NOTES: 'All Races' includes other races not shown separately. *Figure does not meet standard of reliability or precision.

UNITS: Number of persons who had a medically attended injury episode in thousands.

Table 2.32 Restricted Activity Days, 1970 – 1996

	total number of days			days per person		
	Black	White	All Races	Black	White	All Races
1970	365	2,526	2,913	16.2	14.4	14.6
1980	580	3,518	4,165	22.7	18.7	19.1
1985	489	2,899	3,453	17.4	14.5	14.8
1988	487	2,969	3,536	16.6	14.6	14.7
1989	511	3,087	6,693	17.1	15.0	15.2
1992	586	3,384	4,096	18.6	16.2	16.3
1994	608	3,375	4,143	18.4	15.7	16.0
1995	558	3,392	4,097	17.0	15.6	15.6
1996	543	3,154	3,825	16.4	14.3	14.5

SOURCE: U.S. Bureau of the Census, Statistical Abstract of the United States, 1988; p. 105, table 166 (data from the National Health Interview Survey). C 3 134 988

U.S. Department of Health and Human Services, Vital and Health Statistics, Series 10, #173; p. 112, table 69 (data from the National Health Interview Survey). HE 20 6209/4 988

U.S. Department of Health and Human Services, Vital and Health Statistics, Series 10, #176; p. 111, table 69 (data from the National Health Interview Survey). HE 20 6209/4 990

U.S. Department of Health and Human Services, Vital and Health Statistics, Series 10, #179; p. 111, table 69 (data from the National Health Interview Survey). HE 20 6209/4.992

U.S. Department of Health and Human Services, Vital and Health Statistics, Series 10, #193; p. 109, table 69 (data from the National Health Interview Survey). HE 20.6209/4 995

U.S. Department of Health and Human Services, Vital and Health Statistics, Series 10, #199; p. 105, table 69 (data from the National Health Interview Survey). HE 20 6209/4 998

U.S. Department of Health and Human Services, Vital and Health Statistics, Series 10, #200; p. 109, table 69 (data from the National Health Interview Survey). HE 20 6209/4 999

NOTES: 'All Races' includes other races not shown separately. A restricted activity day is a day when a person cuts down on his or her usual activities for the whole day because of illness or injury. Restricted activity days include bed disability days, work-loss days, and school loss days.

UNITS: Total number of days in thousands of days; days per person.

Table 2.33 Percentage of Adults Engaging in Leisure-Time Physical Activity, 1997 - 1998, 2000 - 2003

	Black	White	All Races
1997			
no participation in physical activity	38.2%	27.6%	29.5%
participates in regular, sustained activity	16.3	20.3	19.6
participates in regular, vigorous activity	9.3	14.0	12.9
1998			
no participation in physical activity	33.8%	26.7%	28.7%
participates in regular, sustained activity	17.8	21.6	20.8
participates in regular, vigorous activity	12.3	14.0	13.6
2000			
persons who are physically inactive	34.8%	24.2%	27.6%
persons with insufficient activity	43.3	48.3	46.2
persons who meet recommended activity	21.9	27.5	26.2
2003			
persons who are physically inactive	32.7%	20.9%	24.3%
persons not meeting recommended activity	63.7	51.0	54.0
persons who meet recommended activity	36.3	49.0	46.0

SOURCE: U.S. Bureau of the Census, Statistical Abstract of the United States, 1999; p. 157, table 248; 2000; p. 145, table 232; 2002; p. 127, table 191; 2004; p. 129, table 195 (data from National Center for Chronic Disease Prevention and Health Promotion). C 3 134 (year)

NOTES: 'All Races' includes other races not shown separately. 'Regular, sustained activity' is any type or intensity of activity that occurs 5 or more times per week and 30 minutes or more per occasion. 'Regular, vigorous activity' is rhythmic contraction of large muscle groups performed 3 times per week or more for at least 20 minutes per occasion.
'Recommended activity' is physical activity at least 5 times/week x 30 minutes/time or vigorous physical activity for 20 minutes at a time at least 3 times/week.

UNITS: Percent of persons 18 years of age and over.

Table 2.34 Health Care Visits, 2000 and 2002

	Black	White	All Races
2000			
all places	353	380	374
physician offices	239	315	304
hospital outpatient departments	52	28	31
hospital emergency departments	62	37	40
number of health care visits*			
none	17.3%	16.0%	16.6%
1-3 visits	46.7	45.1	45.4
4-9 visits	23.4	25.3	24.7
10 or more visits	12.6	13.7	13.3
2002			
all places	409	393	384
physician offices	283	330	316
hospital outpatient departments	55	27	29
hospital emergency department	71	36	39
number of health care visits*			
none	15.3%	15.6%	15.9%
1-3 visits	45.8	45.1	45.5
4-9 visits	26.0	25.4	25.2
10 or more visits	13.0	13.8	13.4

SOURCE: U.S. Department of Health and Human Services, Health United States, 2002; pp. 217-219, table 72, pp. 240-241, tables 83 (data from the National Health Interview Survey); 2004; pp. 247-249, table 71; pp. 273-274, table 83. HE 20 6223: (year)

NOTES: 'All Places' includes visits to physician offices and hospital outpatient and emergency departments.
*"Health care visits" include ambulatory and home health care visits during a 12-month period.
Number of visits per 100 persons. All visits per person are age-adjusted.

UNITS: Percentage of persons visiting doctor's offices, emergency departments, and home visit within 12 months.

Table 2.35 Dental Visits in the Past Year by Poverty Status, 2000 and 2002

	Black	White	All Races
2000			
Poor			
2-17 years old	67.5%	63%	61.8%
18-64 years old	45.3	52.1	46.7
65 years old and over	17.3	34.4	30.3
Non-Poor			
2-17 years old	73.9%	82.5%	80.1%
18-64 years old	65.4	73.8	72.0
65 years old and over	55.1	68.3	66.7
2002			
Poor			
2-17 years old	63.3%	69.4%	64.4%
18-64 years old	39.8	48.8	44.6
65 years old and over	23.7	38.2	35.0
Non-Poor			
2-17 years old	72.6%	82.7%	79.6%
18-64 years old	61.4	71.1	69.0
65 years old and over	45.4	66.4	64.6

SOURCE: U.S. Department of Health and Human Services, Health United States, 2002, (Centers for Disease Control and Prevention, National Center for Health Statistics); pp. 235-236, table 80 (data from the National Health Interview Survey); 2004; pp. 265-266, table 79. HE 20 6223 (year)

NOTES: 'All Races' includes other races not shown separately. 'Black' excludes Black Hispanics, 'White' excludes white Hispanics. Data excludes residents of U.S. Territories. Poor persons are defined as below the poverty threshold. Non-poor persons have incomes of 200 percent or greater than the poverty threshold.

UNITS: Percent of persons with a dental visit in the past year.

Table 2.36 Short Stay Hospitals: Discharges, Days of Care, Average Length of Stay, 1989 - 2002

	Black	White	All Races
1989			
discharges	112.0	89.5	91.0
days of care	875.9	580.9	607.1
average length of stay	7.8	6.5	6.7
1999			
discharges	123.1	94.9	119.7
days of care	643.7	369.5	555.1
average length of stay	5.2	3.9	4.6
2000			
discharges	122.3	92.6	120.3
days of care	524.7	356.2	559.1
average length of stay	4.3	3.8	4.6
2001			
discharges	130.3	93.2	122.0
days of care	657.2	369.4	554.2
average length of stay	5.0	4.0	4.5
2002			
discharges	121.2	96.4	122.9
days of care	533.8	343.0	541.0
average length of stay	4.4	3.6	4.4

SOURCE: U.S. Department of Health and Human Services, Health United States, 1988; p. 111, table 66; 1991; p. 224, table 81; 2001; (Centers for Disease Control and Prevention, National Center for Health Statistics); 2002; p. 250, table 90 (data from the National Health Interview Survey); 2003; p. 271, table 89; 2004; p. 289, table 92. HE 20 6223 (year)

NOTES: 'All Races' includes other races not shown separately. Data **are** age adjusted.

UNITS: Discharges and days of care in number per 1,000 population; average length of stay, in average number of days.

Table 2.37 Self-Assessment of Health, 1987 - 2002

	Black	White	All Races
Self-assessment of health			
1987			
excellent	29.5%	42.1%	40.3%
very good	24.4	28.2	27.8
good	29.4	21.1	22.4
fair or poor	16.7	8.5	9.5
1990			
excellent	31.1%	42.1%	40.5%
very good	25.3	29.0	28.5
good	28.5	20.8	22.0
fair or poor	15.1	8.1	8.9
1995			
fair or poor	17.2%	9.7%	10.6%
2000			
fair or poor	14.6%	8.2%	9.0%
2001			
fair or poor	15.4%	8.2%	9.2%
2002			
fair or poor	14.1%	8.6%	9.3%

SOURCE: U.S. Department of Health and Human Services, Health United States, 1988, (Centers for Disease Control and Prevention, National Center for Health Statistics) p. 95, table 50; 1991; p. 202, table 61; 1992; p. 101, table 63; 2001; p. 238, table 58; ; 2002; p. 192, table 59; 2003; p. 208, table 57; 2004; p. 217, table 57 (data from National Health Interview Survey). HE 20 6223· (year)

U.S. Department of Health and Human Services, Vital and Health Statistics, Series 10, #173; p. 114, table 70 (data from the National Health Interview Survey). HE 20 6209/4 988

NOTES: 'All Races' includes other races not shown separately. Data **are** age-adjusted. Data starting in 1997 are not strictly comparable with data for earlier years due to the 1997 questionnaire redesign.

UNITS: Percent of the population.

Table 2.38 Nursing Home and Personal Care Home Residency, by Age, 1977, 1985 and 1999

	residents			residency rate		
	Black	White	All Races	Black	White	All Races
1977						
persons of all ages	61	1,060	1,126	30.7	48.9	47.1
persons 65-74 years old	22	188	211	17.6	14.2	14.4
persons 75-84 years old	20	443	465	33.4	67.0	64.0
persons 85 years old and older	19	429	450	133.6	234.2	225.9
1985						
persons of all ages	82	1,227	1,318	35.0	47.7	46.2
persons 65-74 years old	23	188	212	15.4	12.3	12.5
persons 75-84 years old	31	474	509	45.3	59.1	57.7
persons 85 years old and older	29	566	597	141.5	228.7	220.3
1999						
persons 65-74 years old	30	157	195	18.2	10.0	10.8
persons 75-84 years old	59	441	518	66.5	40.5	43.0
persons 85 years old and older	57	682	757	183.1	181.8	182.5

SOURCE: U.S. Department of Health and Human Services, Health United States, 1987; p. 119, table 69; 1999, p. 260, table 97; 2001, p. 306, table 97; 2002, p. 266, table 97; 2003, p. 286, table 96. HE 20 6223· (year)

NOTES: 'All Races' includes other races not shown separately. 1977 data includes domiciliary care homes. A nursing home is an establishment with three or more beds that provides nursing or personal care to the aged, infirm, or chronically ill. A personal care home without nursing has no residents receiving nursing care. These homes provide administration of medications and treatments in accordance with physicians' orders, supervision of self-administered medications or three or more personal services. A domiciliary care home provides supervisory care and one or two personal services.

UNITS: Residents in thousands of persons; residency rate, residents per 1,000 population.

Table 2.39 Health Care Coverage for Persons Under 65 Years of Age, by Type of Coverage, 1984 – 2002

	Black	White	All Races
1984			
Private insurance	59.2%	80.1%	77.1%
Private insurance obtained through workplace	53.3	72.0	69.2
Medicaid or other public assistance	18.9	4.6	6.7
not covered	20.0	13.4	14.3
1995			
Private insurance	54.9%	74.7%	71.6%
Private insurance obtained through workplace	51.1	68.5	65.6
Medicaid or other public assistance	26.0	8.8	11.3
not covered	18.2	15.3	15.9
2000			
Private insurance	56.9%	75.8%	71.7%
Private insurance obtained through workplace	54.1	70.8	67.0
Medicaid or other public assistance	19.4	7.2	9.4
not covered	20.0	15.2	16.8
2001			
Private insurance	57.4%	75.2%	71.5%
Private insurance obtained through workplace	55.1	70.3	67.0
Medicaid or other public assistance	20.4	8.1	10.3
not covered	19.3	14.7	16.2
2002			
Private insurance	56.1%	73.5%	69.7%
Private insurance obtained through workplace	53.3	68.8	65.2
Medicaid or other public assistance	21.5	9.5	11.8
not covered	19.3	15.3	16.6

SOURCE: U.S. Department of Health and Human Services, Health United States, 2004; pp. 345-346, table 129; pp. 348, table 130; pp. 350, table 131. HE 20 6223· (year)

NOTES: 'Total' includes other races not shown separately. Medicaid includes persons receiving AFDC (Aid to Families with Dependent Children) or SSI (Supplemental Security Income), or those with a current Medicaid card. Not covered includes those persons not covered by private insurance, Medicaid, Medicare, and military plans. Data **are** age-adjusted.
The questionnaire changed in 1997 compared with previous years.

UNITS: Percent of the population.

Table 2.40 Health Care Coverage for Persons 65 Years of Age and Over, by Type of Coverage, 1995 – 2002

	Black	White	All Races
1995			
Private insurance	40.3%	78.3%	74.5%
Private insurance obtained through workplace	24.6	40.4	38.9
Medicaid or other public assistance	28.4	7.4	9.6
Medicare fee-for-service only	29.0	13.5	14.8
Medicare HMO	-	-	-
2000			
Private insurance	35.6%	66.9%	63.1%
Private insurance obtained through workplace	25.0	37.2	35.6
Medicaid or other public assistance	19.6	5.6	7.6
Medicare fee-for-service only	29.6	15.5	16.8
Medicare HMO	14.7	15.2	15.2
2001			
Private insurance	37.6%	66.4%	62.7%
Private insurance obtained through workplace	27.9	37.4	36.0
Medicaid or other public assistance	20.0	6.2	8.1
Medicare fee-for-service only	30.5	16.5	17.9
Medicare HMO	11.2	13.0	12.9
2002			
Private insurance	36.4%	64.0%	60.6%
Private insurance obtained through workplace	26.9	35.9	34.7
Medicaid or other public assistance	19.4	6.3	8.0
Medicare fee-for-service only	na	na	na
Medicare HMO	10.8	11.7	11.9

SOURCE: U.S. Department of Health and Human Services, Health United States, 2004, (Centers for Disease Control and Prevention, National Center for Health Statistics) pp. 352-354, table 132 (data from the National Health Interview Survey). HE 20 6223 (year)

NOTES: 'All Races' includes other races not shown separately. Medicaid includes persons receiving AFDC (Aid to Families with Dependent Children) or SSI (Supplemental Security Income), or those with a current Medicaid card. Medicare fee-for-service only includes persons who are not covered by private insurance, Medicaid or a Medicare HMO. Data are age-adjusted.
The questionnaire changed in 1997 compared with previous years.

UNITS: Percent of the population.

Table 2.41 Overweight Children and Adolescents 6-19 Years of Age, According to Sex and Age, 1971 - 2002

	Black		White		All Races	
	male	female	male	female	male	female
1971-74						
6-11 years old	5.3	3.3	4.1	3.7	4.3	3.6
12-19 years old	5.0	10.1	5.5	6.1	6.1	6.2
1976-80						
6-11 years old	6.7	11.1	6.7	5.7	6.6	6.4
12-19 years old	4.8	10.0	4.6	4.7	4.8	5.3
1988-94						
6-11 years old	12.3	16.7	11.3	9.8	11.6	11.0
12-19 years old	10.4	16.3	12.1	9.0	11.3	9.7
1999-2002						
6-11 years old	17.0	22.8	14.0	13.1	16.9	14.7
12-19 years old	18.7	23.6	14.6	12.7	16.7	15.4

SOURCE: U.S. Department of Health and Human Services, Health United States, 2004, (Centers for Disease Control and Prevention, National Center for Health Statistics) p. 245, table 70. HE 20 6223 (year)

NOTES: 'All Races' includes other races not shown separately. Overweight is defined as body mass (BMI) at or above the sex- and age-specific 95th percentile BMI cutoff points from the revised CDC Growth Charts: United States.

UNITS: Percent of the population.

Table 2.42 Healthy Weight, Overweight, and Obesity Among Persons 20 Years of Age and Over, According to Race and Sex, 1960-2002

	Black		White		All Races	
	male	female	male	female	male	female
1960-62						
healthy	53.5%	36.4%	47.6%	55.4%	48.3%	53.2%
overweight	43.9	58.8	50.2	38.9	45.2	41.2
obesity	14.1	26.6	10.4	14.7	13.5	16.1
1971-74						
healthy	48.5	36.5	43.4	56.1	44.1	54.1
overweight	49.3	58.2	54.3	39.1	53.5	41.0
obesity	16.0	28.7	11.7	15.4	12.0	16.7
1976-80						
healthy	49.5	37.2	46.1	55.9	46.8	53.9
overweight	48.5	60.0	52.5	39.4	51.5	41.6
obesity	15.0	29.8	12.1	15.3	12.3	16.8
1988-94						
healthy	41.5	31.2	38.2	48.8	39.4	45.7
overweight	56.7	66.0	60.6	47.4	59.4	50.7
obesity	20.7	36.7	19.9	22.7	19.5	25.0
1999-2002						
healthy	35.9	21.9	29.2	38.7	30.4	35.4
overweight	61.7	76.8	69.9	58.2	68.6	62.0
obesity	27.5	48.8	28.4	31.3	27.5	33.4

SOURCE: U.S. Department of Health and Human Services, Health United States, 2002; (Centers for Disease Control and Prevention, National Center for Health Statistics) pp. 213-214, table 70; 2004; pp.241-243, table 69. HE 20 6223 (year)

NOTES: 'All Races' includes other races not shown separately. Excludes pregnant women. Percents do not sum to 100 because the percent of persons with BMI less than 18.5 is not shown and the percent of persons with obesity is a subset of the percent with overweight.

UNITS: Percent of the population.

Chapter 3: Education

Table 3.01 School Enrollment, by Age, 2000 and 2002

	enrollment			enrollment rate		
	Black	White	All Races	Black	White	All Races
2000						
all persons 3 years and over	11,503	46,660	72,214	34.0%	25.0%	27.5%
persons 3 and 4 years old	725	2,607	4,097	59.9	54.6	52.1
persons 5 and 6 years old	1,219	4,639	7,648	96.3	95.5	95.6
persons 7 to 9 years old	1,975	7,576	12,083	97.5	98.4	98.1
persons 10 and 13 years old	2,700	10,305	16,213	98.4	98.5	98.3
persons 14 and 15 years old	1,260	5,135	7,885	99.6	98.9	98.7
persons 16 and 17 years old	1,106	4,933	7,341	91.4	94.0	92.8
persons 18 and 19 years old	716	3,337	4,926	57.2	63.9	61.2
persons 20 and 21 years old	416	2,388	3,314	36.6	49.2	44.1
persons 22 to 24 years old	393	1,809	2,731	24.2	24.9	24.6
persons 25 to 29 years old	353	1,286	2,030	14.3	11.1	11.4
persons 30 to 34 years old	252	785	1,292	9.6	6.1	6.7
persons 35 to 44 years old	249	1,092	1,632	4.4	3.4	3.7
persons 45 to 54 years old	97	622	810	2.3	2.2	2.2
persons 55 years old and over	41	147	211	0.8	0.3	0.4
2002						
all persons 3 years and over	11,703	46,725	74,046	34.1%	24.9%	27.3%
persons 3 and 4 years old	702	2,652	4,187	57.5	57.8	54.5
persons 5 and 6 years old	1,159	4,330	7,353	95.7	95.3	95.2
persons 7 to 9 years old	1,981	7,144	11,858	98.1	98.1	98.0
persons 10 and 13 years old	2,789	10,302	16,667	98.1	98.6	98.5
persons 14 and 15 years old	1,254	5,104	8,022	98.2	98.6	98.4
persons 16 and 17 years old	1,216	4,985	7,669	93.3	95.3	94.3
persons 18 and 19 years old	681	3,366	5,007	57.7	67.1	63.3
persons 20 and 21 years old	468	2,605	3,696	43.5	53.1	47.8
persons 22 to 24 years old	391	1,966	3,003	23.5	27.3	25.6
persons 25 to 29 years old	329	1,367	2,196	13.6	12.2	12.1
persons 30 to 34 years old	255	821	1,345	9.8	6.3	6.6
persons 35 to 44 years old	283	1,202	1,772	5.2	4.0	4.1
persons 45 to 54 years old	146	684	979	3.2	2.3	2.4
persons 55 years old and over	48	197	292	0.9	0.4	0.5

SOURCE: U.S. Bureau of the Census, Current Population Reports: School Enrollment, 2000; "(Table) 1. Enrollment Status of the Population 3 Years Old and Over, by Age, Sex, Race, Hispanic 1 Origin, Nativity, and Selected Educational Characteristics: October 2000", published 1 June 2001; 2002; Internet release 9 January 2004; Table 1.

NOTES: 'All Races' includes other races not shown separately. 'White' does not include 'Hispanic'.

UNITS: Enrollment in thousands of persons enrolled. All years: rate as a percent of the civilian non-institutionalized population, by age group.

Table 3.02 School Enrollment, by Level and Control of School, 2002

	Black	White	All Races
Total enrolled	9,359	35,353	57,234
public	8,646	29,521	49,665
private	713	5,832	7,569
nursery school	725	2,881	4,471
public	503	1,172	2,246
private	221	1,709	2,225
kindergarten	598	2,065	3,571
public	543	1,585	2,976
private	55	480	594
elementary school	5,541	20,112	33,100
public	5,207	17,486	29,634
private	335	2,626	3,467
high school	2,495	10,295	16,091
public	2,393	9,279	14,808
private	103	1,016	1,283

SOURCE: U.S. Bureau of the Census, Current Population Reports: School Enrollment, 2002; "(Table) 5. Level of Enrollment Below College for People 3 to 24 Years Old, By Control of School, Sex, Metropolitan Status, Race and Hispanic Origin: October 2002"; Internet release 9 January 2004.

NOTES: 'All Races' includes other races not shown separately. 'White' excludes Hispanic.

UNITS: Enrollment in thousands of persons enrolled; civilian non-institutionalized population.

Table 3.03 Preprimary School Enrollment of Children 3 – 5 Years Old, by Selected Characteristic of the Mother, 2002

	Black	White	All Races
All children 3 and 4 years old enrolled in nursery school	600	2,521	3,858
mother employed part-time	66	551	742
mother employed full-time	328	946	1,569
mother unemployed	42	48	132
mother with 0-8 years of school	8	8	76
with mother high school graduate	200	534	920
with mother with bachelor's degree or more	95	1,099	1,394
All children 3 and 4 years old enrolled in kindergarten	101	131	148
mother employed part-time	17	20	23
mother employed full-time	45	47	43
mother unemployed	13	3	13
mother with 0-8 years of school	-	-	2
with mother high school graduate	33	31	37
with mother with bachelor's degree or more	18	66	53

continued on the next page

Table 3.03 continued

	Black	White	All Races
All children 5 years old enrolled in nursery school	110	336	565
mother employed part-time	3	66	86
mother employed full-time	46	140	226
mother unemployed	17	2	29
mother with 0-8 years of school	-	2	16
with mother high school graduate	21	90	132
with mother with bachelor's degree or more	15	120	149
All children 5 years old enrolled in kindergarten	428	1,625	2,752
mother employed part-time	29	375	491
mother employed full-time	204	560	1,025
mother unemployed	48	44	125
mother with 0-8 years of school	4	8	100
with mother high school graduate	122	407	725
with mother with bachelor's degree or more	50	570	697

SOURCE: U.S. Bureau of the Census, Current Population Reports: School Enrollment, 2002; "(Table) 4. Preprimary School Enrollment of People 3 to 6 Years Old, by Control of School, Mother's Labor Force Status and Education, Family Income, Race, and Hispanic Origin: October 2002"; Internet release 9 January 2004.

NOTES: 'All Races' includes other races not shown separately. 'White' excludes Hispanic. Includes children enrolled in public and non-public nursery school and kindergarten programs. Excludes five year olds enrolled in elementary school. 'All children' includes children whose mothers' labor force status is unknown and children with no mother present in the household. '-' represents or rounds to zero.

UNITS: Enrollment in thousands of children enrolled.

Table 3.04 Estimates of the School Age Population, 1975 – 2002

	Black	White	All Races
1975			
Total	7,199	42,950	51,044
male	3,611	21,956	26,022
female	3,588	20,994	25,022
1980			
Total	6,989	39,002	47,232
male	3,520	19,982	24,135
female	3,469	19,020	23,097
1990			
Total	6,923	36,326	45,325
male	3,505	18,671	23,235
female	3,418	17,655	22,090
2000			
Total	8,073	40,522	51,478
male	4,109	20,804	26,390
female	3,964	19,717	25,088
2002			
Total	8,369	40,872	53,285
male	4,247	20,991	27,293
female	4,122	19,881	25,992

SOURCE: U.S. Department of Education, Center for Education Statistics, Digest of Education Statistics, 2004, p. 23 table 16 (data from U.S. Bureau of the Census, *Current Population Reports*, Series P-25). ED 1 113\(year)

NOTES: 'All Races' includes other races not shown separately. Some data have been revised from previously published figures.

UNITS: Estimates of the civilian non-institutionalized population, 5-17 years old as of July 1, in thousands of persons.

Table 3.05 Enrollment in Public Elementary and Secondary Schools, by State, Fall, 2001

	Black	White	All Races
United States	17.2%	60.3%	100.0%
Alabama	36.5%	60.5%	100.0%
Alaska	4.7	60.4	"
Arizona	4.7	51.3	"
Arkansas	23.3	71.1	"
California	8.4	35.0	"
Colorado	5.7	66.8	"
Connecticut	13.8	69.2	"
Delaware	31.1	59.6	"
District of Columbia	84.4	4.6	"
Florida	24.9	52.5	"
Georgia	38.2	53.8	"
Hawaii	2.4	20.3	"
Idaho	0.8	85.4	"
Illinois	21.2	59.0	"
Indiana	11.8	83.0	"
Iowa	4.1	89.6	"
Kansas	8.9	77.8	"
Kentucky	10.3	87.7	"
Louisiana	47.8	48.7	"
Maine	1.4	96.2	"
Maryland	37.2	52.4	"
Massachusetts	8.6	75.7	"
Michigan	20.0	73.4	"
Minnesota	7.0	82.0	"
Mississippi	51.0	47.3	"
Missouri	17.5	79.0	"
Montana	0.6	85.9	"
Nebraska	6.9	81.8	"
Nevada	10.3	54.5	"
New Hampshire	1.2	95.0	"

continued on the next page

Table 3.05 continued

	Black	White	All Races
New Jersey	17.9	59.4	100.0%
New Mexico	2.4	34.3	"
New York	19.9	54.8	"
North Carolina	31.3	60.0	"
North Dakota	1.1	88.7	"
Ohio	16.7	80.1	"
Oklahoma	10.8	63.7	"
Oregon	3.0	79.1	"
Pennsylvania	15.3	77.7	"
Rhode Island	8.1	73.4	"
South Carolina	41.7	54.7	"
South Dakota	1.3	86.2	"
Tennessee	24.8	71.8	"
Texas	14.4	40.9	"
Utah	1.0	84.7	"
Vermont	1.2	95.8	"
Virginia	27.1	62.8	"
Washington	5.4	73.5	"
West Virginia	4.4	94.5	"
Wisconsin	10.2	80.1	"
Wyoming	1.4	87.3	"

SOURCE: U.S. Department of Education, National Center for Education Statistics, Digest of Education Statistics, 2003, p. 58, table 42. ED 1 113\ (year)

NOTES: 'All Races' includes other races not shown separately. Both 'Black' and 'White' exclude persons of Hispanic origin.

UNITS: Enrollment as a percent of total enrollment, 100.0%.

Table 3.06 Public Elementary and Secondary School Teachers, by Selected Characteristic, 1999 - 2000

	Black	White	All Races
Total number of teachers	228,000	2,532,000	3,002,000
Percent of teachers, by highest degree earned			
bachelor's degree	51.5%	51.6%	na
master's degree	42.0	44.2	na
education specialist	4.0	3.0	na
doctorate	1.6	0.6	na
Percent of teachers, by years of full-time teaching experience			
less than 3 years	20.8%	17.1%	na
3-9 years	22.0	23.2	na
10-20 years	24.5	29.1	na
over 20 years	32.7	30.6	na

SOURCE: U.S. Bureau of Census, Statistical Abstract of the United States, 2003; p. 166, table 249. C 3 134 003

NOTES: 'All Races' includes other races not shown separately. Both 'Black' and 'White' exclude persons of Hispanic origin.

UNITS: Percent, as a percent of all public elementary and secondary school teachers, 100.0%.

Table 3.07 Private Elementary and Secondary School Teachers, by Selected Characteristic, 1999 - 2000

	Black	White	All Races
Total number of teachers	17,000	402,000	449,000
Percent of teachers, by highest degree earned			
bachelor's degree	59.1%	58.3%	na
master's degree	18.7	31.8	na
education specialist	2.1	1.7	na
doctorate	0.7	1.8	na
Percent of teachers, by years of full-time teaching experience			
less than 3 years	37.6%	29.1%	na
3-9 years	24.8	25.0	na
10-20 years	22.5	27.4	na
over 20 years	15.1	18.5	na

SOURCE: U.S. Bureau of Census, Statistical Abstract of the United States, 2003; p. 173, table 263. C 3 134 003

NOTES: 'All Races' includes other races not shown separately. Both 'Black' and 'White' exclude persons of Hispanic origin.

UNITS: Percent, as a percent of all private elementary and secondary school teachers, 100.0%.

Table 3.08 Percent of Students At or Above Selected Reading Proficiency Levels by Age, 1999

	Black	White	All Races
9-year-olds			
level 150	82%	97%	93%
level 200	36	73	64
level 250	4	20	16
13-year-olds			
level 150	99%	100%	100%
level 200	85	96	93
level 250	38	69	61
level 300	5	18	15
17-year-olds			
level 150	100%	100%	100%
level 200	95	98	98
level 250	66	87	82
level 300	17	46	40

SOURCE: U.S. Department of Education, National Center for Education Statistics, Digest of Education Statistics, 2002, p. 138, table 114. ED 1.113 002

NOTES: 'All Races' includes other races not shown separately.

UNITS: Reading level shown as scale score on scale: 150=able to follow brief written directions and carry out simple discrete reading tasks; 200=able to understand, combine ideas, and make inferences based on short uncomplicated passages about specific or sequentially related information; 250=able to search for specific information, interrelate ideas, and make generalizations about literature, science, and social studies materials; 300=able to find, understand, summarize, and explain relatively complicated literary and informational material.

Table 3.09 Percent of Students At or Above Selected Science and Math Proficiency Levels by Age, 1999

	Black	White	All Races
Science Proficiency			
9-year-olds			
level 150	88.9%	99.3%	97.0%
level 200	49.2	86.7	77.4
level 250	9.5	39.2	31.4
level 300	0.3	4.1	3.0
13-year-olds			
level 200	79.1%	97.5%	92.7%
level 250	24.9	69.4	57.9
level 300	1.1	14.3	10.9
level 350	0.0	0.2	0.2
17-year-olds			
level 200	91.9%	99.4%	98.0%
level 250	54.8	92.6	85.0
level 300	12.4	57.2	47.4
level 350	0.4	12.4	9.7
Math Proficiency			
9-year-olds			
level 150	96.4%	99.6%	98.9%
level 200	63.3	88.6	82.5
level 250	12.3	37.1	30.9
level 300	0.2	2.2	1.7
13-year-olds			
level 200	96.5%	99.4%	98.7%
level 250	50.8	86.7	78.8
level 300	4.4	29.0	23.2
level 350	0.0	1.2	0.9
17-year-olds			
level 200	99.9%	100.0%	100.0%
level 250	88.6	98.7	96.8
level 300	26.6	69.9	60.7
level 350	1.0	10.4	8.4

SOURCE: U.S. Department of Education, National Center for Education Statistics, Digest of Education Statistics, 2002; p. 146, table 124; p 151, table 129. ED 1 113 002

NOTES: 'All Races' includes other races not shown separately.

UNITS: Math proficiency scale: 150=performs simple addition and subtraction, 200= use basic operations to solve simple problems, 250=uses intermediate level mathematics skills to solve two-step problems, 300=understands measurement and geometry and solves more complex problems, 350= understands and applies more advanced mathematical concepts. Percent, percentage of students taking this level of mathematics course.

Table 3.10 Student Use of Computers at School, 1993 - 2001

	Black	White	All Races
1993			
Total	51.5%	61.6%	59.0%
Elementary and secondary	50.6	63.8	60.1
College	57.0	54.0	54.7
1997			
Total	66.3%	71.1%	68.8%
Elementary and secondary	66.1	73.9	70.4
College	66.8	62.1	62.9
2001			
Total	82.4%	84.1%	82.9%
Elementary and secondary	83.7	85.9	84.2
under 6 years old	56.9	55.6	56.0
6 to 9 years old	83.6	88.2	85.4
10 to 14 years old	89.4	91.8	90.3
15 years old or over	89.0	89.2	88.0
College	77.7	78.6	78.5

SOURCE: U.S. Department of Education, National Center for Education Statistics, Digest of Education Statistics, 2002, p. 499, table 428. ED 1 113\002

NOTES: 'All Races' includes other races and ethnic groups not shown separately. 'White' excludes persons of Hispanic origin.

UNITS: Percent of students using computers, as of October 1993, October 1997 and September 2001.

Table 3.11 Testing: Students Taking the SAT (Scholastic Aptitude Test), and the ACT (American College Testing Program), 1975 – 2003

	Black	White	All Races
1975			
SAT	7.9%	86.0%	100.0%
ACT	7	77	100.0
1980			
SAT	9.1%	82.1%	100.0%
ACT	8	83	100.0
1985			
SAT	7.5%	81.0%	100.0%
ACT	8	82	100.0
1990			
SAT	10.0%	73.0%	100.0%
ACT	9	79	100.0
1995			
SAT	10.7%	69.2%	100.0%
ACT	10	75	100.0
2000			
SAT	11.2%	66.4%	100.0%
ACT	11	76	100.0
2001			
SAT	11.3%	66.0%	100.0%
ACT	11	75	100.0
2002			
SAT	11.4%	65.0%	100.0%
ACT	12	74	100.0
2003			
SAT	12%	63.8%	100.0%
ACT	12	73	100.0

SOURCE: U.S. Bureau of the Census, Statistical Abstract of the United States, 2001; p. 159, tables 251 and 252; 2002; p. 159, tables 244 and 245; 2003; p. 174, table 264 and 265; 2004; p. 162, table 248 and 249 (data from College Entrance Examination Board, and American College Testing Program, *High School Profile Report*). C 3 134.(year)

NOTES: 'All Races' includes other races not shown separately. Beginning 1990, ACT data not comparable with previous years because a new version of the ACT was introduced.

UNITS: Percent, as a percent of all students taking the respective tests, 100.0%.

Table 3.12 SAT (Scholastic Aptitude Test) Scores, 1975 – 2003

	Black	White	All Races
1975-1976			
SAT-Scholastic Aptitude Test			
verbal score	332	451	431
math score	354	493	472
1980-1981			
SAT-Scholastic Aptitude Test			
verbal score	332	442	424
math score	362	483	466
1990-1991			
SAT-Scholastic Aptitude Test			
verbal score	427	518	499
math score	419	513	500
2000-2001			
SAT-Scholastic Aptitude Test			
verbal score	433	529	506
math score	426	531	514
2001-2002			
SAT-Scholastic Aptitude Test			
verbal score	430	527	504
math score	427	533	516
2002-2003			
SAT-Scholastic Aptitude Test			
verbal score	431	529	507
math score	426	534	519

SOURCE: U.S. Department of Education, Center for Education Statistics, Digest of Education Statistics, 1996; p. 127, table 126; 2003; p. 162, table 248. ED 1.113·(year)

NOTES: 'All races' includes other races not shown separately.

UNITS: Average scores, (minimum score, 200; maximum score 800).

Table 3.13 Labor Force Status of 2004 High School Graduates and 2003-2004 High School Dropouts, October 2004

	Black	White	All Races
2004 high school graduates			
total	204	1,211	1,533
employed	152	1,037	1,282
unemployed	51	174	251
not in labor force	213	900	1,219
2003-2004 high school dropouts			
total	50	196	267
employed	11	140	160
unemployed	39	56	106
not in labor force	42	174	229

SOURCE: U.S. Department Labor, Bureau of Labor Statistics, "(Table) 1. Labor force status of 2004 high school graduates and 2003-2004 high school dropouts 16 to 24 years old by school enrollment, sex, race, and Hispanic origin, October 2004"; <http //stats bls gov/news release/hsgec t01 htm>

NOTES: 'High school dropouts' refers to persons who dropped out of school between October 2003 and October 2004.

UNITS: Number of persons in thousands of persons.

Table 3.14 Percent of High School Dropout Among Persons 16 to 24 Years Old, by Sex, 1975 - 2001

	Black			White			All Races		
	male	female	total	male	female	total	male	female	total
1975	23.0%	22.9%	22.9%	11.0%	11.8	11.4%	13.3%	14.5%	13.9%
1980	20.8	17.7	19.1	12.3	10.5	11.4	15.1	13.1	14.1
1985	16.1	14.3	15.2	11.1	9.8	10.4	13.4	11.8	12.6
1990	11.9	14.4	13.2	9.3	8.7	9.0	12.3	11.8	12.1
1995	11.1	12.9	12.1	9.0	8.2	8.6	12.2	11.7	12.0
1999	12.1	13.0	12.6	7.7	6.9	7.3	11.9	10.5	11.2
2000	15.3	11.1	13.1	7.0	6.9	6.9	12.0	9.9	10.9
2001	13.0	9.0	10.9	7.9	6.7	7.3	12.2	9.3	10.7

SOURCE: U.S. Department of Education, Center for Education Statistics, Digest of Education Statistics 2002, p. 132, table 108. ED 1 113.002

NOTES: 'All Races' includes other races not shown separately. 'White' excludes persons of Hispanic origin. 'Dropouts' are 16- to 24-year-olds who are not enrolled in school and who have not completed a high school program regardless of when they left school.

UNITS: All data are based on October counts.

Table 3.15 Attendance Status of College Students 15 Years Old and Over, October 2000 and 2002

	Black	White	All Races
2000			
total enrolled	2,164	10,636	15,314
year enrolled in college			
1st year	592	2,540	3,823
2nd year	525	2,487	3,609
3rd year	410	1,881	2,711
4th year	314	1,615	2,257
5th year	119	708	994
6th year or higher	205	1,406	1,919
2002			
total enrolled	2,278	11,236	16,497
year enrolled in college			
1st year	709	2,862	4,416
2nd year	517	2,258	3,486
3rd year	399	2,227	3,109
4th year	279	1,735	2,414
5th year	177	765	1,157
6th year or higher	198	1,390	1,915

SOURCE: U.S. Bureau of the Census, Current Population Reports: School Enrollment, 2002; "(Table) 10. Attendance Status of College Students 15 Years Old and Over, by Age, Sex, Year and Type of College, Race and Hispanic Origin: October 2002"; Internet release 9 January 2004.

NOTES: 'All Races' includes other races not shown separately. 'White' excludes Hispanic.

UNITS: College enrollment in thousands of students.

Table 3.16 Enrollment in Institutions of Higher Education, by Type of Institution, 1980 – 2001

	Black	White	All Races
1980			
All institutions	1,106.8	9,883.0	12,086.8
4-year institutions	634.3	6,274.5	7,565.4
2-year institutions	472.5	3,558.5	4,521.4
1990			
All institutions	1,247.0	10,722.5	13,818.6
4-year institutions	722.8	6,768.1	8,578.6
2-year institutions	524.3	3,954.3	5,240.1
1995			
All institutions	1,473.7	10,311.2	14,261.8
4-year institutions	852.2	6,517.2	8,769.3
2-year institutions	621.5	3,794.0	5,492.5
2000			
All institutions	1,730.3	10,462.1	15,312.3
4-year institutions	995.4	6,658.0	9,363.9
2-year institutions	734.9	3,804.1	5,948.4
2001			
All institutions	1,850.4	10,774.5	15,928.0
4-year institutions	1,054.7	6,818.8	9,677.4
2-year institutions	795.7	3,955.7	6,250.6

SOURCE: U.S. Department of Education, Center for Education Statistics, Digest of Education Statistics, 2003, p. 2620, table 210. ED 1 113 (year)

NOTES: 'All Races' includes other races not shown separately. Both 'Black' and 'White' exclude persons of Hispanic origin.

UNITS: Enrollment in thousands of students enrolled.

Table 3.17 Enrollment in Institutions of Higher Education, by State, Fall, 2001

	Black	White	All Races
UNITED STATES	1,850,420	10,774,519	15,927,987
Alabama	65,280	157,489	236,146
Alaska	998	20,356	27,756
Arizona	16,027	252,108	366,485
Arkansas	21,008	93,970	122,282
California	178,091	1,096,589	2,380,090
Colorado	11,217	209,578	269,292
Connecticut	15,545	123,921	165,027
Delaware	8,179	35,067	47,104
District of Columbia	27,112	41,516	87,252
Florida	125,505	448,234	735,554
Georgia	110,516	232,837	376,098
Hawaii	1,747	15,948	62,079
Idaho	529	62,741	69,674
Illinois	99,984	493,721	748,444
Indiana	26,176	283,793	338,715
Iowa	6,219	171,005	194,822
Kansas	9,743	154,191	184,943
Kentucky	17,648	187,946	214,839
Louisiana	66,193	144,650	228,871
Maine	930	56,393	61,127
Maryland	74,165	173,274	288,224
Massachusetts	29,731	312,647	425,071
Michigan	69,655	453,825	585,998
Minnesota	13,872	264,997	308,233
Mississippi	48,888	84,419	137,882
Missouri	35,273	269,035	331,580
Montana	330	38,584	44,932
Nebraska	4,133	99,716	113,817
Nevada	7,113	63,118	93,368
New Hampshire	1,247	58,969	65,031

continued on the next page

Table 3.17 continued

	Black	White	Total
New Jersey	46,232	213,982	346,507
New Mexico	3,178	49,811	112,861
New York	144,170	661,498	1,057,794
North Carolina	94,954	298,827	427,784
North Dakota	504	37,982	42,843
Ohio	60,573	466,724	569,223
Oklahoma	15,802	137,130	189,785
Oregon	4,108	157,613	191,378
Pennsylvania	58,298	508,268	630,299
Rhode Island	4,313	61,984	77,235
South Carolina	51,648	130,386	191,590
South Dakota	455	40,378	45,534
Tennessee	46,026	197,569	258,534
Texas	121,090	598,471	1,076,678
Utah	1,122	158,038	177,045
Vermont	550	33,328	36,351
Virginia	71,242	272,762	389,853
Washington	12,987	250,677	325,132
West Virginia	4,327	82,780	91,319
Wisconsin	14,588	275,572	315,850
Wyoming	274	28,413	31,095

SOURCE: U.S. Department of Education, Center for Education Statistics, Digest of Education Statistics, 2003, p. 262, table 212. ED 1 113· (year)

NOTES: 'All Races' includes other races not shown separately. Both 'White' and 'Black' exclude Hispanic.

UNITS: Enrollment in number of students enrolled.

Table 3.18 Enrollment Rates of 18 – 24 Year Olds in Institutions of Higher Education, 1975 – 2001

	Black	White	All Races
Enrollment as a percent of 18-24 year olds			
1975	20.4%	27.4%	26.3%
1980	19.4	27.3	25.7
1990	25.3	35.2	32.1
1991	23.4	36.8	33.3
1992	25.2	37.3	34.4
1993	24.5	36.8	34.0
1994	27.7	38.1	34.6
1995	27.5	37.9	34.3
1996	27.4	39.5	35.5
1997	29.8	40.6	36.2
1998	29.8	40.6	36.5
1999	30.4	39.4	35.6
2000	30.5	38.7	35.5
2001	31.3	39.3	36.2
Enrollment as a percent of high school graduates			
1975	31.5%	32.3%	32.5%
1980	27.6	32.1	31.8
1985	26.0	34.9	33.7
1990	30.4	39.2	37.7
1991	28.2	41.0	39.3
1992	33.9	42.8	42.0
1993	32.8	42.6	41.6
1994	35.6	43.7	42.3
1995	35.4	44.0	42.3
1996	35.9	45.1	43.4
1997	39.6	46.8	44.6
1998	40.0	46.9	45.2
1999	39.2	45.3	43.7
2000	39.3	44.1	43.2
2001	40.1	45.3	44.2

Source: U.S. Department of Education, National Center for Education Statistics, Digest of Education Statistics, 2002, p. 225, table 186. ED 1 113\002

NOTES: 'All Races' includes other races not shown separately. Both 'White' and 'Black' exclude Hispanic.

UNITS: Percent as a percent of 18-24 year olds, and high school graduates as shown, 100.0%.

Table 3.19 Enrollment of Persons 14 – 34 Years Old in Institutions of Higher Education, by Sex, 1975 – 1999

	Enrollment			percent distribution		
	Black	White	All Races	Black	White	All Races
1975						
Total	927	8,141	9,697	9.6%	84.0%	100.0%
men	433	4,566	5,342	4.5	47.1	55.1
women	494	3,576	4,355	5.1	36.9	44.9
1980						
Total	996	8,453	10,181	9.8%	83.0%	100.0%
men	431	4,225	5,193	4.2	41.5	51.0
women	565	4,228	5,244	5.5	41.5	49.0
1985						
Total	1,036	8,781	10,863	9.5%	80.0%	100.0%
men	458	4,361	5,345	4.2	40.1	49.2
women	578	4,420	5,518	5.3	40.7	50.8
1990						
Total	1,167	8,892	11,303	10.3%	78.7%	100.0%
men	508	4,289	na	4.5	38.0	na
women	659	4,594	na	5.8	40.6	na
1993						
Total	1,227	8,592	11,409	10.8%	75.3%	100.0%
men	515	4,168	na	4.5	36.5	na
women	713	4,424	na	6.2	38.8	na
1999						
Total	1,609	8,853	12,506	12.9%	70.8%	100.0%
men	686	4,310	na	5.5	34.5	na
women	924	4,543	na	7.4	36.3	na

SOURCE: U.S. Department of Education, Center for Education Statistics, Digest of Education Statistics, 2000; p. 243, table 213. ED 1.113\000

NOTES: 'All Races' includes other races not shown separately. Both 'White' and 'Black' exclude Hispanic.

UNITS: Enrollment in thousands of students enrolled; percent as a percentage of 14-34 year olds, by sex as shown, 100.0%.

Table 3.20 School Enrollment by Attendance Status, Type and Control of School, Fall, 2002

	Black	White	All Races
Total enrolled			
two-year college			
full time	396	1,499	2,464
part time	302	1,153	1,914
four-year college			
full time	908	5,245	7,271
part time	297	1,185	1,776
graduate college			
full time	163	929	1,406
part time	211	1,226	1,666
Total public			
two-year college			
full time	365	1,304	2,179
part time	290	1,038	1,768
four-year college			
full time	723	3,878	5,497
part time	232	915	1,385
graduate college			
full time	118	569	916
part time	140	785	1,088
Total private			
two-year college			
full time	32	196	285
part time	12	116	146
four-year college			
full time	185	1,366	1,774
part time	65	270	391
graduate college			
full time	45	360	490
part time	72	441	579

SOURCE: U.S. Bureau of the Census, Current Population Reports: School Enrollment, 2002; "(Table) 9. School Enrollment of the Population 15 Years Old and Over, by Attendance Status, Type and Control of School, Age, Sex, Race and Hispanic Origin: October 2002"; Internet release 9 January 2004.

NOTES: 'All Races' includes other races not shown separately. 'White' excludes Hispanic.

UNITS: Enrollment in thousands of students.

Table 3.21 Traditionally Black Institutions of Higher Education: Enrollment, Fall, 2001, and Earned Degrees Conferred, 2001-2002

	Traditionally Black Institutions				
	public		private		
	4 year	2 year	4 year	2 year	Total
Enrollment, Fall 2001					
total	181,346	28,737	79,201	701	289,985
men	70,261	11,724	30,721	168	112,874
women	111,085	17,013	48,480	533	177,111
full-time enrollment					
total	136,040	14,928	71,084	401	222,453
men	55,721	6,173	27,664	130	89,688
women	80,319	8,755	43,420	271	132,765
part-time enrollment					
total	45,306	13,809	8,117	300	67,532
men	14,540	5,551	3,057	38	23,186
women	30,766	8,258	5,060	262	44,346
Earned degrees conferred, 2001-2002					
Associate degrees					
total	1,034	2,231	89	82	3,436
men	279	765	27	28	1,099
women	755	1,466	62	54	2,337
Bachelor's degrees					
total	19,101	na	9,745	na	28,846
men	6,936	na	3,222	na	10,158
women	12,165	na	6,523	na	18,688
Master's degrees					
total	5,477	na	861	na	6,338
men	1,511	na	262	na	1,773
women	3,966	na	599	na	4,565

continued on the next page

Table 3.21 continued

	Traditionally Black Institutions				
	public		private		
	4 year	2 year	4 year	2 year	Total
Earned degrees conferred, 2001-02 – continued					
Doctor's degrees					
total	204	na	160	na	364
men	82	na	83	na	165
women	122	na	77	na	199
First professional degrees					
total	531	na	896	na	1,427
men	226	na	391	na	617
women	305	na	505	na	810

SOURCE: U.S. Department of Education, National Center for Education Statistics, Digest of Education Statistics, 2003, p. 286, table 224. ED 1 113 (year)

NOTES: Historically black colleges and universities are accredited institutions of higher education established prior to 1964 with the principal mission of educating black Americans. There are some exceptions to the founding date. Most institutions are in the southern and border States.

UNITS: Enrollment in number of students; Earned degrees conferred, number.

Table 3.22 Employment Status of Students 15 – 17 Years of Age, Enrolled in School, 1998-99

	Black	White	All Races
Age 15			
students with an employer job	45.0%	67.4%	59.4%
students who worked during the school year	28.2	50.9	44.1
students who worked Summer only	16.8	16.5	15.3
Age 16			
students with an employer job	66.1%	82.5%	77.4%
students who worked during the school year	52.7	73.1	67.0
students who worked Summer only	13.3	9.4	10.4
Age 17			
students with an employer job	79.3%	90.1%	86.6%
students who worked during the school year	66.1	82.6	77.7
students who worked Summer only	13.2	7.5	8.9

SOURCE: U.S. Bureau of Census, Statistical Abstract of the United States, 2002; p. 150, table 227, (data from U.S. Bureau of Labor Statistics, *Employment Experience of Youths: Results from a Longitudinal Survey*, December 20, 2001). C 3 134·002

NOTES: 'All Races' includes other races not shown separately. Excludes freelance work, such as babysitting or mowing lawns.

UNITS: Percent of students 15 to 17 years old at the beginning of the 1998-99 school year.

Table 3.23 Enrollment in Schools of Medicine, Dentistry and Related Fields, 1980-81 and 2001-2002

	Black	White	All Races
1980-81			
allopathic medicine	5.7%	85.0%	100.0%
osteopathic medicine	1.9	94.9	"
podiatry	4.3	91.3	"
dentistry	4.5	88.5	"
optometry	1.3	91.4	"
pharmacy	4.4	88.6	"
veterinary medicine	2.3	95.2	"
registered nursing	na	na	"
2001-2002			
dentistry	4.9%	65.3%	100.0%
allopathic medicine	7.2	63.2	"
osteopathic medicine	3.7	75.9	"
registered nursing	11.8	78.4	"
optometry	3.2	60.3	"
pharmacy	9.5	58.8	"
podiatry	10.7	62.1	"

SOURCE: U.S. Department of Health and Human Services, Health United States, 2004; pp. 314-315, table 107. HE 20 6223· (year)

NOTES: 'All Races' includes other races not shown separately. Both 'White' and 'Black' exclude Hispanic.

UNITS: Enrollment as a percentage of all students enrolled, 100.0%.

Table 3.24 Earned Degrees Conferred, by Type of Degree, 1991 – 2002

	Black	White	All Races
1991-92			
Bachelor's degrees	72,326	936,771	1,129,833
Master's degrees	18,116	268,371	348,682
Doctor's degrees	1,223	25,813	40,090
First Professional degrees	3,560	59,800	72,129
1997-98			
Bachelor's degrees	98,132	900,317	1,183,033
Master's degrees	30,097	307,587	429,296
Doctor's degrees	2,066	28,747	45,925
First Professional degrees	5,483	59,273	78,353
1999-2000			
Bachelor's degrees	107,891	928,013	1,237,875
Master's degrees	35,625	317,999	457,056
Doctor's degrees	2,220	27,520	44,808
First Professional degrees	5,552	59,601	80,057
2000-2001			
Bachelor's degrees	111,307	927,357	1,244,171
Master's degrees	38,265	320,480	468,476
Doctor's degrees	2,207	27,454	44,904
First Professional degrees	5,416	58,598	79,707
2001-2002			
Bachelor's degrees	116,624	958,585	1,291,900
Master's degrees	40,373	327,635	482,118
Doctor's degrees	2,397	26,905	44,160
First Professional degrees	5,811	58,874	80,698

SOURCE: U.S. Department of Education, Center for Education Statistics, 1998 Education Indicators, pp. 228-229, table 2:5-1. ED 1 109 989
U.S. Department of Education, Center for Education Statistics, Digest of Education Statistics, 1994, pp. 276-288, tables 252-264. 2000; p. 313, table 266; p. 316, table 269; p. 319, table 272; p. 322, table 275; 2001; p. 328, table 269; p. 331, table 272; p. 334, table 275; p. 337, table 278; 2002; p. 323, table 265; p. 326, table 268; p. 329, table 271; p. 332, table 274. 2003; p. 335, table 265; p. 338, table 268; p. 341, table 271; p. 344, table 274. ED 1 113\(year)

NOTES: 'All Races' includes other races not shown separately. Both 'White' and 'Black' exclude Hispanic. 'First professional Degrees' include degrees awarded in chiropractic, dentistry, law, medicine, optometry, osteopathy, pharmacy, podiatry, theology, and veterinary medicine.

UNITS: Earned degrees conferred in number of degrees.

Table 3.25 Associate Degrees Conferred, by Major Field of Study, 2001-2002

	Black	White	All Races
All Fields, Total	67,337	417,739	595,133
agriculture and natural resources	51	6,118	6,494
architecture and related programs	23	331	443
area, ethnic and cultural studies	13	240	319
biological sciences/life sciences	141	1,074	1,517
business	16,052	73,361	108,911
communications	240	2,252	2,819
communications technologies	166	1,518	2,021
computer and information sciences	4,328	19,943	30,965
construction trades	172	2,216	2,639
education	1,397	6,318	9,267
engineering	140	1,284	1,724
engineering related technologies	3,743	22,920	32,895
English language and literature/letters	69	625	864
foreign languages and literatures	13	298	517
health professions and related sciences	9,381	60,300	79,888
home economics	1,792	5,652	9,480
law and legal studies	1,174	4,785	6,825
liberal arts/general studies/humanities	19,935	144,594	207,163
library science	3	85	96
mathematics	28	407	685
mechanics and repairers	824	9,012	12,086
multi/interdisciplinary studies	1,379	8,826	13,204
parks, recreation, and fitness studies	88	629	830
philosophy and religion	21	67	134
physical sciences	205	1,707	2,308
precision production trades	673	8,470	10,818
protective services	1,941	12,276	16,689
psychology	147	1,166	1,705
public administration and services	817	1,862	3,323
military technologies and R.O.T.C.	27	32	62
social sciences and history	650	3,326	5,593
theological studies/religious vocations	68	314	414
transportation	61	901	1,159
visual and performing arts	1,521	14,546	20,911

SOURCE: U.S. Department of Education, National Center for Education Statistics, Digest of Education Statistics, 2003; p. 332, table 262. ED 1 113\(year)

NOTES: 'All Races' includes other races not shown separately. Both 'White' and 'Black' exclude Hispanic.

UNITS: Earned Associate degrees conferred in number of degrees.

Table 3.26 Bachelor's Degrees Conferred, by Major Field of Study, 2001-2002

	Black	White	All Races
All Fields, Total	116,624	958,585	1,291,900
agriculture and natural resources	653	20,659	23,353
architecture and related programs	348	6,518	8,808
area, ethnic and cultural studies	881	3,841	6,557
biological sciences/life sciences	4,807	42,831	60,256
business	28,153	199,906	281,330
communications	5,540	49,483	62,791
communications technologies	149	781	1,110
computer and information sciences	5,030	28,311	47,299
construction trades	6	182	202
education	6,976	90,475	106,383
engineering	3,099	41,192	59,481
engineering related technologies	1,387	10,567	14,117
English language and literature/letters	4,049	43,129	53,162
foreign languages and literatures	622	10,885	15,318
health professions and related sciences	8,011	53,533	70,517
home economics	1,659	14,722	18,153
law and legal studies	303	1,359	1,971
liberal arts/general studies/humanities	4,688	27,786	39,333
library science	0	67	74
mathematics	935	9,190	12,395
mechanics and repairers	18	104	164
multi/interdisciplinary studies	2,739	19,866	27,629
parks, recreation, and fitness studies	1,751	16,795	20,554
philosophy and religion	481	7,661	9,306
physical sciences	1,142	13,900	17,851
precision production trades	25	391	468
protective services	4,484	17,262	25,536
psychology	8,107	55,824	76,671
public administration and services	4,036	12,529	19,392
military technologies and R.O.T.C.	0	3	3
social sciences and history	12,530	96,346	132,874
theological studies/religious vocations	411	6,699	7,785
transportation	220	3,339	4,020
visual and performing arts	3,373	52,224	66,773

SOURCE: U.S. Department of Education, National Center for Education Statistics, Digest of Education Statistics, 2003, p. 335, table 265. ED 1.113\(year)

NOTES: 'All Races' includes other races not shown separately. Both 'White' and 'Black' exclude Hispanic.

UNITS: Earned Bachelor's degrees conferred in number of degrees.

Table 3.27 Master's Degrees Conferred, by Major Field of Study, 2001-2002

	Black	White	All Races
All Fields, Total	40,373	327,635	482,118
agriculture and natural resources	122	3,454	4,519
architecture and related programs	164	2,797	4,566
area, ethnic and cultural studies	130	959	1,578
biological sciences/life sciences	303	4,265	6,205
business	10,434	76,435	120,785
communications	532	3,512	5,510
communications technologies	36	312	549
computer and information sciences	745	5,144	16,113
construction trades	1	2	9
education	13,069	107,793	136,579
engineering	794	11,215	26,015
engineering related technologies	75	583	869
English language and literature/letters	349	5,897	7,268
foreign languages and literatures	55	1,598	2,861
health professions and related sciences	3,249	33,012	43,644
home economics	270	1,911	2,616
law and legal studies	176	1,304	4,053
liberal arts/general studies/humanities	214	2,156	2,754
library science	259	4,280	5,113
mathematics	126	1,727	3,487
multi/interdisciplinary studies	250	2,236	3,211
parks, recreation, and fitness studies	210	2,231	2,754
philosophy and religion	60	1,063	1,334
physical sciences	149	3,056	5,034
precision production trades	0	0	2
protective services	482	2,119	2,935
psychology	1,837	10,931	14,888
public administration and services	4,386	16,889	25,448
social sciences and history	1,022	8,660	14,112
theological studies/religious vocations	334	3,570	4,952
transportation	32	604	709
visual and performing arts	508	7,906	11,595

SOURCE: U.S. Department of Education, National Center for Education Statistics, Digest of Education Statistics, 2003, p. 338, table 268. ED 1 113\(year)

NOTES: 'All Races' includes other races not shown separately. Both 'White' and 'Black' exclude Hispanic.

UNITS: Earned Master's degrees conferred in number of degrees.

Table 3.28 Doctor's Degrees Conferred, by Major Field of Study, 2001-2002

	Black	White	All Races
All Fields, Total	2,397	26,905	44,160
agriculture and natural resources	19	562	1,166
architecture and related programs	8	71	183
area, ethnic and cultural studies	33	125	216
biological sciences/life sciences	117	2,691	4,489
business	71	612	1,158
communications	33	243	374
communications technologies	0	6	9
computer and information sciences	22	288	750
education	900	4,938	6,967
engineering	86	1,696	5,195
engineering related technologies	0	5	15
English language and literature/letters	74	1,101	1446
foreign languages and literatures	17	463	843
health professions and related sciences	124	2,461	3,523
home economics	32	227	355
law and legal studies	1	18	79
liberal arts/general studies/humanities	6	94	113
library science	5	25	45
mathematics	16	396	958
multi/interdisciplinary studies	18	259	384
parks, recreation, and fitness studies	5	107	151
philosophy and religion	17	466	606
physical sciences	77	2,054	3,803
protective services	3	43	49
psychology	257	3,454	4,341
public administration and services	75	386	571
social sciences and history	206	2,485	3,902
theological studies/religious vocations	150	862	1,355
visual and performing arts	25	767	1,114

SOURCE: U.S. Department of Education, National Center for Education Statistics, Digest of Education Statistics, 2003, p. 341, table 271. ED 1 113\(year)

NOTES: 'All Races' includes other races not shown separately. Both 'White' and 'Black' exclude Hispanic.

UNITS: Earned Doctor's degrees conferred in number of degrees.

Table 3.29 First Professional Degrees Conferred, by Field of Study, 2001-2002

	Black	White	All Races
All Fields, Total	5,811	58,874	80,698
Dentistry	155	2,630	4,239
Medicine	1,104	10,148	15,237
Optometry	22	800	1,280
Osteopathic medicine	97	1,825	2,416
Pharmacy	570	4,551	7,076
Podiatry	38	332	474
Veterinary medicine	67	2,055	2,289
Chiropractic medicine	116	2,426	3,284
Law	3,002	30,125	38,981
Theological professions	636	3,782	5,195

SOURCE: U.S. Department of Education, National Center for Education Statistics, Digest of Education Statistics, 2003, p. 344, table 274. ED 1 113\(year)

NOTES: 'All Races' includes other races not shown separately. Both 'White' and 'Black' exclude Hispanic.

UNITS: Earned first professional degrees conferred, in number of degrees.

Table 3.30 Educational Attainment: Years of School Completed by Persons 25 Years Old and Older, 2000 and 2003

	Black	White	All Races
2000			
All persons 25 years old and over	20,036	147,067	175,230
percent of the population:			
not a high school graduate	21.5%	15.1%	15.8%
high school graduate	35.2	33.4	33.1
with some college, no degree	20.0	17.4	17.6
with associate's degree	6.8	8.0	7.8
with bachelor's degree	11.4	17.3	17.0
with advanced degree	5.1	8.8	8.6
2003			
All persons 25 years old and over	20,527	153,188	185,183
percent of the population:			
not a high school graduate	20.0%	14.9%	15.4%
high school graduate	35.2	32.2	32.0
with some college, no degree	19.9	17.0	17.2
with associate's degree	7.5	8.3	8.2
with bachelor's degree	12.2	18.2	17.9
with advanced degree	5.1	9.5	9.3

SOURCE: U.S. Bureau of the Census, Statistical Abstract of the United States, 2001; p. 140, table 217; 2004; p. 142, table 214. C 3.134 (year)

NOTES: 'All Races' includes other races not shown separately. Data as of March.

UNITS: Percent as a percent of the population 25 years old and older; number in thousands of persons 25 years old and older.

Table 3.31 Highest Educational Level and Degree Earned, Persons 18 Years Old and Older, 2000 and 2002

	Black	White	All Races
2000			
Total civilian non-institutional population	23,308	148,091	201,762
less than 7 years of elementary school	637	1,690	6,684
7 or 8 years of elementary school	721	4,024	6,249
1 to 3 years of high school	3,303	11,136	18,394
4 years of high school	560	1,428	2,760
high school graduate	8,195	49,806	66,141
some college	5,042	30,037	39,940
Associate degree	1,449	11,675	14,715
Bachelor's degree	2,389	25,797	31,708
Master's degree	828	8,640	10,527
First professional degree	113	2,200	2,613
Doctorate degree	72	1,659	2,032
2002			
Total civilian non-institutional population	23,449	150,443	209,454
less than 7 years of elementary school	666	1,573	7,157
7 or 8 years of elementary school	657	3,880	6,222
1 to 3 years of high school	3,148	11,075	18,644
4 years of high school	661	1,701	3,400
high school graduate	7,965	49,114	66,682
some college	5,113	29,677	40,282
Associate degree	1,709	12,529	16,183
Bachelor's degree	2,488	27,364	34,368
Master's degree	797	9,514	11,574
First professional degree	142	2,249	2,752
Doctorate degree	105	1,767	2,190

SOURCE: U.S. Department of Education, National Center for Education Statistics, Digest of Education Statistics, 2001; p. 18, table 9; 2003; p. 18, table 9 (data from U.S. Bureau of the Census, *Current Population Reports*, unpublished data.) ED 1.113\(year)

NOTES: 'All Races' includes other races not shown separately. Both 'White' and 'Black' exclude Hispanic.

UNITS: Persons in thousands, by highest educational level attained.

Table 3.32 College Completion, Persons 25 Years Old and Older, 1970 – 2003

	Black	White	All Races
1970			
total	4.5%	11.6%	11.0%
men	4.6	15.0	14.1
women	4.4	8.6	8.2
1980			
total	7.9	17.8	17.0
men	7.7	22.1	20.9
women	8.1	14.0	13.6
1990			
total	11.3	22.0	21.3
men	11.9	25.3	24.4
women	10.8	19.0	18.4
2000			
total	16.6	28.1	25.6
men	16.4	30.8	27.8
women	16.8	25.5	23.6
2002			
total	17.0	27.2	26.7
men	16.4	29.1	28.5
women	17.5	25.4	25.1
2003*			
total	17.6	28.2	27.7
men	16.6	30.0	29.4
women	18.5	26.4	26.1

SOURCE: U.S. Bureau of the Census, Current Population Reports: Educational Attainment in the United States: March 1998 (Update); Series P-20, #513, table 1, pp. 1-5; 2000; #536, pp. 1-8, table 1a; 2002; PPL-169, pp. 1-21, table 1a; 2003; #550, table 1a; 2004; table 1a. C3 186/23 (year)

NOTES: 'All Races' includes other races not shown separately. '*' indicates year in which 'White' and 'Black' as shown are equivalent to 'White Alone' and 'Black Alone' that refer to people who reported 'White' and 'Black' respectively and did not report any other race category.

UNITS: Percent as a percent of all persons 25 years old and older completing four or more years of college (1970-1991) or Bachelor's degree or more (1992 and later).

Table 3.33 Undergraduates Receiving Financial Aid: Average Amount Awarded per Student, by Type and Source of Aid, 1995-96 and 1999-2000

	Black	White	All Races
1995-96			
All full-time, full-year enrolled undergraduates	674	4,500	6,306
undergraduates receiving:			
any aid, total	$ 6,945	$ 6,836	$ 6,832
- from federal source	5,262	5,549	5,362
- from non-federal sources	3,739	3,848	3,883
grants, total	$ 3,904	$ 3,762	$ 3,864
- from federal source	2,122	1,894	2,001
- from non-federal sources	3,533	3,541	3,599
loans, total	$ 4,070	$ 4,437	$ 4,345
- from federal source	4,046	4,366	4,288
- from non-federal sources	2,197	2,912	2,747
work-study funds, total	$ 1,370	$ 1,367	$ 1,371
1999-2000			
All full-time, full-year enrolled undergraduates	NA	NA	6,364
undergraduates receiving:			
any aid, total	$ 8,476	$ 8,659	$ 8,474
- from federal source	6,517	6,261	6,158
- from non-federal sources	4,336	5,288	4,996
grants, total	$4,667	$ 5,053	$ 4,949
- from federal source	2,669	2,382	2,524
- from non-federal sources	3,965	4,658	4,425
loans, total	$5,267	$ 5,483	$5,437
- from federal source	4,950	4,781	4,825
- from non-federal sources	4,295	5,106	4,939
work-study funds, total	$ 1,598	$ 1,658	$ 1,672

SOURCE: U.S. Department of Education, Center for Education Statistics, Digest of Education Statistics, 2001, p. 364, table 321; 2002; p. 358, table 316; p. 359, table 317. ED 1 113\(year)

NOTES: 'All Races' includes other races not shown separately.

UNITS: Average 1995-96 award in dollars per student, for students enrolled in Fall, 1995. Number of undergraduates, in thousands.

Chapter 4: Government, Elections & Public Opinion

Table 4.01 Black Elected Public Officials, by Type of Office Held, 1970 – 2001

	Education	Law enforcement	City & county offices	US & state legislatures	Total
1970 (February)	368	213	719	179	1,479
1980 (July)	1,232	491	2,871	326	4,963
1985 (January)	1,531	685	3,689	407	6,312
1990 (January)	1,645	769	4,481	440	7,335
1995 (January)	1,840	987	4,954	604	8,385
1996 (January)	1,922	994	5,023	606	8,545
1997 (January)	1,952	996	5,056	613	8,617
1998 (January)	2,008	998	5,210	614	8,830
1999 (January)	1,927	997	5,354	618	8,896
2000 (January)	1,923	1,037	5,420	621	9,001
2001 (January)	1,928	1,044	5,456	633	9,061

SOURCE: U.S. Bureau of the Census, Statistical Abstract of the United States, 1994; p. 284, table 443; 2001; p. 250, table 399; 2002; p. 252, table 391; 2003; p. 268, table 417 (data from Joint Center for Political Studies, *Black Elected Officials: A National Roster*). C 3 134 9 (year)

NOTES: 'U.S. and state legislatures' includes elected state administrators; 'city & county officials' includes county commissioners and mayors, councilmen, vice-mayors, aldermen, regional officials and others; 'law enforcement' includes judges, magistrates, sheriffs, justices of the peace, and others; 'education' includes members of state education agencies, college boards, school boards, and others.

UNITS: Number of Black elected public officials.

Table 4.02 Members of Congress, 1981 - 2005

	Black	White	All Races
House of Representatives			
97th Congress, 1981	17	415	434
98th Congress, 1983	21	411	"
99th Congress, 1985	20	412	435
100th Congress, 1987	23	408	433
101st Congress, 1989	24	406	435
102nd Congress, 1991	25	407	"
103rd Congress, 1993	38	393	"
104th Congress, 1995	40	391	"
106th Congress, 1999	39	na	"
107th Congress, 2001	39	na	443
108th Congress, 2003	39	na	435
109th Congress, 2005	na	na	435
Senate			
97th Congress, 1981	0	97	100
98th Congress, 1983	0	98	"
99th Congress, 1985	0	98	"
100th Congress, 1987	0	98	"
101st Congress, 1989	0	98	"
102nd Congress, 1991	0	98	"
103rd Congress, 1993	1	97	"
104th Congress, 1995	1	97	"
106th Congress, 1999	0	na	"
107th Congress, 2001	0	na	"
108th Congress, 2003	0	na	"
109th Congress, 2005	1	96	"

SOURCE: U.S. Bureau of the Census, Statistical Abstract of the United States, 2000, p. 283, table 463; 2002; p. 247, table 382; 2003; p. 263, table 408; 2004; p. 250, table 396 (data from Congressional Quarterly, Inc.). C 3 134 (year)
U.S. Senate HTTP://WWW.SENATE.GOV/

NOTES: 'All Races' includes other races not shown separately.

UNITS: Number of members of the House and Senate respectively, as shown.

Table 4.03 Voting Age Population, Registration, and Voting, 1972 - 2002

	Black	White	All Races
Voting age population			
1972	13.5	121.2	136.2
1974	14.2	125.1	141.3
1976	14.9	129.3	146.5
1978	15.6	133.4	151.6
1980	16.4	137.7	157.1
1982	17.6	143.6	165.5
1984	18.4	146.8	170.0
1986	19.0	149.9	173.9
1988	19.7	152.8	178.1
1990	20.4	155.6	182.1
1992	21.0	157.8	185.7
1994	21.8	160.3	190.3
1996	22.5	162.8	193.7
1998	23.3	165.8	198.2
2000	24.1	168.7	202.6
2002	24.4	174.1	210.4
Presidential election years			
percent reporting registration			
1972	65.5%	73.4%	72.3%
1976	58.5	68.3	66.7
1980	60.0	68.4	66.9
1984	66.3	69.6	68.3
1988	64.5	67.9	66.6
1992	63.9	70.1	68.2
1996	63.5	67.7	65.9
2000	67.5	70.4	69.5
percent reporting voting			
1972	52.1%	64.5%	63.0%
1976	48.7	60.9	59.2
1980	50.5	60.9	59.2
1984	55.8	61.4	59.9
1988	51.5	59.1	57.4
1992	54.0	63.6	61.3
1996	50.6	56.0	54.2
2000	56.8	60.5	59.5

continued on the next page

Table 4.03 continued

	Black	White	All Races
Congressional election years			
percent reporting registration			
1974	54.9%	63.5%	62.6%
1978	57.1	63.8	62.6
1982	59.1	65.6	64.1
1986	64.0	65.3	64.3
1990	58.8	63.8	62.2
1994	58.5	64.6	62.5
1998	60.2	63.9	62.1
2002	58.5	63.1	60.9
percent reporting voting			
1974	33.8%	46.3%	44.7%
1978	37.2	47.3	45.9
1982	43.0	49.9	48.5
1986	43.2	47.0	46.0
1990	39.2	46.7	45.0
1994	37.1	47.3	45.0
1998	39.6	43.3	41.9
2002	39.7	44.1	42.3

SOURCE: U.S. Bureau of the Census, Statistical Abstract of the United States, 1989; p. 257, table 432 , 1999; p. 300, table 487 (data from U.S. Bureau of the Census, *Current Population Reports*, Series P-20). C 3 134 9(year)
U.S. Bureau of the Census, Current Population Reports: Voting and Registration in the Election of November, 1988, Series P-20, #440; pp. 48-49, table 8; 1990, Series P-20, #453; pp. 16-17, table 2; 1992, Series P-20, #466; pp. 4-5, table 2; 1994; Table 1, Table VI; 1996, Series P-20, #504; table 23; 2000, Series P-20, #542; p. 5, Table A; 2002, Series P-20, #552; Table 2.

NOTES: 'All Races' includes other races not shown separately.

UNITS: Voting age population in millions of persons; percent reporting registration and percent reporting voting as a percent of the voting age population.

Table 4.04 Voting Age Population, Selected Characteristics, 1990

	Black	White	All Races
Voting age population, 1990			
by age			
total 18 years and over	20,371	155,587	182,118
18-20 years old	1,671	8,722	10,800
21-24 years old	1,854	11,635	14,031
25-34 years old	5,352	35,682	45,652
35-44 years old	4,153	32,281	37,889
45-54 years old	2,669	21,983	25,648
55-64 years old	2,144	18,477	21,223
65-74 years old	1,609	16,180	18,126
75 years and over	919	10,627	11,748
by sex			
male	9,093	74,625	86,621
female	11,277	80,962	95,496
by years of school completed			
elementary			
0-4 years of school	712	2,617	3,669
5-7 years of school	1,038	5,096	6,445
8 years of school	832	6,564	7,617
high school			
1-3 years high school	3,729	16,733	20,956
4 years high school	8,241	61,342	71,492
college			
1-3 years college	3,714	31,481	36,300
4 years college	1,331	18,900	21,350
5 or more years college	774	12,855	14,288

continued on the next page

Table 4.04 continued

	Black	White	All Races
by family income			
under $5,000	1,981	4,503	6,799
$5,000-$9,999	2,395	6,978	9,808
$10,000-$14,999	2,173	11,049	13,759
$15,000-$19,999	1,439	8,677	10,496
$20,000-$24,999	1,284	10,619	12,304
$25,000-$34,999	2,120	20,827	23,627
$35,000-$49,999	1,852	22,698	25,367
$50,000 and over	1,348	30,330	32,818
income not reported	1,547	9,555	11,576

SOURCE: U.S. Bureau of the Census, Current Population Reports: Voting and Registration in the Election of November, 1990, Series P-20, #453, pp. 16-17, table 2; pp. 47-48, table 8; p. 64, table 13. C 3 186/3-2 990

NOTES: 'All Races' includes other races not shown separately.

UNITS: Voting age population in thousands of persons.

Table 4.05 Selected Characteristics of Persons Registered to Vote, 1990

	Black	White	All Races
Persons registered to vote, 1990			
by age			
total 18 years and over	58.8%	63.8%	62.2%
18-20 years old	30.4	37.0	35.4
21-24 years old	49.1	43.1	43.3
25-34 years old	52.1	53.2	52.0
35-44 years old	63.6	67.2	65.5
45-54 years old	67.0	71.3	69.8
55-64 years old	71.4	74.9	73.5
65-74 years old	72.5	79.7	78.3
75 years and over	68.9	74.8	73.7
by sex			
male	56.0%	63.0%	61.2%
female	60.9	64.6	63.1
by years of school completed			
elementary			
0-4 years of school	50.7%	26.4%	29.5%
5-7 years of school	58.2	38.7	41.1
8 years of school	53.2	54.3	53.3
high school			
1-3 years high school	49.5	48.2	47.9
4 years high school	57.1	61.2	60.0
college			
1-3 years college	65.4	70.2	68.7
4 years college	72.2	77.1	74.5
5 or more years college	80.4	83.5	81.5

continued on the next page

Table 4.05 continued

	Black	White	All Races
by households income			
under $5,000	47.5%	53.1%	50.7%
$5,000-$9,999	53.5	47.6	48.3
$10,000-$14,999	58.6	55.4	54.8
$15,000-$19,999	61.4	57.5	56.8
$20,000-$24,999	58.8	59.0	58.0
$25,000-$34,999	62.3	65.0	63.9
$35,000-$49,999	67.9	69.4	68.3
$50,000 and over	74.4	77.8	76.4
income not reported	55.0	59.7	57.6

SOURCE: U.S. Bureau of the Census, Current Population Reports: Voting and Registration in the Election of November, 1990, Series P-20, #453, pp. 16-17, table 2; pp. 47-48, table 8; p. 64, table 13. C 3 186/3-2 990

NOTES: 'All Races' includes other races not shown separately.

UNITS: Person reporting registration to vote as a percent of the voting age population, 100.0%.

Table 4.06 Selected Characteristics of Persons Voting, 1990

	Black	White	All Races
Persons voting, 1990			
by age			
total 18 years and over	39.2%	46.7%	45.0%
18-20 years old	15.0	19.4	18.4
21-24 years old	24.9	21.8	22.0
25-34 years old	32.4	34.9	33.8
35-44 years old	44.7	50.0	48.4
45-54 years old	45.7	54.9	53.2
55-64 years old	54.0	60.4	58.9
65-74 years old	54.6	65.7	64.1
75 years and over	45.4	55.8	54.5
by sex			
male	37.3%	46.4%	44.6%
female	40.6	46.9	45.4
by years of school completed			
elementary			
0-4 years of school	27.4%	14.8%	16.5%
5-7 years of school	37.9	23.7	25.7
8 years of school	33.3	35.7	34.8
high school			
1-3 years high school	30.7	31.3	30.9
4 years high school	36.2	43.6	42.2
college			
1-3 years college	45.8	51.4	50.0
4 years college	58.1	61.6	59.0
5 or more years college	65.9	69.6	67.8

continued on the next page

Table 4.06 continued

	Black	White	All Races
by household income			
under $5,000	26.8%	35.1%	32.2%
$5,000-$9,999	31.9	31.3	30.9
$10,000-$14,999	38.2	38.5	37.7
$15,000-$19,999	39.2	39.9	38.8
$20,000-$24,999	38.2	42.5	41.3
$25,000-$34,999	42.6	47.5	46.4
$35,000-$49,999	51.2	51.8	51.0
$50,000 and over	54.3	60.5	59.2
income not reported	39.1	45.1	43.3

SOURCE: U.S. Bureau of the Census, Current Population Reports: Voting and Registration in the Election of November, 1990, Series P-20, #453, pp. 16-17, table 2; pp. 47-48, table 8; p. 64, table 13. C 3 186/3-2.990

NOTES: 'All Races' includes other races not shown separately.

UNITS: Persons reporting voting as a percent of the voting age population, 100.0%.

Table 4.07 Voting Age Population, Selected Characteristics, 2000

	Black	White	All Races
Voting age population, 2000			
Total, 18 years and over	24,132	168,733	202,609
by sex			
male	10,771	81,720	97,087
Female	13,361	87,014	105,523
by age			
18-24 years old	3,944	21,295	26,712
25-44 years old	10,816	66,378	81,780
45-64 years old	6,585	52,038	61,352
65-74 years old	1,754	15,493	17,819
75 years and over	1,033	13,529	14,945
by educational attainment			
less than 9th grade	1,497	10,626	12,894
9th to 12th grade, no diploma	3,569	15,822	20,108
high school graduate or GED	8,382	55,530	66,339
some college or associate degree	7,041	45,923	55,308
bachelor's degree	2,545	27,382	32,254
advanced degree	1,096	13,450	15,706
by employment status			
in civilian labor force	16,561	115,103	138,378
unemployed	1,137	3,544	4,944

continued on the next page

Table 4.07 continued

	Black	White	All Races
by family income			
less than $5,000	660	1,405	2,230
$5,000-$9,999	1,299	2,732	4,242
$10,000-$14,999	1,534	5,390	7,286
$15,000-$24,999	2,341	11,568	14,600
$25,000-$34,999	2,292	14,578	17,692
$35,000-$49,999	2,419	18,907	22,349
$50,000-$74.999	2,661	24,250	28,144
$75,000 and over	1,907	31,021	35,030
income not reported	2,311	17,518	20,721

SOURCE: U.S. Bureau of the Census, Current Population Reports: Voting and Registration in the Election of November, 2000; published 27 February 2002;
"(Table 2). Reported Voting and Registration, by Race, Hispanic Origin, Sex, and Age, for the United States: November 2000";
<http://www.census.gov/population/socdemo/voting/p20-542/tab02.txt>;
"(Table 6). Reported Voting and Registration, by Race, Hispanic Origin, Sex, and Educational Attainment: November 2000";
<http://www.census.gov/population/socdemo/voting/p20-542/tab06.txt>
"(Table 7). Reported Voting and Registration, by Race, Hispanic Origin, Sex, Employment Status and Class of Worker: November 2000";
<http://www.census.gov/population/socdemo/voting/p20-542/tab07.txt>
"(Table 9). Reported Voting and Registration of Family Members, by Race, Hispanic Origin, and Family Income: November 2000";
<http://www.census.gov/population/socdemo/voting/p20-542/tab09.txt>

NOTES: 'All Races' includes other races not shown separately.

UNITS: Voting age population in thousands of persons.

Table 4.08 Selected Characteristics of Persons Registered to Vote, 2000

	Black	White	All Races
Voting age population, 2000			
Total, 18 years and over	63.6%	65.6%	63.9%
by sex			
Male	59.6	64.0	62.2
Female	66.8	67.2	65.6
by age			
18-24 years old	48.0	46.3	45.4
25-44 years old	62.0	61.2	59.6
45-64 years old	70.9	72.7	71.2
65-74 years old	75.2	77.3	76.2
75 years and over	73.0	77.2	76.1
by educational attainment			
less than 9th grade	54.5	34.8	36.1
9th to 12th grade, no diploma	54.3	44.8	45.9
high school graduate or GED	59.4	61.3	60.1
some college or associate degree	68.8	71.8	70.0
bachelor's degree	75.5	79.6	76.3
advanced degree	77.7	83.1	79.4
by employment status			
in civilian labor force	64.8	65.5	64.0
Unemployed	54.7	44.9	46.1

continued on the next page

Table 4.08 continued

	Black	White	All Races
by family income			
less than $5,000	58.9%	40.7%	44.0
$5,000-$9,999	59.6	45.3	48.8
$10,000-$14,999	62.1	47.5	49.8
$15,000-$24,999	61.9	55.1	54.9
$25,000-$34,999	65.3	61.9	61.0
$35,000-$49,999	66.5	68.8	67.1
$50,000-$74.999	71.4	75.9	73.8
$75,000 and over	79.4	80.7	78.4
income not reported	53.3	55.5	54.2

SOURCE: U.S. Bureau of the Census, Current Population Reports: Voting and Registration in the Election of November, 2000; published 27 February 2002;
"(Table 2). Reported Voting and Registration, by Race, Hispanic Origin, Sex, and Age, for the United States· November 2000";
<http://www.census.gov/population/socdemo/voting/p20-542/tab02.txt>;
"(Table 6). Reported Voting and Registration, by Race, Hispanic Origin, Sex, and Educational Attainment: November 2000";
<http://www.census.gov/population/socdemo/voting/p20-542/tab06.txt>
"(Table 7). Reported Voting and Registration, by Race, Hispanic Origin, Sex, Employment Status and Class of Worker: November 2000";
<http://www.census.gov/population/socdemo/voting/p20-542/tab07.txt>
"(Table 9). Reported Voting and Registration of Family Members, by Race, Hispanic Origin, and Family Income: November 2000";
<http://www.census.gov/population/socdemo/voting/p20-542/tab09.txt>

NOTES: 'All Races' includes other races not shown separately.

UNITS: Persons registered to vote as a percent of the voting age population, 100.0%.

Table 4.09 Selected Characteristics of Persons Voting, 2000

	Black	White	All Races
Voting age population, 2000			
Total, 18 years and over	53.5%	56.4%	54.7%
by sex			
male	49.5	54.9	53.1
female	56.8	57.7	56.2
by age			
18-24 years old	33.9	33.0	32.3
25-44 years old	52.1	51.2	49.8
45-64 years old	62.9	65.6	64.1
65-74 years old	68.1	71.1	69.9
75 years and over	58.8	66.2	64.9
by educational attainment			
less than 9th grade	41.1	25.8	26.8
9th to 12th grade, no diploma	40.5	32.7	33.6
high school graduate or GED	49.1	50.4	49.4
some college or associate degree	59.0	62.0	60.3
bachelor's degree	69.9	73.4	70.3
advanced degree	73.2	79.3	75.5
by employment status			
in civilian labor force	55.2	56.2	54.8
unemployed	41.2	34.6	35.1

continued on the next page

Table 4.09 continued

	Black	White	All Races
by family income			
less than $5,000	35.0%	27.3%	28.2%
$5,000-$9,999	41.3	32.5	34.7
$10,000-$14,999	48.3	35.6	37.7
$15,000-$24,999	50.5	43.3	43.4
$25,000-$34,999	54.7	51.8	51.0
$35,000-$49,999	58.9	58.8	57.5
$50,000-$74.999	63.7	67.1	65.2
$75,000 and over	73.0	73.8	71.5
Income not reported	45.7	49.6	48.2

SOURCE: U.S. Bureau of the Census, Current Population Reports: Voting and Registration in the Election of November, 2000; published 27 February 2002;
"(Table 2). Reported Voting and Registration, by Race, Hispanic Origin, Sex, and Age, for the United States: November 2000";
<http://www.census.gov/population/socdemo/voting/p20-542/tab02.txt>;
"(Table 6). Reported Voting and Registration, by Race, Hispanic Origin, Sex, and Educational Attainment: November 2000";
<http://www.census.gov/population/socdemo/voting/p20-542/tab06.txt>
"(Table 7). Reported Voting and Registration, by Race, Hispanic Origin, Sex, Employment Status and Class of Worker: November 2000";
<http://www.census.gov/population/socdemo/voting/p20-542/tab07.txt>
"(Table 9). Reported Voting and Registration of Family Members, by Race, Hispanic Origin, and Family Income: November 2000";
<http://www.census.gov/population/socdemo/voting/p20-542/tab09.txt>

NOTES: 'All Races' includes other races not shown separately.

UNITS: Persons reporting voting as a percent of the voting age population, 100.0%.

Table 4.10 Voting Age Population, Selected Characteristics, 2002

	Black	White	All Races
Voting age population, 2002			
Total, 18 years and over	24,445	174,099	210,421
by sex			
male	10,811	84,466	100,939
Female	13,634	89,633	109,481
by age			
18-24 years old	3,930	21,728	27,377
25-44 years old	10,478	66,238	82,228
45-64 years old	7,207	56,204	66,924
65-74 years old	1,618	15,653	17,967
75 years and over	1,212	14,276	15,925
by educational attainment			
less than 9th grade	1,310	10,195	12,333
9th to 12th grade, no diploma	3,748	16,161	20,908
high school graduate or GED	8,869	57,210	68,866
some college or associate degree	6,969	47,538	57,343
bachelor's degree	2,538	28,693	34,095
advanced degree	1,012	14,302	16,877
by employment status			
in civilian labor force	16,338	118,094	142,635
unemployed	1,680	5,488	7,735

continued on the next page

Table 4.10 continued

	Black	White	All Races
by family income			
less than $5,000	716	1,280	2,159
$5,000-$9,999	1,128	2,707	4,051
$10,000-$14,999	1,288	4,960	6,696
$15,000-$24,999	2,290	11,696	14,665
$25,000-$34,999	2,378	13,412	16,868
$35,000-$49,999	2,500	18,200	21,945
$50,000-$74.999	2,535	24,932	28,921
$75,000 and over	1,977	35,540	40,309
income not reported	2,760	18,188	22,278

SOURCE: U.S. Bureau of the Census, Current Population Reports: Voting and Registration in the Election of November, 2002; published July 2004; "(Table 2). Reported Voting and Registration, by Race, Hispanic Origin, Sex, and Age, for the United States: November 2002"; "(Table 6). Reported Voting and Registration, by Race, Hispanic Origin, Sex, and Educational Attainment: November 2002"; "(Table 7). Reported Voting and Registration, by Race, Hispanic Origin, Sex, Employment Status and Class of Worker: November 2002"; "(Table 9). Reported Voting and Registration of Family Members, by Race, Hispanic Origin, and Family Income: November 2002".

NOTES: 'All Races' includes other races not shown separately.

UNITS: Voting age population in thousands of persons.

Table 4.11 Selected Characteristics of Persons Registered to Vote, 2002

	Black	White	All Races
Voting age population, 2002			
Total, 18 years and over	58.5%	63.1%	60.9%
by sex			
Male	53.3	61.3	58.9
Female	62.7	64.8	62.8
by age			
18-24 years old	39.6	39.2	38.2
25-44 years old	55.8	57.4	55.4
45-64 years old	66.9	71.3	69.4
65-74 years old	74.0	77.9	76.1
75 years and over	72.8	76.7	75.5
by educational attainment			
less than 9th grade	48.4	31.6	32.4
9th to 12th grade, no diploma	49.6	41.1	41.6
high school graduate or GED	54.5	58.7	57.1
some college or associate degree	63.6	68.8	66.7
bachelor's degree	72.4	76.7	73.3
advanced degree	69.9	81.3	76.6
by employment status			
in civilian labor force	59.5	62.8	60.9
Unemployed	52.6	48.6	48.1

continued on the next page

Table 4.11 continued

	Black	White	All Races
by family income			
less than $5,000	59.5%	39.5%	45.2%
$5,000-$9,999	47.5	40.1	41.5
$10,000-$14,999	56.8	50.3	49.7
$15,000-$24,999	60.0	51.0	51.3
$25,000-$34,999	56.0	58.5	56.2
$35,000-$49,999	61.4	64.1	62.0
$50,000-$74.999	67.8	72.0	69.8
$75,000 and over	73.8	77.8	75.5
income not reported	49.4	54.4	52.0

SOURCE: U.S. Bureau of the Census, Current Population Reports: Voting and Registration in the Election of November, 2002; published July 2004; "(Table 2). Reported Voting and Registration, by Race, Hispanic Origin, Sex, and Age, for the United States: November 2002"; "(Table 6). Reported Voting and Registration, by Race, Hispanic Origin, Sex, and Educational Attainment: November 2002"; "(Table 7). Reported Voting and Registration, by Race, Hispanic Origin, Sex, Employment Status and Class of Worker: November 2002"; "(Table 9). Reported Voting and Registration of Family Members, by Race, Hispanic Origin, and Family Income: November 2002".

NOTES: 'All Races' includes other races not shown separately.

UNITS: Persons registered to vote as a percent of the voting age population, 100.0%.

Table 4.12 Selected Characteristics of Persons Voting, 2002

	Black	White	All Races
Voting age population, 2002			
Total, 18 years and over	39.7%	44.1%	42.3%
by sex			
male	35.3	43.5	41.4
female	43.1	44.6	43.0
by age			
18-24 years old	19.3	17.4	17.2
25-44 years old	36.1	35.3	34.1
45-64 years old	50.0	54.8	53.1
65-74 years old	57.0	65.1	63.1
75 years and over	51.9	60.1	58.6
by educational attainment			
less than 9th grade	28.7	19.0	19.4
9th to 12th grade, no diploma	27.6	23.1	23.3
high school graduate or GED	34.8	38.3	37.1
some college or associate degree	44.7	47.3	45.8
bachelor's degree	58.9	59.1	56.2
advanced degree	58.1	67.7	63.2
by employment status			
in civilian labor force	40.7	42.7	41.3
unemployed	27.1	28.2	27.2

continued on the next page

Table 4.12 continued

	Black	White	All Races
by family income			
less than $5,000	30.0%	19.6%	22.0%
$5,000-$9,999	23.9	19.8	20.7
$10,000-$14,999	34.5	31.1	30.5
$15,000-$24,999	37.5	31.9	32.0
$25,000-$34,999	37.2	40.2	38.3
$35,000-$49,999	42.9	44.2	42.7
$50,000-$74.999	50.6	51.7	50.1
$75,000 and over	58.3	58.3	56.6
income not reported	37.2	40.5	38.6

SOURCE: U.S. Bureau of the Census, Current Population Reports: Voting and Registration in the Election of November, 2002; published July 2004; "(Table 2). Reported Voting and Registration, by Race, Hispanic Origin, Sex, and Age, for the United States: November 2002"; "(Table 6). Reported Voting and Registration, by Race, Hispanic Origin, Sex, and Educational Attainment: November 2002"; "(Table 7). Reported Voting and Registration, by Race, Hispanic Origin, Sex, Employment Status and Class of Worker: November 2002"; "(Table 9). Reported Voting and Registration of Family Members, by Race, Hispanic Origin, and Family Income: November 2002".

NOTES: 'All Races' includes other races not shown separately.

UNITS: Persons reporting voting as a percent of the voting age population, 100.0%.

Chapter 5: Crime, Law Enforcement & Corrections

Table 5.01 Victimization Rates for Personal Crimes, 2001 - 2003

	Black victims	White victims	Victims of All Races
2001			
crimes of violence	31.2	24.5	25.1
rape/sexual assault	1.1	1.0	1.1
robbery	3.6	2.6	2.8
assault	26.4	20.8	21.2
personal theft	0.8*	0.8	0.8
2002			
crimes of violence	27.9	22.8	23.1
rape/sexual assault	2.5	0.8	1.1
robbery	4.1	1.9	2.2
assault	21.3	20.0	19.8
personal theft	0.7*	0.7	0.7
2003			
crimes of violence	29.1	21.5	22.6
rape/sexual assault	0.8*	0.8	0.8
robbery	5.9	1.9	2.5
assault	22.3	18.8	19.3
personal theft	1.7	0.6	0.8

SOURCE: U.S. Department of Justice, Office of Justice Programs, Criminal Victimization 2001; p. 6, table 2; p.3, table 1; 2002; p. 5, table 3; p. 8, table 6; 2003; p.5-7 table 3 and 6. (data from the *National Crime Victimization Survey*).

NOTES: 'Victims of All Races' includes victims of other races not shown separately. Personal crimes include completed and attempted rape, robbery, assault, and larceny, but exclude homicide.
The National Crime Victimization Survey has been redesigned. Comparisons of estimates of crime based on previous survey procedures (before 1993) are not recommended. * Based on 10 or fewer sample cases.

UNITS: Rates per 1,000 persons, 12 years old and over.

Table 5.02 Victimization Rates for Personal Crimes, by Type of Crime, 2002

	Black	White	All Races
All personal crimes	28.6	23.5	23.7
Crimes of violence	27.9	22.8	23.1
completed	9.4	7.4	7.6
attempted/threatened	18.5	15.4	15.5
rape/sexual assault	2.5	0.8	1.1
rape/attempted rape	1.9	0.5	0.7
- rape	0.7*	0.3	0.4
- attempted rape	1.2	0.2	0.3
sexual assault	0.6*	0.3	0.3
robbery	4.1	1.9	2.2
completed/property taken	3.4	1.4	1.7
- with injury	1.5	0.6	0.7
- without injury	1.9	0.8	0.9
attempted to take property	0.7*	0.5	0.5
- with injury	0.2*	0.2	0.2
- without injury	0.5*	0.3	0.4
assault	21.3	20.0	19.8
aggravated	6.7	4.1	4.3
- with injury	1.6	1.4	1.4
- threatened with weapon	5.1	2.7	2.9
simple	14.6	15.9	15.5
- with minor injury	3.2	4.0	3.9
- without injury	11.4	11.9	11.6
purse snatching/pocket picking	0.7*	0.7	0.7

SOURCE: U.S. Department of Justice, Bureau of Justice Statistics, Sourcebook of Criminal Justice Statistics 2002; table 3.8, table 3.9. J 29 9/2 002

NOTES: The National Crime Victimization Survey has been redesigned. Comparisons of estimates of crime based on previous survey procedures (before 1993) are not recommended. * Based on 10 or fewer sample cases.

UNITS: Rates per 1,000 persons, 12 years old and over.

Table 5.03 Victimization Rates for Personal Crimes, by Sex of the Victim, 2002

	Black		White		All Races	
	male	female	male	female	male	female
All personal crimes	29.3	27.9	26.1	20.9	26.1	21.5
Crimes of violence	29.0	27.0	25.4	20.3	25.5	20.8
completed	8.1	10.4	7.2	7.6	7.3	7.8
attempted/threatened	20.9	16.5	18.1	12.7	18.2	13.0
rape/sexual assault	0.7*	4.0	0.2*	1.5	0.3	1.8
robbery	5.7	2.7	2.5	1.4	2.9	1.6
completed/property taken	4.6	2.4	1.8	1.0	2.1	1.2
- with injury	2.0*	1.1*	0.8	0.4	0.9	0.6
- without injury	2.6	1.3*	1.0	0.6	1.2	0.7
attempted to take property	1.2*	0.3*	0.7	0.3	0.8	0.3
- with injury	0.2*	0.1*	0.3*	0.1*	0.3	0.1*
- without injury	0.9*	0.1*	0.4	0.2*	0.5	0.2*
assault	22.5	20.3	22.7	17.4	22.3	17.4
aggravated	7.4	6.0	5.2	3.1	5.2	3.4
- with injury	1.5*	1.7*	1.5	1.2	1.5	1.3
- threatened with weapon	6.0	4.3	3.6	1.8	3.8	2.1
simple	15.1*	14.3	17.5	14.4	17.1	14.0
- with minor injury	2.1	4.2	3.8	4.3	3.6	4.2
- without injury	13.0	10.1	13.7	10.1	13.4	9.9
purse snatching/pocket picking	0.3*	0.9*	0.7	0.7	0.6	0.7

SOURCE: U.S. Department of Justice, Bureau of Justice Statistics, Sourcebook of Criminal Justice Statistics 2002, table 3.5, table 3.13. J 29 9/2 002

NOTES: 'All Races' includes other races not shown separately. *Based on 10 or fewer sample cases.
The National Crime Victimization Survey has been redesigned. Comparisons of estimates of crime based on previous survey procedures (before 1993) are not recommended.

UNITS: Rates per 1,000 persons, 12 years old and over.

Table 5.04 Victimization Rates for Personal Crimes, by Age of the Victim, 2002

	Black	White	All Races
Persons 12-15 years old			
crimes of violence	39.6	47.5	44.4
completed	9.7*	13.6	12.8
attempted	29.8	33.9	31.7
purse snatching/pocket picking	0.0*	1.2*	0.9*
Persons 16-19 years old			
crimes of violence	73.9	55.6	58.2
completed	28.9	19.9	20.7
attempted	45.0	36.7	37.6
purse snatching/pocket picking	0.0*	0.8*	0.6*
Persons 20-24 years old			
crimes of violence	34.5	49.8	47.4
completed	7.3*	18.0	16.4
attempted	27.2	31.8	31.0
purse snatching/pocket picking	0.0*	1.9*	1.6*
Persons 25-34 years old			
crimes of violence	31.9	26.4	26.3
completed	10.6	9.1	9.0
attempted	21.3	17.2	17.3
purse snatching/pocket picking	1.9*	0.3*	0.5*
Persons 35-49 years old			
crimes of violence	19.5	18.3	18.1
completed	6.0	5.5	5.5
attempted	13.6	12.8	12.6
purse snatching/pocket picking	0.8*	0.7	0.7*

continued on the next page

Table 5.04 continued

	Black	White	All Races
Persons 50-64 years old			
crimes of violence	14.4	10.3	10.7
completed	6.5*	3.1	3.5
attempted	7.9	7.2	7.2
purse snatching/pocket picking	0.0*	0.3*	0.3*
Persons 65 years old and over			
crimes of violence	9.2*	2.8	3.4
completed	6.9*	0.7*	1.2
attempted	2.3*	2.1	2.2
purse snatching/pocket picking	0.8*	0.7*	0.6*

SOURCE: U.S. Department of Justice, Bureau of Justice Statistics, Sourcebook of Criminal Justice Statistics 2002, table 3.7, table 3.14. J 29 9/2 002

NOTES: 'All Races' includes other races not shown separately. *Based on 10 or fewer sample cases. The National Crime Victimization Survey has been redesigned. Comparisons of estimates of crime based on previous survey procedures (before 1993) are not recommended.

UNITS: Rates per 1,000 persons.

Table 5.05 Rate of Murder and Nonnegligent Manslaughter Victimization, 1976-2002

	Black	White	All Races
1976	37.3	5.2	8.8
1980	38.9	6.5	10.2
1985	27.7	5.3	7.9
1986	31.5	5.4	8.6
1987	30.8	5.2	8.3
1988	33.6	5.0	8.4
1989	35.2	5.0	8.7
1990	38.1	5.5	9.4
1991	39.6	5.6	9.8
1992	37.5	5.3	9.3
1993	39.0	5.3	9.5
1994	36.7	5.0	9.0
1995	31.9	4.8	8.2
1996	28.6	4.4	7.4
1997	26.6	3.9	6.8
1998	23.0	3.8	6.3
1999	20.6	3.5	5.7
2000	20.5	3.3	5.5
2001	20.4	3.4	5.6
2002	20.8	3.3	5.6

SOURCE: U.S. Department of Justice, Bureau of Justice Statistics, Sourcebook of Criminal Justice Statistics 2002, table 3.126. J 29.9/2 002

NOTES: 'All Races' includes other races not shown separately.

UNITS: Rates per 100,000 persons.

Table 5.06 Race of Suspected Offender in Hate Crimes, 2000 and 2002

	Black	White	All Races
2000			
Bias motivation			
total	1,021	4,111	9,430
race	644	2,449	5,171
ethnicity	159	616	1,164
religion	39	316	1,556
sexual orientation	168	714	1,486
disability	11	12	36
multiple biases*	0	4	17
2002			
Bias motivation			
total	1,082	3,712	8,832
race	639	2,040	4,393
ethnicity	178	647	1,345
religion	46	327	1,576
sexual orientation	210	679	1,464
disability	9	17	47
multiple biases*	0	2	7

SOURCE: U.S. Department of Justice, Bureau of Justice Statistics, Sourcebook of Criminal Justice Statistics, 2001; p. 303, table 3.124; 2002; table 3.116.
J 29 9/2 (year)

NOTES: 'All Races' includes other races not shown separately. *A hate crime in which two or more offense types were committed as a result of two or more bias motivations.

UNITS: Number of incidents.

Table 5.07 Self Protective Measures Used by Victims of Violent Crime, 1999 and 2002

	Black	White	All Races
1999			
Total	100%	100%	100%
Attacked offender with weapon	1.3*	1.0	1.0
Attacked offender without weapon	14.4	9.8	10.4
Threatened offender with weapon	0.5*	1.3	1.2
Threatened offender without weapon	2.6*	2.4	2.5
Resisted or captured offender	21.8	20.0	20.2
Scared or warned offender	8.0	10.1	9.8
Persuaded or appeased offender	11.5	10.7	10.9
Ran away or hid	14.1	15.2	15.0
Got help or gave alarm	9.0	11.8	11.5
Screamed from pain or fear	2.2*	2.3	2.3
Took other measures	14.5	15.4	15.3
2002			
Total	100%	100%	100%
Attacked offender with weapon	2.6*	0.5*	0.8
Attacked offender without weapon	11.4	9.0	9.4
Threatened offender with weapon	1.3*	0.8	0.8
Threatened offender without weapon	3.4*	1.7	1.9
Resisted or captured offender	28.0	23.8	24.5
Scared or warned offender	8.1	9.2	9.3
Persuaded or appeased offender	9.0	11.3	11.0
Ran away or hid	12.6	14.5	14.1
Got help or gave alarm	9.4	12.6	12.0
Screamed from pain or fear	4.3	2.3	2.7
Took other measures	9.9	14.4	13.5

SOURCE: U.S. Department of Justice, Bureau of Justice Statistics, Sourcebook of Criminal Justice Statistics 2001; p. 201, table 3.21; 2002; table 3.22. J 29 9/2·(year)

NOTES: 'All Races' includes other races not shown separately. *Based on 10 or fewer sample cases. The National Crime Victimization Survey has been redesigned. Comparisons of estimates of crime based on previous survey procedures (before 1993) are not recommended.

UNITS: Percent as a percent of all personal crimes, 100.0%.

Table 5.08 Victimization Rates for Property Crimes, 2001 - 2003

	Black households	White households	All households
2001			
Property crimes	179.7	164.1	166.9
household burglary	42.8	26.6	28.7
motor vehicle theft	16.1	8.2	9.2
theft	120.8	130.3	129.0
2002			
Property crimes	173.7	157.6	159.0
household burglary	41.3	26.0	27.7
motor vehicle theft	17.2	7.5	9.0
theft	115.2	124.1	122.3
2003			
Property crimes	na	na	163.2
household burglary	na	na	29.8
motor vehicle theft	na	na	9.0
theft	na	na	124.4

SOURCE: U.S. Department of Justice, Office of Justice Programs, Criminal Victimization 2001; p. 3, table 1; p. 9, table 7; 2002; p. 5, table 3 (data from the *National Crime Victimization Survey*).
U.S. Department of Justice, Bureau of Justice Statistics, Sourcebook of Criminal Justice Statistics 2002, table 3.29. J 29 9/2 002
U.S. Department of Justice, Bureau of Justice Statistics, Sourcebook of Criminal Justice Statistics 2003, table 3.

NOTES: 'All households' includes households of other races not shown separately.
The National Crime Victimization Survey has been redesigned. Comparisons of estimates of crime based on previous survey procedures (before 1993) are not recommended.

UNITS: Rates per 1,000 households.

Table 5.09 Chances of Going to State or Federal Prison, 1997

	Black	White	All Races
For the first time, by age			
20	4.1%	0.4%	1.1%
25	8.4	0.9	2.4
30	11.6	1.4	3.3
35	13.6	1.7	4.0
40	14.9	2.0	4.4
45	15.4	2.1	4.7
50	15.7	2.3	4.9
55	15.8	2.4	5.0
65	16.0	2.5	5.1
Lifetime	16.2	2.5	5.1
At some time during the rest of life, by age			
birth	16.2%	2.5%	5.1%
20	14.1	2.3	4.5
25	9.6	1.7	3.1
30	6.0	1.2	2.1
35	3.6	0.9	1.4
40	2.0	0.6	0.9
45	1.2	0.4	0.6

SOURCE: U.S. Department of Justice, Bureau of Justice Statistics, Lifetime Likelihood of Going to State or Federal Prison, March 1997, pp. 2-3, tables 1, 2
J29 11/8.997

NOTES: Chances of going to State or Federal Prison for the first time are cumulative percents. These estimates were obtained by sequentially applying age-specific first-incarceration rates and mortality rates for each group to a hypothetical population of 100,000 births. Changes of going to State or Federal Prison at some time are for persons not previously incarcerated. These estimates were obtained by subtracting the cumulative percent first incarcerated for each age from the lifetime likelihood of incarceration. 'White' and 'Black' exclude persons of Hispanic origin.

UNITS: Percent of all resident population.

Table 5.10 Victimization Rates for Property Crimes, by Type of Crime, 2002

	Black households	White households	All Races households
All property crimes	173.7	157.6	159.0
Household burglary	41.3	26.0	27.7
completed	31.7	22.6	23.5
- forcible entry	18.6	7.9	9.2
- unlawful entry without force	13.1	14.7	14.3
attempted forcible entry	9.6	3.4	4.2
Theft	115.2	124.1	122.3
completed	111.1	119.9	118.2
- less than $50.	29.2	39.6	37.9
- $50-$249	42.7	40.3	40.4
- $250 or more	28.3	30.0	29.6
- amount not available	10.9	10.0	10.2
attempted	4.1	4.1	4.1
Motor vehicle theft	17.2	7.5	9.0
completed	13.7	6.0	7.1
attempted	3.6	1.6	1.9

SOURCE: U.S. Department of Justice, Bureau of Justice Statistics, Sourcebook of Criminal Justice Statistics 2002, table 3.25. J29 9/2 002

NOTES: 'All households' includes households of other races not shown separately. The National Crime Victimization Survey has been redesigned. Comparisons of estimates of crime based on previous survey procedures (before 1993) are not recommended.

UNITS: Rates per 1,000 households.

Table 5.11 Victimization Rates for Property Crimes, by Locality of Residence, 1999 and 2002

	Black households	White households	All Races households
1999			
All areas	249.9	190.0	198.0
Urban	299.0	247.5	256.3
Suburban	207.1	177.9	181.4
Rural	175.0	157.2	159.8
2002			
All areas	173.7	157.6	159.0
Urban	211.7	220.0	215.3
Suburban	150.4	145.9	145.3
Rural	95.7	120.6	118.3

SOURCE: U.S. Department of Justice, Bureau of Justice Statistics, Sourcebook of Criminal Justice Statistics 2001; p. 198, table 3.15; 2002; table 3.28, table 3.29. J29 9/2 (year)

NOTES: 'All Races' includes other races not shown separately. The National Crime Victimization Survey has been redesigned. Comparisons of estimates of crime based on previous survey procedures (before 1993) are not recommended.

UNITS: Rates per 1,000 households.

Table 5.12 Victimization Rates for Property Crimes: Type of Crime, by Housing Tenure, 1994

	Black households	White households	All households
Owner households			
All property crimes	342.4	264.8	272.2
Household burglary	58.3	43.7	45.5
completed	48.1	37.8	39.1
- forcible entry	26.8	12.2	13.4
- unlawful entry without force	21.3	25.6	25.6
attempted forcible entry	10.2	5.9	6.5
Theft	253.9	208.3	212.2
completed	246.7	199.4	203.4
- less than $50.	80.7	89.9	89.0
- $50. - $249	88.6	63.3	65.7
- $250. or more	55.7	34.5	36.3
- amount not available	21.6	11.6	12.5
attempted	7.3	8.9	8.7
Motor vehicle theft	30.2	12.8	14.5
completed	24.4	8.1	9.7
attempted	5.8	4.7	4.9
Renter households			
All property crimes	340.4	379.6	371.2
Household burglary	80.5	68.5	70.3
completed	64.0	55.3	56.7
- forcible entry	34.8	21.1	23.7
- unlawful entry without force	29.3	34.2	32.9
attempted forcible entry	16.5	13.2	13.6

continued on the next page

Table 5.12 continued

	Black households	White households	All households
Renter households - continued			
Theft	236.1	289.5	278.1
completed	226.5	275.9	265.4
- less than $50.	69.5	107.8	100.3
- $50. - $249.	90.9	103.8	100.3
- $250. or more	50.5	53.1	52.8
- amount not available	15.6	11.3	12.0
attempted	9.6	13.5	12.6
Motor vehicle theft	23.9	21.5	22.8
completed	16.2	14.5	15.2
attempted	7.6	7.0	7.7

SOURCE: U.S. Department of Justice, Bureau of Justice Statistics, Criminal Victimization in the United States, 1994; p. 54, table 56, (data from the *National Crime Victimization Survey*). J 29 9/2·994

NOTES: 'All households' includes households of other races not shown separately.
*Based on 10 or fewer sample cases.
The National Crime Victimization Survey has been redesigned. Comparisons of estimates crime based on previous survey procedures (before 1993) are not recommended.

UNITS: Rates per 1,000 households.

Table 5.13 Lifetime Likelihood of Victimization by Crime, by Type of Crime and Number of Likely Victimizations, 1997

	Black	White	All Races
All violent crimes			
both sexes			
one or more victimizations	87%	82%	83%
one victimization	26	31	30
two victimization	27	26	27
three or more victimizations	34	24	25
male			
one or more victimizations	92	88	89
one victimization	21	25	24
two victimization	26	27	27
three or more victimizations	45	37	38
female			
one or more victimizations	81	71	73
one victimization	31	36	35
two victimization	26	22	23
three or more victimizations	24	13	14
All completed violent crimes			
both sexes			
one or more victimizations	53	41	42
one victimization	35	31	32
two victimization	13	8	9
three or more victimizations	4	2	2

continued on the next page

Table 5.13 continued

	Black	White	All Races
rape (female victimization)			
one or more victimizations	11%	8%	8%
one victimization	10	7	8
two victimization	1	*	*
three or more victimizations	*	*	*
robbery			
one or more victimizations	51	27	30
one victimization	35	23	25
two victimization	12	4	5
three or more victimizations	4	*	1
assault			
one or more victimizations	73	74	74
one victimization	35	35	35
two victimization	25	24	24
three or more victimizations	12	16	15
Personal theft			
both sexes			
one or more victimizations	99	99	99
one victimization	5	9	4
two victimization	12	9	8
three or more victimizations	81	87	87
male			
one or more victimizations	99	99	99
one victimization	5	3	3
two victimization	10	8	8
three or more victimizations	84	88	88
female			
one or more victimizations	98	99	99
one victimization	7	4	4
two victimization	15	10	10
three or more victimizations	76	86	84

SOURCE: U.S. Department of Justice, Bureau of Justice Statistics, Technical Report: Lifetime Likelihood of Victimization, March 1997; p. 2, table 1, (data from the *National Crime Survey*). NCJ 160092

NOTES: 'All Races' includes other races not shown separately.

UNITS: Percent of persons who will be victimized by crime, starting at 12 years of age. *less than 0.5%.

Table 5.14 Death Rates for Firearm-Related Injuries, 2000 and 2002

	Black		White		All Races
	male	female	male	female	both sexes
2000					
All ages	34.2	3.9	15.9	2.7	10.2
1-14 years	36.1	na	1.0	na	0.7
15-24 years	1.8	7.6	19.6	2.8	16.8
25-44 years	89.3	6.5	18.0	3.9	13.1
45-64 years	18.4	3.1	17.4	3.5	10.0
65 years and over	13.8	1.3	28.2	2.4	12.2
2002					
All ages	36.0	4.1	16.2	2.7	10.4
1-14 years	1.8	na	0.8	na	0.7
15-24 years	87.1	8.1	19.4	2.6	16.7
25-44 years	60.6	6.7	18.5	3.8	13.7
45-64 years	18.6	3.0	18.7	3.6	10.6
65 years and over	14.2	1.2	28.9	2.2	12.4

SOURCE: U.S. Department of Health and Human Services, Health United States, 2004; pp. 200-202, table 47 (Centers for Disease Control and Prevention, National Center for Health Statistics). HE 20 6223 (year)

NOTES: 'All Races' includes other races not shown separately.

UNITS: Death rate per 100,000 population.

Table 5.15 Murder Victims, 2003

	Black	White	All Races
All murders and nonnegligent homicides, 2003	6,887	6,913	14,408
by age of the victim			
under 1 year old	73	139	225
1-4 years old	131	165	307
5-8 years old	34	44	82
9-12 years old	34	33	69
13-16 years old	202	150	369
17-19 years old	689	549	1,283
20-24 years old	1,585	1,165	2,855
25-29 years old	1,234	839	2,148
30-34 years old	842	692	1,594
35-39 years old	605	636	1,286
40-44 years old	484	589	1,114
45-49 years old	362	552	951
50-54 years old	226	382	630
55-59 years old	113	236	365
60-64 years old	57	148	226
65-69 years old	32	122	164
70-74 years old	42	105	153
75 years old and older	61	247	323
age unknown	81	120	264

SOURCE: U.S. Federal Bureau of Investigation, Crime in the United States 2004; table 2.4 (data from the Uniform Crime Reporting program).
J 1 14/7 (year)

NOTES: 'All Races' includes other races not shown separately. *Data covers only those murders and nonnegligent homicides in which there was a single offender and single victim.

UNITS: Number of murders and nonnegligent homicides known to police.

Table 5.16 Law Enforcement Officers Killed, 1978 - 2002

	Black	White	All Races	
1978	9%	91%	100%	(93)
1979	9	88	"	(106)
1980	13	86	"	(104)
1981	14	85	"	(91)
1982	15	84	"	(92)
1983	13	84	"	(80)
1984	14	85	"	(72)
1985	10	88	"	(78)
1986	11	89	"	(66)
1987	10	90	"	(73)
1988	9	91	"	(78)
1989	11	89	"	(66)
1990	18	80	"	(65)
1991	13	87	"	(71)
1992	16	82	"	(62)
1993	14	86	"	(70)
1994	14	84	"	(76)
1995	12	84	"	(74)
1996	15	80	"	(55)
1997	17	80	"	(65)
1998	11	87	"	(61)
1999	7	88	"	(42)
2000	22	76	"	(51)
2001	11	87	"	(70)*
2002	7	91	"	(56)

SOURCE: U.S. Department of Justice, Bureau of Justice Statistics, Sourcebook of Criminal Justice Statistics, 2000; p. 312, table 3.174; 2001; p. 330, table 3.168; 2002; table 3.161, table 3.162 (data from Federal Bureau of Investigation, *Law Enforcement Officers Killed and Assaulted, {annual}*). J 29 9/6·(year)

NOTES: 'All Races' includes other races not shown separately. Data have been revised since last publication. (xx) where xx denotes the total. '*' does not include the deaths of 72 law enforcement officers (12 Black and 59 White) resulting from the events of Sept. 11, 2001.

UNITS: Percent distribution of law enforcement officers killed as a percent of total, 100.0% (total number of law enforcement officers killed shown in parenthesis).

Table 5.17 Arrests, by Offense Charged, 1985

	number of arrests			percent distribution		
	Black	White	All Races	Black	White	All Races
All arrests	2,721	7,338	10,239	26.6%	71.7%	100.0%
Arrests for crime index crimes	713.3	1,365.6	2,118.5	33.7	64.5	"
arrests for violent crimes	202.1	221.3	429.3	47.1	51.5	"
arrests for property crimes	511.2	1,144.3	1,689.2	30.3	67.7	"
arrests for violent crimes:						
murder and nonnegligent homicide	7.6	7.8	15.6	48.4	50.1	"
forcible rape	14.7	16.5	31.6	46.5	52.2	"
robbery	73.9	44.8	119.9	61.7	37.4	"
aggravated assault	105.9	152.2	262.2	40.4	58.0	"
arrests for property crimes:						
burglary	110.1	265.1	380.6	28.9	69.7	"
larceny-theft	360.1	790.9	1,177.0	30.6	67.2	"
motor vehicle theft	37.2	75.6	114.9	32.4	65.8	"
arson	3.8	12.6	16.7	22.8	75.7	"

SOURCE: U.S. Department of Justice, Bureau of Justice Statistics, Sourcebook of Criminal Justice Statistics, 1986; p. 300, table 4.8, (data from the Uniform Crime Reporting program). J 29 9/6 986

NOTES: 'All Races' includes other races not shown separately. Crime index crimes are made up of the four violent crimes (murder and nonnegligent homicide, rape, robbery, and aggravated assault), and four property crimes (burglary, larceny-theft, motor vehicle theft, and arson) which are tracked by the FBI.

UNITS: Arrests in thousands of arrests; percent distribution as a percent of total, 100.0%

Table 5.18 Arrests, by Offense Charged, 2003

	number of arrests			percent distribution		
	Black	White	All Races	Black	White	All Races
All arrests	2,570,770	6,723,093	9,529,469	27.0%	70.6%	100.0%
Arrests for violent crimes	155,199	252,366	416,850	37.2	60.5	"
Arrests for property crimes	330,225	773,757	1,133,766	29.1	68.2	"
arrests for violent crimes:						
murder and nonnegligent manslaughter	4,395	4,454	9,063	48.5	49.1	"
forcible rape	6,114	11,766	18,355	33.3	64.1	"
robbery	40,993	33,070	75,387	54.4	43.9	"
aggravated assault	103,697	203,076	314,045	33.0	64.7	"
arrests for property crimes:						
burglary	56,050	143,889	202,035	27.5	70.5	"
larceny-theft	233,806	572,515	821,542	28.8	68.5	"
motor vehicle theft	38,012	64,625	105,902	35.9	61.3	"
arson	2,357	9,067	11,287	20.9	77.5	"

SOURCE: U.S. Federal Bureau of Investigation, Crime in the United States 2003, p. 288, table 43 (data from the Uniform Crime Reporting program). J1 14/7: (year)

NOTES: 'All Races' includes other races not shown separately. Crime index crimes are made up of the four violent crimes (murder and nonnegligent manslaughter, rape, robbery, and aggravated assault), and four property crimes (burglary, larceny-theft, motor vehicle theft, and arson) which are tracked by the FBI.

UNITS: Number of arrests; percent distribution as a percent of total, 100.0%

Table 5.19 Arrests, by Offense Charged, Persons Under 18 Years of Age, 1985

	number of arrests			percent distribution		
	Black	White	All Races	Black	White	All Races
All arrests	407.8	1,317.8	1,758.8	23.2%	74.9%	100.0%
Arrests for crime index crimes	187.1	452.4	653.4	28.6	69.2	"
arrests for violent crimes	37.8	33.5	72.3	52.4	46.3	"
arrests for property crimes	149.2	418.9	581.1	25.7	72.1	"
arrests for violent crimes:						
murder and nonnegligent homicide	0.6	0.6	1.3	50.7	48.2	"
forcible rape	2.4	2.3	4.8	50.6	48.3	"
robbery	20.1	9.6	30.0	66.8	32.1	"
aggravated assault	14.7	20.9	36.2	40.7	57.8	"
arrests for property crimes:						
burglary	32.6	109.9	144.8	25.5	75.9	"
larceny-theft	103.1	273.1	385.8	27.7	07.8	"
motor vehicle theft	12.6	30.1	43.6	28.9	69.1	"
arson	0.9	5.8	6.9	13.6	84.7	"

SOURCE: U.S. Department of Justice, Bureau of Justice Statistics, Sourcebook of Criminal Justice Statistics, 1986; p. 301, table 4.8, (data from the Uniform Crime Reporting program). J 29 9/6 986

NOTES: 'All Races' includes other races not shown separately. Crime index crimes are made up of the four violent crimes (murder and nonnegligent homicide, rape, robbery, and aggravated assault), and four property crimes (burglary, larceny-theft, motor vehicle theft, and arson) which are tracked by the FBI.

UNITS: Arrests in thousands of arrests; percent distribution as a percent of total, 100.0%

Table 5.20 Arrests, by Offense Charged, Persons Under 18 Years of Age, 2003

	number of arrests			percent distribution		
	Black	White	All Races	Black	White	All Races
All arrests	413,236	1,098,012	1,555,801	26.6%	70.6%	100.0%
arrests for violent crimes	29,012	34,012	64,483	45.0	52.7	"
arrests for property crimes	90,682	225,612	327,052	27.7	69.0	"
arrests for violent crimes:						
murder and nonnegligent manslaughter	375	381	779	48.1	48.9	"
forcible rape	988	1,895	2,958	33.4	64.1	"
robbery	11,208	6,278	17,849	62.8	35.2	"
aggravated assault	16,441	25,458	42,897	38.3	59.3	"
arrests for property crimes:						
burglary	15,581	42,586	59,657	26.1	71.4	"
larceny-theft	61,715	161,082	230,876	26.7	69.8	"
motor vehicle theft	12,417	17,281	30,785	40.3	56.1	"
arson	969	4,663	5,734	16.9	81.3	"

SOURCE: U.S. Federal Bureau of Investigation, Crime in the United States 2003; p. 289, table 43 (data from the Uniform Crime Reporting program). J1 14/7· (yea)

NOTES: 'All Races' includes other races not shown separately. Crime index crimes are made up of the four violent crimes (murder and nonnegligent manslaughter, rape, robbery, and aggravated assault), and four property crimes (burglary, larceny-theft, motor vehicle theft, and arson) which are tracked by the FBI.

UNITS: Number of arrests; percent distribution as a percent of total, 100.0%

Table 5.21 Arrests in Cities, by Offense Charged, 1985

	number of arrests			percent distribution		
	Black	White	All Races	Black	White	All Races
All arrests	2,325.6	5,443.9	7,916.9	29.4%	68.8%	100.0%
Arrests for crime index crimes	614.5	1,067.6	1,716.6	35.8	62.2	"
arrests for violent crimes	171.7	158.8	335.3	51.2	474.	"
arrests for property crimes	442.8	908.8	1,381.3	32.1	65.8	"
arrests for violent crimes:						
murder and nonnegligent homicide	6.3	4.9	11.3	55.6	42.8	"
forcible rape	12.4	10.9	23.7	52.4	46.2	"
robbery	65.5	36.6	103.2	63.5	35.5	"
aggravated assault	87.9	106.4	197.0	44.4	54.0	"
arrests for property crimes:						
burglary	91.6	186.9	282.6	32.4	66.1	"
larceny-theft	315.4	658.2	997.3	31.6	66.0	"
motor vehicle theft	32.5	54.8	89.0	36.5	61.6	"
arson	3.2	9.0	12.5	26.1	72.2	"

SOURCE: U.S. Department of Justice, Bureau of Justice Statistics, Sourcebook of Criminal Justice Statistics, 1986; p. 304, table 4.10, (data from the Uniform Crime Reporting program). J 29 9/6 986

NOTES: 'All Races' includes other races not shown separately. Crime index crimes are made up of the four violent crimes (murder and nonnegligent homicide, rape, robbery, and aggravated assault), and four property crimes (burglary, larceny-theft, motor vehicle theft, and arson) which are tracked by the FBI.

UNITS: Arrests in thousands of arrests; percent distribution as a percent of total, 100.0%

Table 5.22 Arrests in Cities, by Offense Charged, 2003

	number of arrests			percent distribution		
	Black	White	All Races	Black	White	All Races
All arrests	2,078,041	4,826,952	7,081,879	29.3%	68.2%	100.0%
arrests for violent crimes	129,674	184,742	321,419	40.3	57.5	"
arrests for property crimes	278,694	613,157	916,999	30.4	66.9	"
arrests for violent crimes:						
murder and nonnegligent manslaughter	3,664	2,815	6,619	55.4	42.5	"
forcible rape	5,074	7,699	13,105	38.7	58.7	"
robbery	35,072	27,116	63,284	55.4	42.8	"
aggravated assault	85,864	147,112	238,411	36.0	61.7	"
arrests for property crimes:						
burglary	45,498	99,228	147,633	30.8	67.2	"
larceny-theft	198,485	460,710	679,004	29.2	67.9	"
motor vehicle theft	32,826	47,254	82,374	39.8	57.4	"
arson	1,885	5,965	7,988	23.6	74.7	"

SOURCE: U.S. Federal Bureau of Investigation, Crime in the United States 2003; p. 297, table 49 (data from the Uniform Crime Reporting program). J1.14/7. (year)

NOTES: 'All Races' includes other races not shown separately. Crime index crimes are made up of the four violent crimes (murder and nonnegligent manslaughter, rape, robbery, and aggravated assault), and four property crimes (burglary, larceny-theft, motor vehicle theft, and arson) which are tracked by the FBI.

UNITS: Number of arrests; percent distribution as a percent of total, 100.0%

Table 5.23 Prisoners Under Jurisdiction of Federal and State Correctional Authorities, 1995 - 1997, 2000 - 2002

	Black	White	All Races
December 31, 1995			
total	544,005	455,021	1,126,287
federal institutions	37,055	60,261	100,250
state institutions	506,950	394,760	1,026,037
December 31, 1996			
total	565,549	478,308	1,180,524
federal institutions	40,323	61,885	105,544
state institutions	525,226	416,423	1,074,980
December 31, 1997			
total	590,454	505,513	1,240,962
federal institutions	43,786	65,539	112,973
state institutions	546,668	439,974	1,127,989
June 30, 2000			
total	587,300	453,300	1,305,253
federal institutions	44,800	29,800	110,974
state institutions	506,408	395,637	1,101,202
December 31, 2001			
total	na	na	1,404,032
federal institutions	na	na	156,993
state institutions	na	na	1,247,039
December 31, 2002			
total	na	na	1,440,655
federal institutions	na	na	163,528
state institutions	na	na	1,277,127

SOURCE: U.S. Department of Justice, Bureau of Justice Statistics, Sourcebook of Criminal Justice Statistics, 1995; p. 562, table 6.26; 1996; p. 524, table 6.26; 1998; p. 498, table 6.44; 1999; p. 510, table 6.34; 2001; p. 496, table 5.25; 2002; table 6.24, table 6.28.
J 29 9/6·(year)

NOTES: 'All Races' includes other races not shown separately.

UNITS: Number of prisoners under jurisdictional authority.

Table 5.24 Criminal History Profile of Prisoners Under Sentence of Death, 2003

	Black	White	All Races
U.S. Total	1,404	1,541	3,374
Prior felony convictions			
Yes	899	879	2,007
No	389	544	1,103
Not reported	na	na	264
Prior homicide convictions			
Yes	117	125	272
No	1,252	1,387	3,032
Not reported	na	na	70
Legal status at time of capital offense			
Charges pending	101	120	239
Probation	151	132	327
Parole	222	199	501
Prison escapee	12	23	42
Prison inmate	33	52	95
Other status	7	7	17
None	730	850	1,809
Not reported	na	na	344

SOURCE: U.S. Department of Justice, Bureau of Justice Statistics, Capital Punishment 2003; p. 8, table 8; issued November 2004, revised February 2005. NCJ 201848

NOTES: 'All Races' includes other races not shown separately.

UNITS: Number of jail inmates.

Table 5.25 Jail Inmates, 1990 - 2004

	Black	White	All Races
1990	42.5%	41.8%	100%
1991	43.4	41.1	100
1992	44.1	40.1	100
1993	44.2	39.3	100
1994	43.9	39.1	100
1995	43.5	40.1	100
1996	41.1	41.6	100
1997	42.0	40.6	100
1998	41.2	41.3	100
1999	41.5	41.3	100
2000	42.3	41.9	100
2001	40.6	43.0	100
2002	39.8	43.8	100
2003	39.2	43.6	100
2004	38.6	44.4	100

SOURCE: U.S. Department of Justice, Bureau of Justice Statistics, Prison and Jail Inmates 2001; p. 9, table 11; 2004; p. 8, table 10.

NOTES: 'All Races' includes other races not shown separately.

UNITS: Percent of local jail inmates.

Table 5.26 Type of Offense by Juvenile Offenders, 1999 and 2000

	Black	White	All Races
1999			
All offenses	28.4%	68.2%	100%
Person	34.3	62.7	100
Property	25.8	70.1	100
Drug	26.6	71.1	100
Public order	28.0	69.0	100
2000			
All offenses	28.1	68.6%	100%
Person	35.1	61.9	100
Property	26.3	69.7	100
Drug	22.2	75.4	100
Public order	27.3	69.6	100

SOURCE: U.S. Department of Justice, Bureau of Justice Statistics, Sourcebook of Criminal Justice Statistics, 2001; p. 455, table 5.59; 2002; table 5.61. J 29 9/6 (year)

NOTES: 'All Races' includes other races not shown separately. Cases disposed by juvenile courts.

UNITS: Percent of all offenses committed by juvenile offenders, as disposed by juvenile courts.

Table 5.27 Juvenile Court Cases, by Type of Case and Outcome, 2000

	Black	White	All Races
Type of offense			
Total	100%	100%	100%
crimes against persons	28.5	20.6	22.8
crimes against property	38.4	41.6	40.9
drug law violations	9.5	13.2	12.0
offenses against public order	23.6	24.6	24.2
Case outcome			
Delinquency cases			
detained prior to court disposition	23.8	17.5%	19.5%
petitioned	64.5	55.1	57.8
Petitioned cases			
adjudicated delinquent	64.2	67.2	66.2
transferred/waived to adult court	0.8	0.5	0.6
Adjudicated cases			
placed out of home	26.9	22.8	24.0
placed on probation	61.9	63.6	63.1
dismissed	3.4	2.2	2.5
other	7.8	11.4	10.3

SOURCE: U.S. Department of Justice, Bureau of Justice Statistics, Sourcebook of Criminal Justice Statistics, 2002; table 5.62, table 5.63.
J 29 9/6·002

NOTES: 'All Races' includes other races not shown separately. Data based on national estimates of delinquency cases disposed by juvenile courts.

UNITS: Percent, as a percent of total shown, 100.0%.

Table 5.28 Prisoners Under Sentence of Death, and Elapsed Time from Sentence to Execution, 1980 - 2004

	Black	White	All Races
Prisoners under sentence of death			
1980	268	425	697
1990	940	1,368	2,346
April, 1995	1,217	1,455	3,009
April, 1996	1,272	1,493	3,122
April, 1998	1,420	1,611	3,387
April, 1999	1,516	1,657	3,565
April, 2000	1,574	1,698	3,670
April, 2001	1,593	1,700	3,711
April, 2002	1,593	1,678	3,701
April, 2004	1,462	1,591	3,487
Average elapsed time (in months) from sentence to execution			
1990	91	97	95
1995	144	128	134
1996	153	112	125
1997	147	126	133
1998	132	128	130
1999	141	143	143
2000	142	134	137
2001	166	134	142
2002	120	130	127

SOURCE: U.S. Bureau of the Census, Statistical Abstract of the United States, 1989, p. 187, table 325. C 3 134 989

U.S. Department of Justice, Bureau of Justice Statistics, Sourcebook of Criminal Justice Statistics, 1993; p. 666, table 6.108; p. 667, table 6.110; 1994; p. 587, table 6.70, 1995; p. 604, table 6.74, 1997; p. 527, table 6.76; 1998; p. 526, table 6.81; 1999; p. 547, table 6.83; 2000; p. 547, table 6.83; 2001; p.531, table 6.76; 2002; table 6.77.

U.S. Department of Justice, Bureau of Justice Statistics, Bureau of Justice Statistics Bulletin: Capital Punishment 2002; p. 11, table 11. J 29 11 002

NOTES: 'All Races' includes other races not shown separately.

UNITS: Number of prisoners under sentence of death; Average elapsed time from sentence to execution in months.

Table 5.29 Prisoners Executed Under Civil Authority, 1930 - 2003

	Black	White	All Races
All years, 1930-2003			
all executions	2,369	2,319	4,744
for murder	1,933	2,232	4,219
1930-1939			
all executions	816	827	1,667
for murder	687	803	1,514
1940-1949			
all executions	781	490	1,284
for murder	595	458	1,064
1950-1959			
all executions	376	336	717
for murder	280	316	601
1960-1967			
all executions	93	98	191
for murder	68	87	155
1968-1976			
all executions	na	na	na
for murder	na	na	na
1977-2003			
all executions	303	568	885
for murder	303	568	885

continued on the next page

Table 5.29 continued

	Black	White	All Races
2000			
all executions	35	49	85
for murder	35	49	85
2001			
all executions	17	48	66
for murder	17	48	66
2002			
all executions	18	53	71
for murder	18	53	71
2003			
all executions	20	44	65
for murder	20	44	65

SOURCE: U.S. Bureau of the Census, Statistical Abstract of the United States, 2004, p. 209, table 341. C 3 134 (year)

NOTES: 'All Races' includes other races not shown separately. Since 1965 the only executions that have taken place have been for murder.

UNITS: Number of prisoners executed under civil authority.

Table 5.30 Attitudes Toward the Police, 2002

Question: Do you think the police in your community treat all races fairly or do they tend to treat one or more of these groups unfairly?

	Black	White	All Races
Treat all races fairly	43%	61%	57%
Treat one or more groups unfairly	56	27	33
Not sure	1	10	9

Question: Are you sometimes afraid that the police will stop and arrest you when you are completely innocent, or not?

	Black	White	All Races
Yes, sometimes afraid	42%	16%	21%
No, not afraid	56	84	78

SOURCE: U.S. Department of Justice, Bureau of Justice Statistics, Sourcebook of Criminal Justice Statistics, 2002; table 2.24, table 2.25.
J 29 9/6.002

NOTES: Table constructed by Sourcebook staff from data provided by Harris Interactive, Inc.

UNITS: Percent of persons taking survey who answered with given response.

Table 5.31 Attitudes Toward the Death Penalty, 2003

Question: "Are you in favor of the death penalty for a person convicted of murder?"

	Black	White	All Races
Yes, in favor	35%	75%	70%
No, not in favor	58	23	28
Don't know / refused	7	2	2

Question: "Generally speaking, do you believe the death penalty is applied fairly or unfairly in this country today?"

	Black	White	All Races
Applied fairly	26%	65%	60%
Applied unfairly	71	32	37
Don't know / refused	3	3	3

SOURCE: U.S. Department of Justice, Bureau of Justice Statistics, Sourcebook of Criminal Justice Statistics, 2002; table 2.50, table 2.52. J 29 9/6 002

NOTES: Table constructed by Sourcebook staff from data provided by The Gallup Organization, Inc.

UNITS: Percent of persons taking survey who answered with given response.

Table 5.32 Inmates Ever Tested for HIV and Results – 1996, 1997 and 2002

	Black	White	All Races
1996			
Local jails			
number	125,259	110,023	289,991
percent HIV positive	2.6%	1.4%	2.2%
1997			
State prisons			
number	384,870	257,919	790,128
percent HIV positive	2.8%	1.4%	2.2%
Federal prisons			
number	28,178	21,128	70,902
percent HIV positive	0.8%	0.3%	0.6%
2002			
State prisons			
number	163,219	136,069	374,711
percent HIV positive	1.2%	0.8%	1.3%

SOURCE: U.S. Department of Justice, Bureau of Justice Statistics, HIV in Prisons and Jails, 1996; p. 14, table 8. <www ojp usurlobj gov/bjs/pub/pdf/hivpj96 pdf> Accessed October 11, 1999; 2002; p. 8, table 9; NCJ 205333.

NOTES: 'All Races' includes other races not shown separately.

UNITS: Percent of inmates tested for HIV (Human Immunodeficiency Virus) and reporting the results.

Chapter 6: The Labor Force, Employment & Unemployment

Table 6.01 Labor Force Participation of the Civilian Noninstitutional Population 16 Years Old and Over, by Age, 1980 - 2004

	Black	White	All Races
1980			
civilian noninstitutional population			
all persons 16 years old and over	17,824	146,122	167,745
- persons 16-19 years old	2,289	13,854	16,543
- persons 20 years old and over	15,535	132,268	151,202
- persons 65 years old and over	2,030	22,050	24,350
civilian labor force			
all persons 16 years old and over	10,865	93,600	106,940
- persons 16-19 years old	891	8,312	9,378
- persons 20 years old and over	9,975	85,286	97,561
- persons 65 years old and over	257	2,759	3,054
labor force participation rate			
all persons 16 years old and over	61.0%	64.1%	63.8%
- persons 16-19 years old	38.9	60.0	56.7
- persons 20 years old and over	64.1	64.5	64.5
- persons 65 years old and over	13.0	12.5	12.5

continued on the next page

Table 6.01 continued

	Black	White	All Races
1990			
civilian noninstitutional population			
all persons 16 years old and over	21,300	160,415	188,049
- persons 16-19 years old	2,150	11,095	13,794
- persons 20 years old and over	19,150	149,320	174,255
- persons 65 years old and over	2,506	26,643	29,730
civilian labor force			
all persons 16 years old and over	13,493	107,177	124,787
- persons 16-19 years old	831	6,374	7,410
- persons 20 years old and over	12,662	100,803	117,377
- persons 65 years old and over	279	3,189	3,535
labor force participation rate			
all persons 16 years old and over	63.3%	66.8%	66.4%
- persons 16-19 years old	38.6	57.5	53.7
- persons 20 years old and over	59.4	62.8	62.4
- persons 65 years old and over	11.1	12.0	11.9

continued on the next page

Table 6.01 continued

	Black	White	All Races
2000			
civilian noninstitutional population			
all persons 16 years old and over	25,218	174,428	209,699
- persons 16-19 years old	2,468	12,707	16,042
- persons 65 years old and over	2,778	28,947	32,705
civilian labor force			
all persons 16 years old and over	16,603	117,574	140,863
- persons 16-19 years old	967	7,075	8,369
- persons 65 years old and over	322	3,749	4,200
labor force participation rate			
all persons 16 years old and over	65.8%	67.4%	67.2%
- persons 16-19 years old	39.2	55.7	52.2
- persons 65 years old and over	11.6	13.0	12.8

continued on the next page

Table 6.01 continued

	Black	White	All Races
2004			
civilian noninstitutional population			
all persons 16 years old and over	26,065	182,643	223,357
- persons 16-19 years old	2,423	12,599	16,222
- persons 65 years old and over	2,899	30,245	34,609
civilian labor force			
all persons 16 years old and over	16,638	121,086	147,401
- persons 16-19 years old	762	5,929	7,114
- persons 65 years old and over	380	4,408	4,998
labor force participation rate			
all persons 16 years old and over	63.8%	66.3%	66.0%
- persons 16-19 years old	31.4	47.1	43.9
- persons 65 years old and over	13.1	14.6	14.4

SOURCE: U.S. Department of Labor, Bureau of Labor Statistics, Handbook of Labor Statistics, 1989, pp. 13-30, tables 3-5. L 2.3/5 989
U.S. Department of Labor, Bureau of Labor Statistics, *Employment and Earnings*, January, 1991; pp. 164-166, table 3; January, 2001; pp. 168-170, table 3; January, 2002; pp. 166-169, table 3; January, 2005; pp. 196-199, table 3 (data from the Current Population Survey). L2 41/2·(vol)/1 (year)

NOTES: 'All Races' includes other races not shown separately.

UNITS: Civilian noninstitutional population and civilian labor force in thousands of persons; participation rate as a percent (the civilian noninstitutional population divided by the civilian labor force).

Table 6.02 Labor Force Participation of the Civilian Noninstitutional Population 16 Years Old and Over, by Sex and Age, 1980 - 2004

	Black		White		All Races	
	male	female	male	female	male	female
1980						
civilian noninstitutional population						
all persons 16 years old and over	7,944	9,880	69,634	76,489	79,398	88,348
- persons 16-19 years old	1,110	1,180	6,941	6,914	8,260	8,283
- persons 20 years old and over	6,834	8,700	62,694	69,575	71,138	80,065
- persons 65 years old and over	822	1,208	9,027	13,022	9,979	14,372
civilian labor force						
all persons 16 years old and over	5,612	5,253	54,473	39,127	61,453	45,487
- persons 16-19 years old	479	412	4,424	3,888	4,999	4,381
- persons 20 years old and over	5,134	4,841	50,049	35,239	56,455	41,106
- persons 65 years old and over	138	119	1,727	1,032	1,893	1,161
labor force participation rate						
all persons 16 years old and over	70.3%	53.1%	78.2%	51.2%	77.4%	51.5%
- persons 16-19 years old	43.2	34.9	63.7	56.2	60.5	52.9
- persons 20 years old and over	75.1	55.6	79.8	50.6	79.4	51.3
- persons 65 years old and over	16.9	10.2	19.1	7.9	19.0	8.1

continued on the next page

Table 6.02 continued

	Black male	Black female	White male	White female	All Races male	All Races female
1990						
civilian noninstitutional population						
all persons 16 years old and over	9,567	11,773	77,082	83,332	89,650	98,399
- persons 16-19 years old	1,065	1,085	5,600	5,495	6,947	6,847
- persons 20 years old and over	8,502	10,648	71,482	77,837	82,703	91,552
- persons 65 years old and over	1,012	1,493	11,129	15,514	12,392	17,337
civilian labor force						
all persons 16 years old and over	6,708	6,785	58,298	47,879	68,234	56,554
- persons 16-19 years old	433	398	3,329	3,046	3,866	3,544
- persons 20 years old and over	6,275	6,387	54,969	44,833	64,368	53,010
- persons 65 years old and over	131	148	1,865	1,325	2,033	1,502
labor force participation rate						
all persons 16 years old and over	70.1%	57.8%	76.9%	57.5%	76.1%	57.5%
- persons 16-19 years old	40.6	36.7	59.4	55.4	55.7	51.8
- persons 20 years old and over	73.8	60.0	78.3	57.6	77.8	57.9
- persons 65 years old and over	13.0	9.9	16.8	8.5	16.4	8.7

continued on the next page

Table 6.02 continued

	Black male	Black female	White male	White female	All Races male	All Races female
2000						
civilian noninstitutional population						
all persons 16 years old and over	11,320	13,898	84,647	89,781	100,731	108,968
- persons 16-19 years old	1,213	1,255	6,496	6,211	8,151	7,890
- persons 65 years old and over	1,105	1,673	12,390	16,557	13,925	18,780
civilian labor force						
all persons 16 years old and over	7,816	8,787	63,861	53,714	75,247	65,616
- persons 16-19 years old	473	494	3,679	3,396	4,317	4,051
- persons 65 years old and over	157	165	2,198	1,550	2,439	1,762
labor force participation rate						
all persons 16 years old and over	69.0%	63.2%	75.4%	59.8%	74.7%	60.2%
- persons 16-19 years old	39.0	39.4	56.6	54.7	53.0	51.3
- persons 65 years old and over	14.2	9.9	17.7	9.4	17.5	9.4

continued on the next page

Table 6.02 continued

	Black		White		All Races	
	male	female	male	female	male	female
2004						
civilian noninstitutional population						
all persons 16 years old and over	11,656	14,409	89,044	93,599	107,710	115,647
- persons 16-19 years old	1,195	1,227	6,429	6,169	8,234	7,989
- persons 65 years old and over	1,111	1,789	12,946	17,299	14,684	19,925
civilian labor force						
all persons 16 years old and over	7,773	8,865	65,994	55,092	78,980	68,421
- persons 16-19 years old	359	403	3,050	2,879	3,616	3,498
- persons 65 years old and over	188	192	2,478	1,930	2,787	2,211
labor force participation rate						
all persons 16 years old and over	66.7%	61.5%	74.1%	58.9%	73.3%	59.2%
- persons 16-19 years old	30.0	32.8	47.4	46.7	43.9	43.8
- persons 65 years old and over	17.0	10.7	19.1	11.2	19.0	11.1

SOURCE: U.S. Department of Labor, Bureau of Labor Statistics, Handbook of Labor Statistics, 1989, pp. 13-30, tables 3-5. L 2 3/5 989
U.S. Department of Labor, Bureau of Labor Statistics, *Employment and Earnings*, January, 1991; pp. 164-166, table 3; January, 2001; pp. 168-170, table 3; January, 2002; pp. 166-168, table 3; January, 2005; pp. 196-199, table 3 (data from the Current Population Survey). L2 41/2 (vol)/1 (year)

NOTES: 'All Races' includes other races not shown separately.

UNITS: Civilian noninstitutional population and civilian labor force in thousands of persons; participation rate as a percent (the civilian noninstitutional population divided by the civilian labor force).

Table 6.03 Civilian Labor Force and Civilian Labor Force Participation Rates: Projections for 2008 and 2012

	Black	White	All Races
2008			
civilian labor force			
total	19.1	126.7	154.6
men	8.9	67.7	81.1
women	10.2	59.0	73.4
labor force participation rate			
total	66.3%	67.9%	67.6%
men	68.3	74.5	73.7
women	64.6	61.5	61.9
2012			
civilian labor force			
total	19.8	130.4	162.3
men	9.3	70.6	85.3
women	10.4	59.8	77.0
labor force participation rate			
total	66.3%	66.2%	67.2%
men	69.1	73.5	73.1
women	64.0	59.2	61.6

SOURCE: U.S. Bureau of the Census, Statistical Abstract of the United States, 2000; p. 403, table 644; 2002; p. 367, table 561; 2004; p. 371, table 570 (data from U.S. Department of Labor, Bureau of Labor Statistics)
C 3 134 (year)

NOTES: 'All Races' includes other races not shown separately.

UNITS: Civilian labor force population 16 years old and over in millions of persons; labor force participation rate as a percent (the civilian noninstitutional population divided by the civilian labor force).

Table 6.04 Employed Members of the Civilian Labor Force, by Sex and Age, 1980 - 2004

	Black		White		All Races	
	male	female	male	female	male	female
1980						
all employed persons 16 years old and over	4,798	4,515	51,127	36,587	57,186	42,177
- persons 16-19 years old	299	248	3,708	3,314	4,085	3,625
- persons 20 years old and over	4,498	4,267	47,419	33,275	53,101	38,492
- persons 65 years old and over	126	113	1,684	1,001	1,835	1,125
1990						
all employed persons 16 years old and over	5,915	6,051	56,432	45,654	64,435	53,479
- persons 16-19 years old	294	279	2,856	2,662	3,237	3,024
- persons 20 years old and over	5,621	5,780	53,576	42,992	61,198	50,455
- persons 65 years old and over	125	139	1,812	1,288	1,972	1,455
2000						
all employed persons 16 years old and over	7,180	8,154	61,696	51,780	72,293	62,915
- persons 16-19 years old	348	380	3,227	3,043	3,713	3,563
- persons 65 years old and over	147	155	2,130	1,512	2,357	1,713
2004						
all employed persons 16 years old and over	6,912	7,997	62,712	52,527	74,524	64,728
- persons 16-19 years old	231	289	2,553	2,486	2,952	2,955
- persons 65 years old and over	180	179	2,390	1,870	2,683	2,135

SOURCE: U.S. Department of Labor, Bureau of Labor Statistics, Handbook of Labor Statistics, 1989, pp. 63-68, table 15, (data from the Current Population Survey). L 2.3/5 989

U.S. Department of Labor, Bureau of Labor Statistics, *Employment and Earnings*, January, 1991, pp. 164-166, table 3; January, 2001, pp. 168-170, table 3 (data from the Current Population Survey); January, 2002, pp. 166-169, table 3; January, 2005, pp. 196-199, table 3 (data from the Current Population Survey). L2 41/2.(vol)/1·(year)

NOTES: 'All Races' includes other races not shown separately. Data covers members of the civilian labor force.

UNITS: Employed members of the civilian labor force in thousands of persons, by age group as shown.

Table 6.05 Employment Status of Families, 2001 - 2003

	Black	White	All Races
2001			
Total families	8,737	59,943	71,980
With employed member(s)	6,988	49,804	59,699
some usually work full time	6,425	46,429	55,599
With no employed member	1,749	10,140	12,281
With unemployed member(s)	1,000	3,506	4,775
some member(s) employed	601	2,629	3,441
some usually work full time	538	2,351	3,076
2002			
Total families	8,845	61,494	74,169
With employed member(s)	6,987	50,785	61,121
some usually work full time	6,390	47,193	56,742
With no employed member	1,858	10,709	13,048
With unemployed member(s)	1,162	4,275	5,809
some member(s) employed	689	3,164	4,126
some usually work full time	611	2,808	3,668
2003			
Total families	8,869	61,995	75,301
With employed member(s)	6,906	51,002	61,761
some usually work full time	6,270	47,356	57,229
With no employed member	1,963	10,993	13,540
With unemployed member(s)	1,213	4,411	6,079
some member(s) employed	695	3,245	4,285
some usually work full time	612	2,873	3,790

SOURCE: U.S. Department Labor, Bureau Labor Statistics, Employment Characteristics of Families, 2001; "(Table) 1. Employment and unemployment in families, by race and Hispanic origin, 2000-2001 annual averages"; <http://stats bls gov/news release/famee t01htm>, (accessed 4 March 2003)
U.S. Department of Labor, Bureau Labor Statistics, "Employment and unemployment in families by race and Hispanic or Latino ethnicity, 2002-2003 annual averages"; <http://stats bls gov/news release/famee t01htm>, (accessed 15 June 2004)

NOTES: 'All Races' includes other races not shown separately.

UNITS: Number of families in thousands of families.

Table 6.06 Work at Home, 2001

	Black	White	All Races
2001			
worked at home	173	3,138	3,436
percent who worked less than 8 hours	24.4%	24.4%	24.5%
8 hours or more			
total	48.1	48.0	47.6
35 hours or more	28.9	15.0	15.7
mean hours:			
worked at home	23.2	17.7	18.0

SOURCE: U.S. Department of Labor, Bureau of Labor Statistics, "Table 3: Hours of paid job-related work at home on primary job among wage and salary workers, May 2001"; pp. 1-2, table 3. <http://stats bls gov/news release/homey t03 htm> accessed 5 March, 2003

NOTES: Data refer to employed persons in nonagricultural industries who reported that they usually work at home at least once per week as part of their primary job excluding self-employed. Detail for the above race and Hispanic-origin groups will not sum to totals because data for the "other races" group are not presented and Hispanics are included in both the white and black population groups.

UNITS: Numbers in thousands of persons. Percent as a percent of persons working at home.

Table 6.07 Unemployed Jobseekers by Active Job Search Methods Used, 2001 - 2004

	Black	White	All Races
2001			
Total unemployed	1,450	4,923	6,742
Total jobseekers	1,303	4,063	5,693
Methods used as a percent of total jobseekers			
Employer directly	61.5%	63.0%	62.4%
Sent out resumes or filled out applications	50.5	51.7	51.5
Placed or answered ads	27.7	32.5	15.8
Friends or relatives	26.7	31.8	15.6
Public employment agency	45.5	36.1	19.2
Private employment agency	17.2	16.7	8.6
Other	7.6	12.5	11.4
2004			
Total unemployed	1,729	5,847	8,149
Total jobseekers	1,599	5,029	7,151
Methods used as a percent of total jobseekers			
Employer directly	63.4%	62.6%	62.7%
Sent out resumes or filled out applications	52.9	55.0	54.5
Placed or answered ads	14.5	17.4	16.4
Friends or relatives	17.0	18.1	18.0
Public employment agency	25.5	18.4	19.9
Private employment agency	7.6	7.5	7.7
Other	9.4	12.4	11.8

SOURCE: U.S. Department of Labor, Bureau of Labor Statistics, *Employment and Earnings*, January, 2002, p. 205, table 33; January, 2005, p. 244, table 33 (data from the Current Population Survey). L 2 41/2 40/1(year)

NOTES: 'All Races' includes other races not shown separately. "Jobseekers" does not include persons on temporary layoff.

UNITS: Persons in thousands of persons.

Table 6.08 Employed Black Persons as Percent of All Employed Persons in the Civilian Labor Force, by Selected Occupation, 2004

	Black	All Races
2004		
All occupations	10.7%	139,252
Management occupations	5.9	14,555
chief executive	3.2	1,680
general and operations managers	5.8	795
computer and information systems managers	4.9	337
financial managers	7.8	1,045
education administrators	12.8	757
medical and health services managers	8.8	508
Business and financial operations occupations	9.6	5,680
accountants and auditors	8.6	1,723
insurance underwriters	8.4	98
wholesale and retail buyers, except farm products	5.0	212
Computer and mathematical occupations	7.5	3,140
computer scientists and systems analysts	9.8	700
database administrators	5.5	94
operations research analysts	9.4	90
Architecture and engineering occupations	4.9	2,760
architects, except naval	2.6	207
aerospace engineers	4.4	113
chemical engineers	4.4	63
civil engineers	7.7	293
engineering technicians, except drafters	5.9	416
Life, physical, and social science occupations	5.6	1,365
medical scientists	5.1	93
environmental scientists and geoscientists	5.1	86
psychologists	3.3	185
Legal occupations	6.4	1,554
lawyers	4.7	954
judges, magistrate, and other judicial workers	12.8	64
Education, training and library occupations	9.4	7,900
Healthcare practitioner and technical occupations	10.0	6,721
dentists	5.0	167
physicians and surgeons	6.1	830
registered nurses	10.1	2,464

continued on the next page

Table 6.08 continued

	Black	All Races
Arts, design, entertainment, sports and media occupations	6.1	2,687
Healthcare support occupations	25.9	2,921
Protective service occupations	17.9	2,847
fire fighters	8.4	268
police and sheriff's patrol officers	15.7	664
Food preparation and serving related occupations	11.5	7,279
Building and grounds cleaning and maintenance	14.9	5,185
Personal care and service occupations	14.9	4,488
Sales and related occupations	9.0	15,983
cashiers	15.6	2,971
retail salespersons	10.9	3,130
real estate brokers and sales agents	5.7	912
Office and administrative occupations	12.8	19,481
Farming, fishing and forestry occupations	5.4	991
Construction and extraction occupations	6.7	8,522
carpenters	5.2	1,764
construction laborers	8.9	1,234
electricians	6.5	781
Installation, maintenance and repair	7.6	5,069
Production occupations	11.9	9,462
electrical and electronic assemblers	12.0	226
machinist	6.0	445
printing machine operators	8.7	195
medical, dental, ophthalmic laboratory technicians	8.4	92
Transportation and material moving	16.1	8,491
aircraft pilots and flight engineers	1.7	118
bus drivers	24.4	602
industrial truck and tractor operators	22.2	530
refuse and recyclable material collectors	29.5	81

SOURCE: U.S. Department of Labor, Bureau of Labor Statistics, *Employment and Earnings*, January, 2005, pp. 209-214, table 11 (data from the Current Population Survey). L 2 41/2 408/1· (year)

NOTES: Only selected subcategories of occupational groups displayed.

UNITS: Employed Black persons as a percent of all employed persons, by occupation. Employed persons in thousands.

Table 6.09 Employed Black Persons as Percent of All Employed Persons in the Civilian Labor Force, by Industry Group, 2004

	Black	All Races
2004		
All industries	10.7%	139,252
agriculture, forestry, fishing, and hunting	2.4	2,232
mining	4.8	539
construction	5.9	10,768
manufacturing	9.4	16,484
durable goods	8.2	10,329
nondurable goods	11.6	6,155
wholesale and retail trade	9.4	20,869
wholesale trade	7.4	4,600
retail trade	10.0	16,269
transportation and warehousing	16.7	5,844
utilities	9.5	1,168
information	10.8	3,463
finance and insurance	10.6	6,940
real estate and rental and leasing	8.2	3,029
legal services	6.5	1,591
architectural, engineering and related services	4.7	1,361
scientific research and development services	3.8	509
management, administrative and waste services	13.5	5,722
educational services	10.7	12,058
hospitals	15.4	5,700
health services, except hospitals	15.4	8,118
social assistance	19.7	2,844
arts, entertainment, and recreation	8.9	2,690
accommodation and food services	11.1	9,131
services	10.6	6,903
public administration	16.3	6,365

SOURCE: U.S. Department of Labor, Bureau of Labor Statistics, *Employment and Earnings*, January, 2005, pp. 226-230, table 18 (data from the Current Population Survey). L 2 41/2 40/1 (year)

NOTES: Only selected subcategories of industry groups are displayed.

UNITS: Employed Black persons as a percent of all employed persons, by industry group. Employed persons in thousands.

Table 6.10 Full-Time and Part-Time Status of Employed Persons in Nonagricultural Industries, 1980 - 2004

	Black	White	All Races
1980			
All employed persons in nonagricultural industries	8,502	79,614	90,209
full-time	6,998	64,835	73,590
part-time	1,504	14,780	16,619
part time for economic reasons	601	3,375	4,064
1990			
All employed persons in nonagricultural industries	11,184	93,886	108,697
full-time	9,358	76,697	89,081
part-time	1,826	17,188	19,616
part time for economic reasons	721	3,989	4,860
2000			
All employed persons in nonagricultural industries	14,590	105,736	126,433
full-time	11,692	81,132	97,701
part-time	2,897	24,604	28,732
part time for economic reasons	488	2,404	3,045

continued on the next page

Table 6.10 continued

	Black	White	All Races
2001			
All employed persons in nonagricultural industries	14,561	105,653	126,513
full-time	11,487	79,747	96,176
part-time	3,073	25,907	30,337
part time for economic reasons	553	2,784	3,529
2003			
All employed persons in nonagricultural industries	14,129	107,595	130,096
full-time	11,160	81,207	98,810
part-time	2,969	26,388	31,286
part time for economic reasons	630	3,643	4,596
2004			
All employed persons in nonagricultural industries	14,332	108,593	131,637
full-time	11,325	81,736	99,836
part-time	3,007	26,857	31,801
part time for economic reasons	665	3,507	4,469

SOURCE: U.S. Department of Labor, Bureau of Labor Statistics, Handbook of Labor Statistics, 1989, pp. 121-123, table 23, (data from the Current Population Survey). L 2.3/5:989

U.S. Department of Labor, Bureau of Labor Statistics, *Employment and Earnings*, January, 1991; p. 201, table 32; p. 202, table 33; January, 2001, p. 197, table 22; January, 2002, p. 195, table 22; January, 2004, p. 232, table 22; January, 2005, p. 233, table 22 (data from the Current Population Survey). L 2.41/2·(vol)/1 (year)

NOTES: 'All Races' includes other races not shown separately. Economic reasons for persons who are employed part-time are: slack work; material shortages; repairs to plant or equipment; start or termination of a job during the week; and inability to find full time work.

UNITS: Employed members of the civilian labor force in thousands of persons, by status, as shown.

Table 6.11 Unemployment Rates for the Civilian Labor Force, by Age, 1980 - 2004

	Black	White	All Races
1980			
unemployment rate			
all ages	14.3%	6.3%	7.1%
- persons 16-19 years old	38.5	15.5	17.8
- persons 20 years old and over	12.1	5.4	6.1
- persons 65 years old and over	6.9	2.7	3.1
1985			
unemployment rate			
all ages	15.1%	6.2%	7.2%
- persons 16-19 years old	40.2	15.7	18.6
- persons 20 years old and over	13.1	5.5	6.4
- persons 65 years old and over	7.0	2.9	3.2
1990			
unemployment rate			
all ages	11.3%	4.7%	5.5%
- persons 16-19 years old	31.3	13.4	15.5
- persons 20-24 years old	19.9	7.2	8.8
- persons 25-54 years old	9.0	3.9	4.5
- persons 55-64 years old	4.6	3.2	3.3
- persons 65 years old and over	5.3	2.8	3.0

continued on the next page

Table 6.11 continued

	Black	White	All Races
2000			
unemployment rate			
all ages	7.6%	3.5%	4.0%
- persons 16-19 years old	24.7	11.4	13.1
- persons 20-24 years old	15.0	5.8	7.1
- persons 25-54 years old	5.6	2.7	3.1
- persons 55-64 years old	3.0	2.4	2.5
- persons 65 years old and over	6.1	2.8	3.1
2003			
unemployment rate			
all ages	10.8%	5.2%	6.0%
- persons 16-19 years old	33.0	15.2	17.5
- persons 20-24 years old	19.8	8.4	10.0
- persons 25-54 years old	8.7	4.4	5.0
- persons 55-64 years old	6.3	3.8	4.1
- persons 65 years old and over	5.4	3.7	3.8
2004			
unemployment rate			
all ages	10.4%	4.8%	5.5%
- persons 16-19 years old	31.7	15.0	17.0
- persons 20-24 years old	18.4	7.9	9.4
- persons 25-54 years old	8.5	4.0	4.6
- persons 55-64 years old	5.6	3.6	3.8
- persons 65 years old and over	5.5	3.3	3.6

SOURCE: U.S. Department of Labor, Bureau of Labor Statistics, Handbook of Labor Statistics, 1989, pp. 136-141, table 28, (data from the Current Population Survey). L 2 3/5.989

U.S. Department of Labor, Bureau of Labor Statistics, *Employment and Earnings*, January, 1991, pp. 164-166, table 3; January, 2001, pp. 168-170, table 3; January, 2002, pp. 166-169, table 3; January, 2004, pp. 196-199, table 3; January, 2005, pp. 196-199, table 3 (data from the Current Population Survey). L2 41/2:(vol)/1 (year)

NOTES: 'All Races' includes other races not shown separately. Data covers members of the civilian labor force.

UNITS: Unemployment rate, by age group as shown.

Table 6.12 Unemployment Rates for the Civilian Labor Force, by Sex and Age, 1980 - 2004

	Black		White		All Races	
	male	female	male	female	male	female
1980						
unemployment rate						
all ages	14.5%	14.0%	6.1%	6.5%	6.9%	7.4%
- persons 16-19 years old	37.5	39.8	16.2	14.8	18.3	17.2
- persons 20 years old and over	12.4	11.9	5.3	5.6	5.9	6.4
- persons 65 years old and over	8.7	4.9	2.5	3.0	3.1	3.1
1985						
unemployment rate						
all ages	15.3	14.9%	6.1%	6.4%	7.0%	7.4%
- persons 16-19 years old	41.0	39.2	16.5	14.8	19.5	17.6
- persons 20 years old and over	13.2	13.1	5.4	5.7	6.2	6.6
- persons 65 years old and over	8.9	5.2	2.7	3.1	3.1	3.3
1990						
unemployment rate						
all ages	11.3%	10.8%	4.8%	4.6%	5.6%	5.4%
- persons 16-19 years old	31.1	30.0	14.2	12.6	16.3	14.7
- persons 20-24 years old	19.9	19.7	7.6	6.8	9.1	8.5
- persons 25-54 years old	9.0	8.7	3.9	3.9	4.5	4.5
- persons 55-64 years old	4.6	3.7	3.6	2.7	3.8	2.8
- persons 65 years old and over	5.3	5.8	2.8	2.8	3.0	3.1

continued on the next page

Table 6.12 continued

	Black		White		All Races	
	male	female	male	female	male	female
2000						
unemployment rate						
all ages	8.1%	7.2%	3.4%	3.6%	3.9%	4.1%
- persons 16-19 years old	26.4	23.0	12.3	10.4	14.0	12.1
- persons 20-24 years old	16.7	13.5	5.9	5.8	7.3	7.0
- persons 25-54 years old	5.9	5.4	2.5	2.9	2.9	3.3
- persons 55-64 years old	2.7	3.3	2.4	2.4	2.4	2.5
- persons 65 years old and over	6.3	6.0	3.1	2.4	3.4	2.8
2003						
unemployment rate						
all ages	11.6%	10.2%	5.6%	4.8%	6.3%	5.7%
- persons 16-19 years old	36.0	30.3	17.1	13.3	19.3	15.6
- persons 20-24 years old	20.9	18.8	9.1	7.6	10.6	9.3
- persons 25-54 years old	9.2	8.2	4.6	4.1	5.2	4.8
- persons 55-64 years old	6.8	5.9	4.2	3.4	4.5	3.7
- persons 65 years old and over	5.6	5.3	3.8	3.5	4.0	3.6
2004						
unemployment rate						
all ages	11.1%	9.8%	5.0%	4.7%	5.6%	5.4%
- persons 16-19 years old	35.6	28.2	16.3	13.6	18.4	15.5
- persons 20-24 years old	20.3	16.6	8.5	7.1	10.1	8.7
- persons 25-54 years old	8.8	8.3	4.0	3.9	4.6	4.6
- persons 55-64 years old	6.4	4.8	3.7	3.5	3.9	3.6
- persons 65 years old and over	4.2	6.8	3.5	3.1	3.7	3.4

SOURCE: U.S. Department of Labor, Bureau of Labor Statistics, Handbook of Labor Statistics, 1989; pp. 151-153, table 37, (data from the Current Population Survey). L 2 3/5 989

U.S. Department of Labor, Bureau of Labor Statistics, *Employment and Earnings*, January, 1991, pp. 164-166, table 3; January, 2001, pp. 168-170, table 3; January, 2002, pp. 166-169, table 3; January, 2004, pp. 196-199, table 3; January, 2005, pp. 196-199, table (data from the Current Population Survey). L2.41/2·(vol)/1 (year)

NOTES: 'All Races' includes other races not shown separately. Data covers members of the civilian labor force.

UNITS: Unemployment rate, by age group as shown.

Table 6.13 Unemployment, by Reason for Unemployment, 1990 - 2004

	Black	White	All Races
1990			
Total	1,527	5,091	6,874
job losers	678	2,534	3,322
job leavers	187	787	1,014
re-entrants to the labor force	461	1,346	1,883
new entrants to the labor force	201	423	654
2000			
Total	1,269	4,099	5,655
job losers	514	1,866	2,492
job leavers	145	593	775
re-entrants to the labor force	494	1,356	1,957
new entrants to the labor force	115	284	431
2001			
Total	1,450	4,923	6,742
job losers	676	2,576	3,428
job leavers	155	635	832
re-entrants to the labor force	500	1,412	2,029
new entrants to the labor force	118	301	453
2004			
Total	1,729	5,847	8,149
job losers	828	3,105	4,197
job leavers	142	654	858
re-entrants to the labor force	590	1,638	2,408
new entrants to the labor force	169	450	686

SOURCE: U.S. Department of Labor, Bureau of Labor Statistics, *Employment and Earnings*, January, 1991, p. 176, table 12; January, 2001, p. 203, table 28; January, 2002, p. 201, table 28); January, 2005; p. 239, table 27; p.240, table 29. (data from the Current Population Survey).
L2 41/2:(vol)/1 (year)

NOTES: 'All Races' includes other races not shown separately. Data covers members of the civilian labor force.

UNITS: Unemployed members of the civilian labor force in thousands of persons, by reason for unemployment as shown.

Table 6.14 Duration of Unemployment, by Region of Residence, 2000 and 2002

	Black	White	All Races
2000			
Northeast			
less than 5 weeks	35.0%	42.0%	40.1%
5-14 weeks	32.1	31.9	32.1
15 weeks and over	32.9	26.1	27.9
27 weeks and over	18.4	13.0	14.3
52 weeks and over	11.5	7.4	8.5
Midwest			
less than 5 weeks	37.9%	50.1%	47.4%
5-14 weeks	34.9	31.1	32.0
15 weeks and over	26.8	18.8	20.6
27 weeks and over	14.5	8.4	9.8
52 weeks and over	na	na	4.5
South			
less than 5 weeks	37.5%	49.1%	45.2%
5-14 weeks	34.2	31.6	32.4
15 weeks and over	28.3	19.4	22.5
27 weeks and over	14.3	8.8	10.8
52 weeks and over	7.6	4.8	5.9
West			
less than 5 weeks	43.0%	47.1%	46.0%
5-14 weeks	27.1	31.3	31.2
15 weeks and over	30.8	21.6	22.9
27 weeks and over	17.8	10.5	11.5
52 weeks and over	10.3	5.1	5.7

continued on the next page

Table 6.14 continued

	Black	White	All Races
2002			
Northeast			
less than 5 weeks	25.7%	31.9%	30.3%
5-14 weeks	30.3	30.2	30.4
15 weeks and over	44.0	37.9	39.4
27 weeks and over	25.0	20.7	21.6
52 weeks and over	13.0	8.9	9.7
Midwest			
less than 5 weeks	28.4%	36.4%	34.9%
5-14 weeks	30.5	31.9	31.5
15 weeks and over	41.1	31.8	33.6
27 weeks and over	20.5	15.5	16.5
52 weeks and over	11.1	6.6	7.5
South			
less than 5 weeks	28.7%	39.0%	35.3%
5-14 weeks	30.9	31.2	31.1
15 weeks and over	40.3	29.8	33.6
27 weeks and over	22.0	15.4	17.8
52 weeks and over	11.2	7.2	8.4
West			
less than 5 weeks	30.7%	37.6%	36.4%
5-14 weeks	30.1	30.1	30.0
15 weeks and over	39.8	32.3	33.6
27 weeks and over	23.5	17.3	18.4
52 weeks and over	11.4	8.1	8.7

SOURCE: U.S. Department of Labor, Bureau of Labor Statistics, Geographic Profile of Employment and Unemployment, 2000; table 11; 2002; table 11.
L 2 3/12·(year)

NOTES: 'All Races' includes other races not shown separately.

UNITS: Duration of unemployment by region as a percent of total unemployment in each region, 100.0%.

Table 6.15 Labor Force Status of the Civilian Noninstitutional Population 16 - 24 Years of Age, by School Enrollment, 2001 and 2003

	Black	White	All Races
2001			
All persons enrolled in school	2,759	14,906	18,949
civilian labor force	1,009	7,531	9,047
- employed	817	6,911	8,174
- unemployed	193	619	873
all persons enrolled in school below college level	1,480	7,027	na
civilian labor force	349	2,862	na
- employed	247	2,530	na
- unemployed	102	332	na
all persons enrolled in school on college level	1,279	7,879	9,958
civilian labor force	660	4,669	5,721
- employed	570	4,381	5,311
- unemployed	91	288	470
persons not enrolled in school	2,497	13,107	16,246
civilian labor force	1,898	10,995	13,411
- employed	1,482	9,901	11,822
- unemployed	416	1,094	1,588

continued on the next page

Table 6.15 continued

	Black	White	All Races
2003			
All persons enrolled in school	2,835	15,573	20,114
civilian labor force	951	7,309	8,932
- employed	758	6,712	8,069
- unemployed	193	597	863
all persons enrolled in school below college level	1,580	7,333	na
civilian labor force	351	2,510	na
- employed	234	2,185	na
- unemployed	116	326	na
all persons enrolled in school on college level	1,253	8,239	10,503
civilian labor force	600	4,798	5,914
- employed	524	4,527	5,538
- unemployed	77	271	376
persons not enrolled in school	2,345	12,570	15,903
civilian labor force	1,742	10,449	12,926
- employed	1,288	9,350	11,235
- unemployed	454	1,100	1,691

SOURCE: U.S. Bureau of the Census, Statistical Abstract of the United States, 2002; p. 371, table 567; 2004; p. 375, table 576 (data from U.S. Department of Labor, Bureau of Labor Statistics). C 3 134.(year)

NOTES: 'All Races' includes other races not shown separately.

UNITS: Civilian noninstitutional population, civilian labor force, employed and unemployed, in thousands of persons.

Table 6.16 Educational Attainment of Persons 16 Years and Over, by Labor Force Status and Sex, 2000 and 2004

	Black		White		All Races	
	male	female	male	female	male	female
2000						
High school graduate						
Employed	2,524	2,676	16,710	14,588	22,377	19,681
Unemployed	254	268	697	535	1,136	951
Not in labor force	966	1,480	5,577	11,677	7,173	14,757
Bachelor's degree						
Employed	900	1,097	10,789	9,363	13,028	11,786
Unemployed	27	19	171	172	250	225
Not in labor force	122	215	1,896	3,292	2,248	4,032
2004*						
High school graduate						
Employed	2,558	2,678	18,351	15,198	21,950	18,800
Unemployed	388	308	1,370	855	1,853	1,231
Not in labor force	1,241	1,712	6,917	13,288	8,482	15,749
Bachelor's degree						
Employed	921	1,271	11,993	10,627	14,064	12,954
Unemployed	30	57	410	315	490	422
Not in labor force	142	294	2,434	4,232	2,810	5,087

SOURCE: U.S. Bureau of the Census, Current Population Reports: Educational Attainment in the United States: March 2000 (Update); Series P-20, #536, pp. 1-7, 11, 12, table 5a; 2003; #550, table 5a; 2004; table 5a. <www census gov>

NOTES: 'All Races' includes other races not shown separately. '*' indicates year in which 'White' and 'Black' as shown are equivalent to 'White Alone' and 'Black Alone' that refer to people who reported 'White' and 'Black' respectively and did not report any other race category.

UNITS: Number of persons in thousands.

Table 6.17 Unemployment Rates of the Civilian Labor Force 25 - 64 Years of Age, by Educational Attainment, 1990 - 2003

	Black	White	All Races
1990			
Total	8.6%	3.8%	4.4%
less than 4 years of high school	13.3	7.6	8.5
4 years of high school only	9.5	4.2	4.9
1-3 years of college	6.8	3.2	3.7
4 or more years of college	3.0	2.1	2.2
2000			
Total	5.4%	3.0%	3.3
number	731	2,644	3,589
less than a high school diploma	10.4	7.5	7.9
high school graduate, no college	6.3	3.3	3.8
less than a bachelor's degree	4.3	2.7	3.0
college graduate	2.5	1.4	1.5
2001			
Total	6.5%	3.1%	3.5%
number	890	2,995	4,072
less than a high school diploma	14.0	7.2	8.1
high school graduate, no college	7.7	3.6	4.2
less than a bachelor's degree	4.3	2.7	2.9
college graduate	3.3	1.8	2.0
2003			
Total	8.3%	4.3%	4.8%
number	1,157	4,389	6,028
less than a high school diploma	13.9	7.8	8.8
high school graduate, no college	9.3	4.8	5.5
less than a bachelor's degree	7.9	4.2	4.8
college graduate	4.5	2.8	3.1

SOURCE: U.S. Bureau of the Census, Statistical Abstract of the United States, 1992; p. 400, table 637; 2001; p. 389, table 604; 2002; p. 390, table 598; 2004; p. 396, table 608 (data from U.S. Department of Labor, Bureau of Labor Statistics). C 3 134 (year)

NOTES: 'All Races' includes other races not shown separately. Data is for persons 25 years old and over.

UNITS: Unemployment rates (percent of the civilian labor force that is unemployed) as a percent of the total civilian labor force. Number in thousands.

Table 6.18 Self-Employed Workers, 1980 - 2004

	Black	White	All Races
1980	342	8,116	8,642
1985	379	8,659	9,269
1990	461	9,377	10,160
1991	475	9,512	10,341
1992	452	9,215	10,017
1993	468	9,486	10,335
1994	458	8,179	9,003
1995	488	8,105	8,902
1996	481	8,106	8,971
1997	471	8,153	9,056
1998	497	8,030	8,962
1999	520	7,846	8,790
2000	583	7,692	8,674
2001	544	7,639	8,594
2002	582	7,914	8,923
2003	593	8,160	9,344
2004	600	8,252	9,467

SOURCE: U.S. Bureau of the Census, Statistical Abstract of the United States, 1989; p. 380, table 627 (data from U.S. Department of Labor, Bureau of Labor Statistics, *Employment and Earnings*). C 3 134:989

U.S. Department of Labor, Bureau of Labor Statistics, *Employment and Earnings*, January, 1991; p. 210, table 41; January, 1992; p. 210, table 41; January, 1993; p. 220, table 41; January, 1994; p. 230, table 41; January, 1999; p. 184, table 12; January, 2000; p. 184, table 12; January, 2001; p. 184, table 12; January, 2002; p. 182, table 12; January, 2004; p. 215, table 12; January, 2005; p. 216, table 12 (data from the Current Population Survey). L2 41/2.(vol)/1 (year)

NOTES: 'All Races' includes other races not shown separately.

UNITS: Self-employed workers in thousands of persons.

Table 6.19 Labor Force Participation Rates for Wives in Married Couple Families, by Age of Own Youngest Child, 1980 - 2003

	Black	White	All Races
1980			
All wives in married couple families	59.3%	49.3%	50.2%
wives with no children under 18	51.2	45.5	46.0
wives with children under 18	65.6	53.2	54.3
with children under 6	63.4	43.5	45.3
with children under 3	57.7	40.0	41.5
- 1 year or under	52.9	37.7	39.0
- 2 years old	71.0	46.1	48.1
with children 3-5	72.3	49.4	51.7
- 3 years old	73.4	48.4	51.5
- 4 years old	66.4	49.8	51.4
- 5 years old	77.8	50.4	52.4
with children 6-13 years	71.8	61.4	62.6
with children 14-17 years	58.4	60.6	60.5
1990			
All wives in married couple families	64.7%	57.6%	58.2%
wives with no children under 18	52.9	50.8	51.1
wives with children under 18	75.6	65.6	66.3
with children under 6	73.1	57.8	58.9
with children under 3	67.5	54.9	55.5
- 1 year or under	64.4	53.3	53.9
- 2 years old	75.4	60.3	60.9
with children 3-5	80.4	62.5	64.1
- 3 years old	74.5	62.3	63.1
- 4 years old	80.6	63.2	65.1
- 5 years old	86.2	62.0	64.5
with children 6-13 years	77.6	72.6	73.0
with children 14-17 years	78.8	74.9	75.1

continued on the next page

Table 6.19 continued

	Black	White	All Races
2000			
All wives in married couple families	70.9%	61.3%	62.0%
wives with no children under 18	60.9	54.4	54.7
wives with children under 18	80.9	69.8	70.6
with children under 6	78.0	61.5	62.8
with children under 3	74.2	57.5	59.0
- 1 year or under	72.3	57.6	58.3
- 2 years old	80.1	59.8	61.9
with children 3-5	82.5	67.4	68.4
- 3 years old	80.4	65.2	66.0
- 4 years old	82.0	68.7	69.7
- 5 years old	88.0	69.4	70.6
with children 6-13 years	84.3	75.0	75.8
with children 14-17 years	79.6	81.0	80.6
2003			
All wives in married couple families	68.7%	61.3%	61.8%
wives with no children under 18	58.5	55.5	55.7
wives with children under 18	79.2	68.7	69.2
with children under 6	70.5	59.4	59.8
with children under 3	66.4	56.1	56.5
- 1 year or under	63.6	54.6	54.7
- 2 years old	77.7	60.5	61.3
with children 3-5	75.2	64.3	64.8
- 3 years old	75.0	63.2	63.6
- 4 years old	72.3	63.9	64.1
- 5 years old	75.9	65.7	66.9
with children 6-13 years	85.5	74.4	75.1
with children 14-17 years	86.3	80.9	81.2

SOURCE: U.S. Bureau of the Census, Statistical Abstract of the United States, 1992; p. 388, table 621; 1994; p. 402, table 627; 2001; p. 373, table 578; 2002; p. 373, table 571; 2004; p. 377, table 580 (data from the Current Population Survey).
C 3 134 (year)

NOTES: 'All Races' includes other races not shown separately. Civilian noninstitutional population, 16 years old and over.

UNITS: Participation rates in percent.

Table 6.20 Workers Paid Hourly Rates With Earnings at or Below the Minimum Wage, 2001 and 2003

	Black	White	All Races
2001			
Number of workers			
All workers paid hourly rates	10,014	59,152	72,486
at or below $5.15 per hour	297	1,861	2,238
at $5.15 per hour	114	502	636
below $5.15 per hour	183	1,359	1,602
Percent of all workers paid hourly rates			
All at or below $5.15 per hour	3.0%	3.1%	3.1%
at $5.15 per hour	1.1	0.8	0.9
below $5.15 per hour	1.8	2.3	2.2
Median hourly earnings	$9.66	$10.25	$10.17
2003			
Number of workers			
All workers paid hourly rates	9,419	59,109	72,946
at or below $5.15 per hour	250	1,746	2,100
at $5.15 per hour	105	421	545
below $5.15 per hour	145	1,325	1,555
Percent of all workers paid hourly rates			
All at or below $5.15 per hour	2.7%	3.0%	2.9%
at $5.15 per hour	1.1	0.7	0.7
below $5.15 per hour	1.5	2.2	2.1
Median hourly earnings	7.89	10.97	10.85

SOURCE: U.S. Bureau of the Census, Statistical Abstract of the United States, 2003; p. 405, table 617; 2004; p. 413, table 627 (data from the U.S. Bureau of Labor Statistics). C3 134 (year)

NOTES: 'All Races' includes other races not shown separately. Workers 16 years and over.

UNITS: Number of workers in thousands; 'percent of all workers paid hourly rates' in percent, as a percent of total, 100.0%; median hourly earnings of workers paid hourly rates in dollars per hour.

Table 6.21 Union Membership, by Sex, 2004

	Black	White	All Races
Men			
total employed	6,409	53,432	64,145
members of unions			
number	1,085	7,260	8,878
as a percent of total employed	16.9%	13.6%	13.8%
represented by unions			
total	1,185	7,854	9,638
as a percent of total employed	18.5%	14.7%	15.0%
Women			
total employed	7,681	47,908	59,408
members of unions			
number	1,045	5,121	6,593
as a percent of total employed	13.6%	10.7%	11.1%
represented by unions			
total	1,170	5,803	7,450
as a percent of total employed	15.2%	12.1%	12.5%

SOURCE: U.S. Department of Labor, Bureau of Labor Statistics, *Employment and Earnings*, January 2005, p. 255, table 40, (data from the Current Population Survey). L 2 41/2.40/1: (year)

NOTES: 'All Races' includes other races not shown separately. 'Members of unions' includes members of a labor union or an employee association similar to a union. 'Represented by unions' includes members of a labor union or an employee association similar to a union as well as workers who report no union affiliation but whose jobs are covered by a union or an employee association contract.

UNITS: Total employed, members of unions and represented by unions in thousands of persons 16 years old and older; percent as shown.

Chapter 7: Earnings, Income, Poverty & Wealth

Table 7.01 Money Income of Households, 1980 – 2003

	Black	White	All Races
Median income			
1980	$22,760	$39,506	$37,447
1985	24,163	40,614	38,510
1990	25,488	42,622	40,865
1995	26,842	42,871	40,845
2000	31,690	46,910	44,853
2001	30,625	46,261	43,882
2002*	29,691	46,119	43,381
2003*	29,645	45,631	43,318
Mean income			
1980	$29,539	$46,334	$44,537
1985	31,527	49,339	47,394
1990	33,865	53,105	51,046
1995	36,439	56,012	53,865
2000	41,849	63,294	61,031
2001	40,786	62,883	60,488
2002*	40,928	61,544	59,177
2003*	40,131	61,587	59,067

SOURCE: U.S. Bureau of the Census, Current Population Reports: Income 2003; "Table H-5: Households by Total Money Income, Race, and Hispanic Origin of Householder: 1967 to 2003.

NOTES: 'All Races' includes other races not shown separately. '*' indicates a change in race classification: 'White' or 'White alone' refers to people who reported White and not any other race category.

UNITS: Median and mean money income in 2003 CPI-U-RS 28/ adjusted dollars, as shown.

Table 7.02 Money Income of Households, by Selected Household Characteristic, 1990 and 2001

	Black	White	All Races
1990			
Number of households	10,671	80,968	94,312
percent of households with current dollar incomes of:			
under $5,000	14.1%	4.0%	5.2%
$5,000-$9,999	16.7	8.8	9.7
$10,000-$14,999	11.6	9.2	9.5
$15,000-$24,999	19.1	17.7	17.7
$25,000-$34,999	13.5	16.1	15.8
$35,000-$49,999	13.1	18.0	17.5
$50,000-$74,999	8.1	15.8	14.9
$75,000-$99,999	2.7	5.7	5.4
$100,000 and over	1.1	4.7	4.3
mean income	$24,814	$38,912	$37,403
median income	$18,676	$31,231	$29,943
Median income by:			
type of residence			
nonfarm	$18,734	$31,216	$29,901
farm	na	31,819	21,589
inside metropolitan area	20,121	33,460	31,823
outside metropolitan area	13,119	24,887	23,709
type of household			
family households	$21,899	$37,219	$35,707
married couple families	33,893	40,433	39,996
non-family households	11,789	18,449	17,690
male householder living alone	13,126	20,900	19,964
female householder living alone	7,674	13,094	12,548
age of householder			
15-24 years old	$ 9,816	$19,662	$18,002
25-34 years old	18,339	31,859	30,359
35-44 years old	26,011	40,423	38,561
45-54 years old	26,910	44,098	41,922
55-64 years old	19,226	34,249	32,365
65 years old and over	9,902	17,539	16,855

continued on the next page

Table 7.02 continued

	Black	White	All Races
1990 - continued			
size of household			
one person	$ 10,156	$15,981	$15,344
two persons	20,122	32,561	31,358
three persons	21,474	38,930	36,765
four persons	25,683	43,363	41,473
five persons	24,342	40,715	39,275
six persons	26,742	40,420	38,159
seven or more persons	22,361	40,822	36,108
number of earners			
no earners	$ 5,870	$12,395	$11,159
one earner	17,040	25,801	24,575
two earners or more	36,404	45,705	44,887
work experience of the householder			
all civilian householders	$18,471	$31,242	$29,945
worked	25,683	37,441	36,329
worked year-round full-time	31,042	42,010	40,976
did not work	7,249	15,144	13,820
housing tenure			
owner occupied	$27,377	$36,810	$36,298
renter occupied	13,929	21,962	20,722

continued on the next page

Table 7.02 continued

	Black	White	All Races
2001			
Number of households	13,315	90,682	109,297
percent of households with current dollar incomes of:			
under $5,000	6.8%	2.4%	3.1%
$5,000-$9,999	10.9	5.2	5.9
10,000-$14,999	8.7	6.7	6.9
$15,000-$24,999	16.5	13.0	13.3
$25,000-$34,999	14.3	12.2	12.4
$35,000-$49,999	14.9	15.5	15.4
$50,000-$74,999	15.4	18.8	18.4
$75,000-$99,999	6.8	11.4	10.8
$100,000 and over	5.6	14.8	13.8
median income	$29,470	$44,517	$42,228
mean income	$39,248	$60,512	$58,208
Median income by:			
type of residence			
inside metropolitan area	$30,726	$47,759	$45,219
outside metropolitan area	21,328	34,971	33,601
type of household			
family households	$35,080	$55,051	$52,275
married couple families	51,557	61,137	60,471
non-family households	20,610	26,114	25,631
male householder living alone	22,544	29,049	28,283
female householder living alone	15,508	18,199	17,868
age of householder			
15-24 years old	$18,386	$30,860	$28,196
25-34 years old	30,206	47,412	45,080
35-44 years old	36,794	56,642	53,320
45-54 years old	36,824	61,643	58,045
55-64 years old	30,281	47,907	45,864
65 years old and over	16,761	23,769	23,118

continued on the next page

Table 7.02 continued

	Black	White	All Races
2001 - continued			
size of household			
one person	$18,176	$22,079	$21,761
two persons	29,936	47,109	45,245
three persons	33,752	58,007	54,481
four persons	42,425	65,815	62,595
five persons	42,655	62,931	59,898
six persons	50,465	59,573	57,548
seven or more persons	40,695	57,488	54,560
number of earners			
no earners	$9,142	$16,765	$15,452
one earner	26,115	35,830	34,104
two earners or more	56,453	69,522	68,106
work experience of the householder			
all civilian householders	$29,470	$44,517	$42,228
worked	37,436	55,618	53,002
worked year-round full-time	42,343	60,783	58,608
did not work	12,505	22,192	20,887

SOURCE: U.S. Bureau of the Census, Current Population Reports: Income 2000; published September 2001; "(Table) 1. Median Income of Households by Selected Characteristics, Race, and Hispanic Origin of Householder: 2000, 1999, and 1998"; "(Table) 2. Selected Characteristics – Households by Total Money Income in 2000".
U.S. Bureau of the Census, Current Population Reports: Income 2001; published September 2002; "(Table) 1. Median Income of Households by Selected Characteristics, Race, and Hispanic Origin of Householder: 2001, 2000 and 1999"; "(Table) H-17. Households by Total Money Income, Race, and Hispanic Origin of Householder: 1967 to 2001".

NOTES: 'All Races' includes other races not shown separately. Number of households as of March of the following year. 'Occupation of the householder' represents the longest job held by the householder.

UNITS: Number of households in thousands; mean and median income in current dollars.

Table 7.03 Money Income of Families, 1980 – 2003

	Black	White	All Races
Median income			
1980	$25,788	$44,569	$42,776
1985	26,339	45,742	43,518
1990	28,135	48,480	46,429
1995	29,956	49,191	46,843
1996	29,792	50,275	47,516
1997	31,457	51,421	49,017
1998	31,890	53,168	50,689
1999	33,755	54,411	51,996
2000	34,616	54,509	52,148
2001	33,598	54,067	51,407
2002*	33,525	54,633	51,680
2003*	34,369	55,768	52,680
Mean income			
1980	$32,161	$50,744	$48,781
1985	33,514	53,937	51,692
1990	36,187	58,484	56,015
1995	39,231	61,821	59,234
1996	39,243	63,127	60,295
1997	40,148	65,536	62,582
1998	41,824	67,659	64,628
1999	45,455	69,272	66,533
2000	45,078	70,386	67,609
2001	43,938	69,856	66,863
2002*	45,485	69,803	66,970
2003*	45,278	71,770	68,563

SOURCE: U.S. Bureau of the Census, Current Population Reports: Historical Income Tables - Families, "(Table) F-23. Families by Total Money Income, Race, and Hispanic Origin of Householder: 1967 to 2003;" published September 2003.
U.S. Bureau of the Census, Current Population Reports: Income 2003; "(Table) FINC-01. Selected Characteristics of Families by Total Money Income in 2003.

NOTES: 'Total' includes other races and ethnic groups not shown separately. '*' indicates year in which 'White' and 'Black' as shown are respectively equivalent to 'White Alone' and 'Black Alone' that refer to people who reported 'White' or 'Black' and did not report any other race category.

UNITS: Median and mean money income in 2001 CPI-U-RS 28/ adjusted dollars, as shown except for 2002 and 2003 that are in current dollars.

Table 7.04 Money Income of Families, by Selected Family Characteristic, 1985

	Black	White	All Races
Families			
Number of families	6,921	54,991	63,558
percent of families with incomes:			
under $2,500	4.2%	1.6%	1.9%
$2,500-$4,499	9.3	2.1	2.9
$5,000-$7,499	9.4	3.6	4.2
$7,500-$9,999	7.7	3.9	4.3
$10,000-$12,499	7.9	4.8	5.2
$12,500-$14,999	6.4	4.9	5.0
$15,000-$19,999	13.0	10.3	10.5
$20,000-$24,999	9.0	10.4	10.3
$25,000-$34,999	14.3	19.2	18.6
$35,000-$49,999	11.8	19.7	18.8
$50,000 and over	7.0	19.6	18.3
median income	$16,786	$29,152	$27,735
mean income	$21,359	$34,375	$32,944
Mean family income by:			
occupation of the householder			
managerial, professional specialty	$38,870	$52,649	$51,820
technical, sales, administrative support	24,732	38,798	37,436
service occupations	19,485	26,604	24,846
farming, forestry, fishing	16,185	21,305	21,285
precision production, craft, repair	30,315	33,691	33,507
operators, fabricators, laborers	24,223	29,449	28,725
work experience of the householder			
worked at full time jobs	$28,022	$39,510	$38,437
worked 50-52 weeks	30,281	41,992	40,968

continued on the next page

Table 7.04 continued

	Black	White	All Races
Mean family income - continued			
type of family			
married couple families	$28,163	$36,911	$36,267
wife in paid labor force	33,120	41,818	41,058
wife not in paid labor force	19,306	31,934	30,650
male householder, no wife present	18,205	29,041	27,525
female householder, no husband present	13,050	19,468	17,647
type of income			
wages and salaries	$21,651	$31,277	$30,258
non-farm self-employment	10,165	14,565	14,420
farm self employment	na	4,593	4,557
property income	1,042	3,486	3,327
- interest income	722	2,440	2,328
transfer payments and all other income	5,491	7,776	7,469
- social security or railroad retirement income	5,801	7,684	7,488
-public assistance and supplemental income	3,475	3,416	3,498

SOURCE: U.S. Bureau of the Census, Current Population Reports: Money Income of Households Families and Persons in the United States; March 1985, Series P-60, #156, pp. 26-29, tables 9, 10; pp. 40-46, tables 13, 14; pp. 56-64, table 17; pp. 86-88, table 25. C3 186:P-60/156

NOTES: 'All Races' includes other races not shown separately. Number of families as of March of the following year. 'Occupation of the householder' represents the longest job held by the householder. 'Property income' includes interest, dividends, net rental income, income from trusts and estates, and net royalty income.

UNITS: Number of families and families with income, in thousands of families; percent as a percent as shown; mean and median income in current dollars.

Table 7.05 Money Income of Families, by Selected Family Characteristic, 1990

	Black	White	All Races
Families			
Number of families	7,471	58,803	66,322
percent of families with current dollar incomes of:			
under $5,000	11.5%	2.5%	3.6%
$5,000-$9,999	14.1	4.7	5.8
$10,000-$14,999	11.3	7.0	7.5
$15,000-$24,999	19.5	16.0	16.4
$25,000-$34,999	14.0	16.5	16.2
$35,000-$49,999	15.0	20.8	20.0
$50,000-$74,999	9.8	19.3	18.2
$75,000-$99,999	3.4	7.3	6.9
$100,000 and over	1.3	5.9	5.4
mean income	$27,554	$44,532	$42,652
median income	$21,423	$36,915	$35,353
Median income by:			
type of residence			
nonfarm	$21,467	$36,974	$35,376
farm	na	34,476	34,171
inside metropolitan area	22,924	40,086	37,893
outside metropolitan area	15,677	29,693	28,272
type of family			
married couple families	$33,784	$40,331	$39,895
wife in paid labor force	40,038	47,247	46,777
wife not in paid labor force	20,333	30,781	30,265
male householder, no wife present	21,848	30,570	29,046
female householder, no husband present	12,125	19,528	16,932

continued on the next page

Table 7.05 continued

	Black	White	All Races
Median income by:			
age of householder			
15-24 years old	$ 7,218	$18,234	$16,219
25-34 years old	17,130	33,457	31,497
35-44 years old	27,025	42,632	41,061
45-54 years old	30,847	49,249	47,165
55-64 years old	25,442	40,416	39,035
65 years old and over	16,585	25,864	25,049
size of family			
two persons	$19,020	$31,734	$30,428
three persons	20,602	38,858	36,644
four persons	25,758	43,352	41,451
five persons	22,455	41,037	39,452
six persons	26,926	40,387	38,379
seven or more persons	22,501	39,845	35,363
number of earners			
no earners	$ 6,305	$17,369	$15,047
one earner	16,308	27,670	25,878
two earners or more	36,741	46,261	45,462

SOURCE: U.S. Bureau of the Census, Current Population Reports: Money Income of Households, Families, and Persons in the United States: March 1990, Series P-60, #174, pp. 52-54, table 13; p. 56, table 14. C3 186/2 990

NOTES: 'All Races' includes other races not shown separately. Number of families as of March of the following year.

UNITS: Number of families and families with income, in thousands of families; percent as a percent as shown; mean and median income in current dollars.

Table 7.06 Money Income of Families, by Selected Family Characteristic, 2003

	Black	White	All Races
Families			
Number of families	8,914	62,620	76,232
with current dollar incomes of:			
under $5,000	593	1,382	2,151
$5,000-$9,999	628	1,302	2,095
$10,000-$14,999	692	2,234	3,120
$15,000-$24,999	1,408	6,610	8,489
$25,000-$34,999	1,187	7,049	8,657
$35,000-$49,999	1,402	9,366	11,443
$50,000-$74,999	1,458	12,936	15,352
$75,000-$99,999	772	8,784	10,157
$100,000 and over	775	12,953	14,768
median income	34,369	55,768	52,680
mean income	45,278	71,770	68,563
Median income by:			
type of residence			
inside metropolitan area	36,060	59,846	56,200
outside metropolitan area	26,893	44,492	42,532
type of family			
married couple families	52,556	63,038	62,281
wife in paid labor force	61,902	76,259	75,170
wife not in paid labor force	32,345	41,334	41,122
male householder, no wife present	29,788	39,286	38,032
female householder, no husband present	21,336	29,120	26,550

continued on the next page

Table 7.06 continued

	Black	White	All Races
Median income by:			
age of householder			
15-24 years old	15,230	29,188	26,198
25-34 years old	28,993	49,844	46,554
35-44 years old	38,268	61,956	59,122
45-54 years old	45,637	74,163	70,149
55-64 years old	41,016	62,455	60,976
65 years old and over	28,407	36,121	35,310
size of family			
two persons	30,201	47,353	45,254
three persons	33,700	58,693	54,664
four persons	42,050	68,480	65,093
five persons	39,719	63,889	60,422
six persons	45,879	60,723	58,263
seven or more persons	40,776	61,422	59,858
number of earners			
no earners	10,324	24,183	21,878
one earner	25,339	39,127	36,661
two earners or more	60,030	75,142	73,483

SOURCE: U.S. Bureau of the Census, Current Population Reports: Income 2003; "(Table) FINC-01. Selected Characteristics of Families by Total Money Income in 2003".

NOTES: 'All Races' includes other races not shown separately. Number of families as of March of the following year. 'White' and 'Black' as shown are respectively equivalent to 'White Alone' and 'Black Alone' that refer to people who reported 'White' or 'Black' and did not report any other race category.

UNITS: Number of families and families with income, in thousands of families; mean and median income in current dollars.

Table 7.07 Median Weekly Earnings of Families, by Type of Family and Number of Earners, 1985, 1990, 1993

	Black	White	All Races
1985			
All families with earners	$378	$543	$522
married couple families	487	589	582
with one earner	257	395	385
with two or more earners	622	723	715
families maintained by women	259	311	297
families maintained by men	360	475	450
1990			
All families with earners	$459	$681	$653
married couple families	601	745	732
with one earner	304	473	455
with two or more earners	748	892	880
families maintained by women	314	382	363
families maintained by men	397	539	514
1993			
All families with earners	$490	$739	$707
married couple families	674	816	804
with one earner	344	492	481
with two or more earners	846	984	973
families maintained by women	334	415	393
families maintained by men	413	547	523

SOURCE: U.S. Department of Labor, Bureau of Labor Statistics, Handbook of Labor Statistics, 1989; p. 200, table 44 (data from the Current Population Survey). L 2.3/5.989
U.S. Department of Labor, Bureau of Labor Statistics, *Employment and Earnings*, January, 1991; p. 219, table 52; January, 1994; p. 239, table 52 (data from the Current Population Survey). L 2 41/2:37/1 (year)

NOTES: 'All Races' includes other races not shown separately. Data excludes families in which there is no wage or salary earner, or in which the husband, wife, or other person maintaining the family is either self-employed or in the armed forces.

UNITS: Median weekly earnings in dollars.

Table 7.08 Money Income of Persons 15 Years Old and Older, by Selected Characteristic, 1985

	Black		White		All Races	
	male	female	male	female	male	female
Number of persons	9,309	11,263	76,617	82,345	88,474	96,354
persons with incomes:						
under $2,000	909	1,301	5,180	14,024	6,304	15,848
$2,000-$2,999	400	871	1,808	4,420	2,297	5,425
$3,000-$3,999	407	993	2,190	4,856	2,671	5,958
$4,000-$4,999	479	946	2,095	4,635	2,642	5,693
$5,000-$5,999	351	540	2,169	4,201	2,595	4,848
$6,000-$6,999	353	556	2,278	3,992	2,708	4,648
$7,000-$8,499	584	707	3,402	5,006	4,132	5,855
$8,500-$9,999	365	416	2,896	3,779	3,353	4,288
$10,000-$12,499	737	788	5,895	6,579	6,859	7,576
$12,500-$14,999	598	530	4,527	4,672	5,245	5,339
$15,000-$17,499	673	531	4,940	4,359	5,739	5,012
$17,500-$19,999	453	363	3,869	2,980	4,423	3,432
$20,000-$24,999	672	483	7,521	4,839	8,410	5,513
$25,000-$29,999	454	336	6,374	2,759	7,018	3,194
$30,000-$34,999	301	135	5,324	1,437	5,767	1,633
$35,000-$49,999	289	99	7,730	1,450	8,211	1,585
$50,000-$74,999	80	14	3,421	484	3,588	509
$75,000 and over	32	4	1,603	169	1,669	177
median income	$10,768	$ 6,277	$17,111	$ 7,357	$16,311	$ 7,217
mean income	$13,376	$ 9,001	$21,523	$10,317	$20,652	$10,173
Mean income by:						
occupation						
managerial, professional specialty	$25,575	$18,273	$34,711	$17,763	$34,201	$17,857
technical, sales, administrative support	16,026	11,645	24,050	10,988	23,293	11,076
service occupations	10,270	6,800	13,161	5,935	12,549	6,104
farming, forestry, fishing	4,800	na	8,241	3,865	8,024	3,762
precision production, craft, repair	$16,314	$11,217	$20,593	$12,998	$20,277	$12,595
operators, fabricators, laborers	13,808	9,649	16,378	9,528	15,971	$9,548
work experience						
worked at full time jobs	$16,618	$12,988	$24,531	$14,556	$23,767	$14,364
worked 50-52 weeks	19,940	15,448	28,140	17,249	27,414	17,028

continued on the next page

Table 7.08 continued

	Black		White		All Races	
	male	female	male	female	male	female
educational attainment						
less than 8 years of school	$ 7,962	$ 4,684	$10,593	$ 5,809	$10,016	$ 5,582
high school graduates	15,392	10,155	21,584	10,121	20,916	10,120
1-3 years of college	18,658	12,687	25,768	12,763	24,987	12,754
4 or more years of college	27,210	19,587	38,460	18,367	37,570	18,410
type of income						
wages and salaries	$14,446	$10,668	$21,848	$11,295	$21,056	$11,239
non-farm self-employment	10,222	5,565	16,083	5,885	15,834	5,867
farm self employment	na	na	4,234	1,654	4,184	1,695
property income	709	708	1,866	2,021	1,794	1,937
- interest income	505	483	1,305	1,454	1,254	1,395
transfer payments and all other income	4,777	3,641	6,812	4,428	6,572	4,318
- social security or railroad retirement	4,757	3,620	5,803	4,330	5,701	4,261
-public assistance and supplemental income	2,383	2,922	2,526	2,881	2,560	2,919

SOURCE: U.S. Bureau of the Census, Current Population Reports: Money Income of Households in the United States: March 1985, Series P-60, #156, pp. 107-109, table 31; pp. 135-138, table 35; pp. 141-143, table 37; pp. 160-163, tables 40, 41. C3 186 P-60/156

NOTES: 'All Races' includes other races not shown separately. Number of persons as of March of the following year. Data is based on persons living in households. Persons with incomes under $2,000 includes those with a loss. Occupation represents the longest job held by the person during the year. Educational attainment covers persons 25 years old and older; income covers persons 15 years old and older. 'Property income' includes interest, dividends, net rental income, income from trusts and estates, and net royalty income.

UNITS: Number of persons and persons by income in thousands of persons; median and mean income in dollars.

Table 7.09 Money Income of Persons 15 Years Old and Older, by Selected Characteristic, 1990

	Black		White		All Races	
	male	female	male	female	male	female
Number of persons	10,074	12,124	79,555	85,012	92,240	100,680
persons with incomes:						
under $5,000	1,866	3,455	8,539	22,062	10,820	26,337
$5,000-$9,999	1,643	2,561	9,249	16,358	11,312	19,563
$10,000-$14,999	1,323	1,487	9,529	11,652	11,253	13,566
$15,000-$24,999	1,859	1,793	16,679	15,162	19,166	17,516
$25,000-$34,999	1,112	883	12,707	7,547	14,185	8,707
$35,000-$49,999	716	392	10,531	3,895	11,604	4,457
$50,000-$74,999	237	83	5,973	1,382	6,433	1,535
$75,000 and over	64	32	3,274	509	3,446	565
median income	$12,868	$ 8,328	$21,170	$10,317	$20,293	$10,070
mean income	$16,985	$12,049	$27,142	$14,138	$26,041	$13,913
Mean income by:						
work experience						
worked at full time jobs	$20,729	$16,992	$30,498	$19,269	$29,524	$19,010
worked 50-52 weeks	24,021	19,976	34,300	22,198	33,334	21,977
educational attainment						
less than 8 years of school	$13,719	$ 7,565	$15,057	$ 8,598	$14,914	$ 8,602
high school graduates	18,879	14,146	25,520	13,955	24,727	13,999
1-3 years of college	23,877	17,499	31,235	17,148	30,340	17,188
4 or more years of college	33,404	26,195	45,709	25,230	44,864	25,388
age						
15-24 years old	$ 7,254	$ 6,105	$ 8,915	$ 7,161	$ 8,693	$ 6,998
25-34 years old	16,948	12,436	25,442	15,317	24,365	14,955
35-44 years old	23,266	17,271	35,723	17,724	34,468	17,667
45-54 years old	24,268	16,963	38,632	17,845	37,182	17,831
55-64 years old	18,585	11,234	33,396	14,159	31,899	13,834
65 years old and over	10,954	7,136	20,918	11,864	20,011	11,441

continued on the next page

Table 7.09 continued

	Black		White		All Races	
	male	female	male	female	male	female
Mean income by:						
marital status						
single	$11,997	$10,306	$16,902	$14,504	$16,112	$13,656
married	21,648	13,711	32,362	13,828	31,488	13,858
spouse present	22,457	14,261	32,627	13,805	31,888	13,883
spouse absent	16,790	11,910	25,396	14,255	23,158	13,508
widowed	10,873	8,985	18,528	13,822	17,440	13,190
divorced	19,120	16,781	26,830	19,448	25,787	19,058

SOURCE: U.S. Bureau of the Census, Current Population Reports: Money Income of Households, Families, and Persons in the United States· March 1990, Series P-60, #174, pp. 104-105, table 24; p. 108, table 25; pp. 112-119, table 26; pp. 124-127, table 28; pp. 128-149, table 29; pp. 160-163, table 31. C3 186/2 990

NOTES: 'All Races' includes other races not shown separately. Number of persons as of March of the following year. Data is based on persons living in households. Persons with incomes under $5,000 includes those with a loss. Educational attainment covers persons 25 years old and older; income covers persons 15 years old and older. Single persons are those who were never married.

UNITS: Number of persons and persons with income, in thousands of persons; percent as a percent as shown; mean and median income in current dollars.

Table 7.10 Money Income of Persons 15 Years Old and Older, by Selected Characteristic, 2003

	Black		White		All Races	
	male	female	male	female	male	female
Total with income	10,003	12,564	84,405	83,852	100,769	102,713
persons with incomes:						
$1-$2,499 or loss	676	938	4,144	8,679	5,233	10,431
$2,500-$4,999	481	782	2,197	4,713	2,937	5,903
$5,000-$7,499	711	1,280	2,983	6,800	3,987	8,585
$7,500-$9,999	583	1,025	3,008	6,064	3,861	7,570
$10,000-$12,499	618	999	4,470	6,398	5,391	7,838
$12,500-$14,999	427	748	3,584	4,557	4,263	5,571
$15,000-$17,499	534	807	4,196	4,866	5,062	6,042
$17,500-$19,999	491	554	3,242	3,417	3,946	4,201
$20,000-$22,499	604	726	4,213	4,248	5,142	5,284
$22,500-$24,999	358	495	2,865	3,110	3,416	3,764
$25,000-$27,499	514	657	3,815	3,664	4,607	4,581
$27,500-$29,999	285	392	2,206	2,372	2,612	2,897
$30,000-$32,499	533	525	4,377	3,548	5,167	4,315
$32,500-$34,999	163	241	1,789	1,713	2,072	2,066
$35,000-$37,499	356	372	3,182	2,682	3,767	3,243
$37,500-$39,999	199	232	1,729	1,494	2,037	1,820
$40,000-$42,499	421	337	3,409	2,291	4,108	2,807
$42,500-$44,999	132	133	1,422	1,167	1,623	1,369
$45,000-$47,499	247	174	2,317	1,413	2,744	1,677
$47,500-$49,999	120	126	1,263	920	1,467	1,121
$50,000-$52,499	260	182	2,742	1,445	3,210	1,778
$52,500-$54,999	106	84	1,108	700	1,267	819
$55,000-$57,499	136	102	1,672	760	1,900	911
$57,500-$59,999	63	37	796	407	903	476

continued on the next page

Table 7.10 continued

	Black		White		All Races	
	male	female	male	female	male	female
$60,000-$62,499	148	90	2,002	879	2,317	1,041
$62,500-$64,999	52	67	760	371	845	469
$65,000-$67,499	95	54	1,126	544	1,311	669
$67,500-$69,999	33	37	640	320	708	384
$70,000-$72,499	67	49	1,196	590	1,379	682
$72,500-$74,999	34	28	481	190	554	233
$75,000-$77,499	58	37	1,045	368	1,177	451
$77,500-$79,999	36	29	449	192	513	236
$80,000-$82,499	61	32	891	292	1,034	355
$82,500-$84,999	14	13	370	162	415	199
$85,000-$87,499	48	8	625	229	725	253
$87,500-$89,999	20	12	314	127	350	151
$90,000-$92,499	55	17	653	174	761	212
$92,500-$94,999	18	8	276	85	324	102
$95,000-$97,499	13	10	339	129	368	155
$97,500-$99,999	14	4	194	77	223	87
$100,000 and over	218	122	6,317	1,694	7,044	1,964
median income	21,986	16,581	30,732	17,422	29,931	17,259
mean income	28,869	22,369	43,030	24,897	41,483	24,630

SOURCE: U.S. Bureau of the Census and Bureau of Labor Statistics, Annual Demographic Survey, March Supplement, 2003; "(Table) PINC-01 Selected Characteristics of People 15 Years and Over, by Total Money Income in 2003, Work Experience in 2003, Race, Hispanic Origin, and Sex".

NOTES: 'All Races' includes other races not shown separately. Number of persons as of March of the following year.

UNITS: Number of persons with income, in thousands of persons; mean and median income in current dollars.

Table 7.11 Median Weekly Earnings of Full-Time Wage and Salary Workers, by Sex and Age, 1990-2004

	Black		White		All Races	
	male	female	male	female	male	female
1990						
All full-time wage and salary workers	$360	$308	$497	$355	$485	$348
workers 16-24 years old	na	na	na	na	283	254
workers 25 years old and over	na	na	na	na	514	370
2000						
All full-time wage and salary workers	$503	$429	$669	$500	$646	$491
workers 16-24 years old	na	na	na	na	376	342
workers 25 years old and over	na	na	na	na	700	515
2003						
All full-time wage and salary workers	$555	$491	$715	$567	$695	$552
workers 16-24 years old	na	na	na	na	398	371
workers 25 years old and over	na	na	na	na	744	584
2004						
All full-time wage and salary workers	$569	$505	$732	$584	$713	$573
workers 16-24 years old	na	na	na	na	400	375
workers 25 years old and over	na	na	na	na	762	599

SOURCE: U.S. Bureau of the Census, Statistical Abstract of the United States, 1991, p. 415, table 678, (data from *the Current Population Survey*). C 3 134 991
U.S. Department of Labor, Bureau of Labor Statistics, *Employment and Earnings*, January, 2002, p. 209, table 37; January, 2004, p. 247, table 37 ; January, 2005, p. 248, table 37 (data from the Current Population Survey). L 2 41/2·38/1.(year)

NOTES: 'All Races' includes other races not shown separately.

UNITS: Median weekly earning in dollars.

Table 7.12 Median Income of Year-Round, Full-Time Workers, by Sex, 1980 - 2003

	Black		White		All Races	
	male	female	male	female	male	female
1980	$23,094	$18,193	$32,658	$19,224	$31,729	$19,088
1985	22,791	18,656	32,678	20,596	31,548	20,372
1990	22,665	19,365	31,002	21,521	29,711	21,278
1995	24,798	21,079	33,515	24,264	32,199	23,777
1996	27,136	21,990	34,741	25,358	33,538	24,935
1997	26,897	22,764	36,118	26,470	35,248	26,029
1998	27,472	23,864	37,196	27,304	36,252	26,855
1999	30,297	25,142	39,331	28,023	37,574	27,370
2000	30,893	25,745	40,350	29,659	39,020	28,823
2001	31,921	27,297	40,790	30,849	40,136	30,420
2002	31,932	27,625	41,375	31,400	40,507	30,970
2003	33,429	27,622	42,142	32,192	41,503	31,653

SOURCE: U.S. Bureau of the Census, Current Population Reports: Money Income of Households, Families, and Persons in the United States: March 1992, Series P-60, #184; p. B 36, table B-17; 1996, Series P-60, #197, pp.28-29, table 7. C3 186/2:(year)
U.S. Bureau of the Census, Current Population Reports: Income Poverty, and Valuation of Noncash Benefits: 1994, Series P-60, #189, pp. 15-16, table 5. C3 186/2 994
U.S. Bureau of the Census, Current Population Reports: Money Income in the United States: 1999, Series P-60, #209, pp. 30-31, table 7. <www census gov>
U.S. Bureau of the Census, Current Population Reports: Income 2001; "(Table) 7. Median Income of People by Selected Characteristics: 2001, 2000, and 1999;" published September 2002.
U.S. Bureau of the Census and Bureau of Labor Statistics, Annual Demographic Survey, March Supplement, 2002, "(Table) PINC-01 Selected Characteristics of People 15 Years and Over, by Total Money Income in 2002, Work Experience in 2002, Race, Hispanic Origin, and Sex";2003; 2004.

NOTES: 'All Races' includes other races not shown separately. Data covers the earnings of wage and salary workers who usually worked 35 or more hours per week for 50 to 52 weeks during the year. Data prior to 1989 are for civilian workers only.

UNITS: Median money earnings.

Table 7.13 Per Capita Money Income, 1985 - 1997

	Black	White	All Races
1985	$10,203	$17,409	$16,427
1986	10,554	18,088	17,090
1987	10,801	18,569	17,507
1988	11,221	18,853	17,804
1989	11,322	19,281	18,193
1990	11,073	18,745	17,667
1991	10,806	18,277	17,225
1992	10,569	18,058	16,985
1993	10,955	18,660	17,524
1994	11,534	19,073	17,929
1995	11,566	19,277	18,143
1996	12,172	19,621	18,552
1997	12,351	20,425	19,241

SOURCE: U.S. Bureau of the Census, Current Population Reports: Measuring 50 Years of Economic Change, Series P-60, #203; p. C-6, table C-3.

NOTES: 'All Races' includes other races not shown separately.

UNITS: Income in 1997 CPI-U adjusted dollars.

Table 7.14 Families Below the Poverty Level, 1980 – 2003

	Black	White	All Races
Number below the poverty level			
1980	1,826	4,195	6,217
1985	1,983	4,983	7,223
1990	2,193	4,622	7,098
1995	2,127	4,994	7,532
2000	na	na	6,400
2001	na	na	6,813
2002	na	na	7,229
2003	na	na	7,607
Percent below the poverty level			
1980	28.9%	8.0%	10.3%
1985	28.7	9.1	11.4
1990	29.3	8.1	10.7
1995	26.4	8.5	10.8
2000	na	na	8.7
2001	na	na	9.2
2002	na	na	9.6
2003	na	na	10.0

SOURCE: U.S. Bureau of the Census, Current Population Reports: Poverty in the United States, 1999; Series P-60, #210, pp. B-11 - B-17, table B-3; 2002; "Table B-2. People and Families in Poverty by Selected Characteristics: 2001 and 2002".
U.S. Bureau of the Census, Current Population Reports: Income, Povery, and Health Insurance Coverage in the United States: 2003; Series P-60, #226; Table B-3; issued August 2004.

NOTES: 'All Races' includes other races not shown separately. Families as of March of the following year.

UNITS: Number below the poverty level in thousands of families; percent as a percent of all families, by race, as shown.

Table 7.15 Families Below the Poverty Level by Type of Family and Presence of Related Children, 2002 and 2003

	Black	White	All Races
2002			
Total Families	8,932	62,313	75,616
Families below poverty level	1,923	4,862	7,229
Married-couple families	331	2,510	3,052
Male householder, no wife present	160	349	564
Female householder, no husband present	1,433	2,004	3,613
Total families with children under 18 years	5,747	30,501	38,846
Families below poverty level	1,567	3,488	5,397
Married-couple families	194	1,494	1,831
Male householder, no wife present	106	250	395
Female householder, no husband present	1,267	1,744	3,171
2003			
Total Families	8,914	62,620	76,232
Families below poverty level	1,986	5,058	7,607
Married-couple families	321	2,504	3,115
Male householder, no wife present	192	383	636
Female householder, no husband present	1,473	2,171	3,856
Total families with children under 18 years	5,799	30,443	39,029
Families below poverty level	1,666	3,698	5,772
Married-couple families	200	1,499	1,885
Male householder, no wife present	146	287	470
Female householder, no husband present	1,320	1,912	3,416

SOURCE: U.S. Bureau of the Census, Current Population Reports: Poverty in the United States: 2002; "Table POV44: Region, Division and Type of Residence – Poverty Status for Families by Family Structure: 2002, Below 100% of Poverty"; Table POV45: Region, Division and Type of Residence – Poverty Status for Families With Related Children Under 18 by Family Structure: 2002, Below 100% of Poverty"; 2003.

NOTES: 'All Races' includes other races not shown separately. 'White' and 'Black' as shown are respectively equivalent to 'White Alone' and 'Black Alone' that refer to people who reported 'White' or 'Black' and did not report any other race category.

UNITS: Number in thousands of families

Table 7.16 Persons Below the Poverty Level, 1980 – 2003

	Black	White	All Races
Number below the poverty level			
1980	8,579	19,699	29,272
1985	8,926	22,860	33,064
1990	9,837	22,326	33,585
1995	9,872	24,423	36,425
1996	9,694	24,650	36,529
1997	9,116	24,396	35,574
1998	9,091	23,454	34,476
1999	8,360	21,922	32,258
2000	7,901	21,291	31,139
2001	8,136	22,739	32,907
2002*	8,602	23,466	34,570
2003*	8,781	24,272	35,861
Percent below the poverty level			
1980	32.5%	10.2%	13.0%
1985	31.3	11.4	14.0
1990	31.9	10.7	13.5
1995	29.3	11.2	13.8
1996	28.4	11.2	13.7
1997	26.5	11.0	13.3
1998	26.1	10.5	12.7
1999	23.6	9.8	11.8
2000	22.1	9.4	11.3
2001	22.7	9.9	11.7
2002*	24.1	10.2	12.1
2003*	24.4	10.5	12.5

SOURCE: U.S. Bureau of the Census, Current Population Reports: Poverty in the United States, 2001; P60-219, pp. 21-24, table A-1; 2002; "Table 1. Number in Poverty and Poverty Rate by Race and Hispanic Origin: 2001 and 2002". U.S. Bureau of the Census, Current Population Reports: Income, Poverty, and Health Insurance Coverage in the United States: 2003; Series P-60, #226; Table B-1; issued August 2004.

NOTES: 'All Races' includes other races not shown separately. '*' denotes year(s) in which 'White' and 'Black' as shown are respectively equivalent to 'White Alone' and 'Black Alone' that refer to people who reported 'White' or 'Black' and did not report any other race category.

UNITS: Number below the poverty level in thousands of persons; percent as a percent of all persons, by race, as shown.

Table 7.17 Children Below the Poverty Level, 1980 - 2003

	Black	White	All Races
Number below the poverty level			
1980	3,961	7,181	11,543
1985	4,157	8,253	13,010
1990	4,550	8,232	13,431
1995	4,761	8,981	14,665
2000	3,526	7,328	11,633
2001	3,492	7,527	11,733
2002*	3,645	7,549	12,133
2003*	3,877	7,985	12,866
Percent below the poverty level			
1980	42.3%	13.9%	18.3%
1985	43.6	16.2	20.7
1990	44.8	15.9	20.6
1995	41.9	16.2	20.8
2000	30.9	13.0	16.2
2001	30.2	13.4	16.3
2002*	32.3	13.6	16.7
2003*	34.1	14.3	17.6

SOURCE: U.S. Bureau of the Census, Current Population Reports: Poverty in the United States, 2000; Series P-60, #214 pp. 23-25, table A-2; 2001; pp. 26-30, table A-2.

U.S. Bureau of the Census, Current Population Reports: Income, Poverty, and Health Insurance Coverage in the United States: 2003; Series P-60, #226; Table B-2; issued August 2004.

NOTES: 'All Races' includes other races not shown separately. '*' indicates the year in which 'White' and 'Black' as shown are respectively equivalent to 'White Alone' and 'Black Alone' that refer to people who reported 'White' or 'Black' and did not report any other race category.

UNITS: Number below the poverty level in thousands of children; percent as a percent of all children under 18 years, by race, as shown

Table 7.18 Persons 65 Years Old and Over Below Poverty Level, 1970 - 2003

	Black	White	All Races
Number below the poverty level			
1970	735	4,011	4,793
1985	717	2,698	3,456
1990	860	2,707	3,658
1995	629	2,572	3,318
2000	607	2,584	3,323
2001	626	2,656	3,414
2002*	680	2,739	3,576
2003*	680	2,666	3,552
Percent below the poverty level			
1970	47.7%	22.6%	24.6%
1985	31.5	11.0	12.6
1990	33.8	10.1	12.2
1995	25.4	9.0	10.5
2000	21.8	8.7	10.2
2001	21.9	8.9	10.1
2002*	23.8	9.1	10.4
2003*	23.7	8.8	10.2

SOURCE: U.S. Bureau of the Census, Statistical Abstract of the United States, 1994; p. 476, table 731; 2000; p. 476, table 757; 2001, p. 443, table 682; 2002; p. 442, table 671. C 3 134·9 (year)
U.S. Bureau of the Census, Current Population Reports: Income, Poverty, and Health Insurance Coverage in the United States: 2003; Series P-60, #226; Table B-2; issued August 2004.

NOTES: 'All Races' includes other races not shown separately. Persons as of March of following year. '*' denotes year(s) in which 'White' and 'Black' as shown are respectively equivalent to 'White Alone' and 'Black Alone' that refer to people who reported 'White' or 'Black' and did not report any other race category.

UNITS: Number below the poverty level in thousands of persons; percent as a percent of all persons, by race, as shown.

Table 7.19 Income of Households from Specified Sources, 1992

	Black	White	All Races
All households	11,190	82,083	96,391
one or more members received:			
Social Security	25.1%	28.5%	27.7%
AFDC or other non-SSI cash assistance	15.5	3.7	5.2
SSI	10.2	3.2	4.1
food stamps	25.0	6.6	8.8
housing assistance	14.5	3.3	4.6
free or reduced-price school lunches	20.5	5.5	7.4
employer subsidized health insurance	43.4	54.3	52.9
Medicare	23.1	26.6	25.9
Medicaid	30.9	10.1	12.8
Mean household income from:			
Social Security	$6,597	$8,980	$8,708
AFDC or other non-SSI cash assistance	3,379	3,444	3,489
SSI	3,415	3,651	3,666
food stamps	1,791	1,430	1,564
housing assistance	2,129	1,957	2,022
free or reduced-price school lunches	558	547	553
employer subsidized health insurance	2,777	3,163	3,139
Medicare	2,305	3,652	3,511
Medicaid	1,297	1,696	1,595

SOURCE: U.S. Bureau of the Census, Current Population Reports: Measuring the Effect of Benefits and Taxes on Income and Poverty: 1992, Series P60-186RD, pp. 52-54, table 7. C 3 186/P-60/186RD

NOTES: 'All Races' includes other races not shown separately.

UNITS: Number of households in thousands. Percent as a percent of all households, 100.0%. Mean amount of income from specified source per household receiving that source.

Table 7.20 Income of Persons from Specified Sources, 2003

	Black	White	All Races
All persons, 15 years and over	22,567	168,257	203,482
Number with income from:			
Earnings	16,662	125,350	151,880
Unemployment compensation	1,011	6,647	8,219
Workers' compensation	252	1,659	2,022
Social Security	4,050	35,066	40,632
SSI (Supplemental Security Income)	1,338	3,438	5,173
Public assistance (total)	803	1,432	2,428
Veterans' benefits	270	1,938	2,323
Survivors benefits	168	2,397	2,649
Disability benefits	309	1,265	1,642
Pensions	1,301	14,041	15,809
Interest	6,083	86,898	98,565
Dividends	1,527	32,494	35,947
Rents, royalties, estates or trusts	514	10,118	11,255
Educational assistance	1,247	6,554	8,466
Child support	996	4,202	5,443
Alimony	17	378	401
Mean income, total from:	$25,250	$33,993	$32,976
Earnings	28,420	37,282	36,323
Unemployment compensation	4,347	4,518	4,493
Workers' compensation	6,376	6,587	6,573
Social Security	8,518	10,185	9,977
SSI (Supplemental Security Income)	5,229	5,444	5,417
Public assistance (total)	3,371	3,054	3,154
Veterans' benefits	12,134	9,068	9,516
Survivors benefits	10,124	11,835	11,719
Disability benefits	8,860	11,220	10,825
Pensions	13,224	15,157	14,987
Interest	975	1,575	1,507
Dividends	1,580	2,558	2,484
Rents, royalties, estates or trusts	2,929	5,783	5,650
Educational assistance	4,620	5,094	5,129
Child support	3,948	4,828	4,616
Alimony	na	11,722	11,498

SOURCE: U.S. Bureau of the Census and Bureau of Labor Statistics, Annual Demographic Survey, March Supplement, 2003; "(Table) PINC-09. Source of Income in 2003--Number With Income and Mean Income of Specified Type in 2003 of People 15 Years Old and Over".

NOTES: 'All Races' includes other races not shown separately. Persons 15 years old and older as of March the following year. "White" and "Black" as shown are equivalent to "White Alone" and "Black Alone" respectively.

UNITS: Number of persons in thousands, mean income in dollars.

Table 7.21 Child Support Payments Agreed to or Awarded Custodial Parents, 2001

	Black	White	All Races
All Custodial Parents	3,331	9,535	13,383
Child support agreed to or awarded	1,718	5,915	7,916
Supposed to receive child support	1,500	5,212	6,924
Received payments	951	4,032	5,119
Full Payments	563	2,472	3,099
Partial Payments	388	1,560	2,020
Did not receive payments	548	1,180	1,804
All Custodial Mothers	3,010	7,843	11,291
Child support agreed to or awarded	1,612	5,258	7,110
Supposed to receive child support	1,400	4,624	6,212
Received payments	896	3,622	4,639
Full Payments	541	2,222	2,821
Partial Payments	355	1,401	1,818
Did not receive payments	503	1,002	1,573
All Custodial Fathers	321	1,692	2,092
Child support agreed to or awarded	105	657	807
Supposed to receive child support	100	588	712
Received payments	55	410	480
Full Payments	22	251	278
Partial Payments	33	159	202
Did not receive payments	45	178	232

SOURCE: U.S. Bureau of the Census, Current Population Reports: Custodial Mothers and Fathers and Their Child Support: 2001, Series P-60, #225, "Table 4. Child Support Payments Agreed to or Awarded Custodial Parents by Selected Characteristics and Sex: 2001", published in October 2003. C3 186 P-60/003

NOTES: 'All Races' includes other races not shown separately.

UNITS: Numbers in thousands.

Chapter 8: Special Topics

Table 8.01 Social Security Benefits and Beneficiaries, 1980, 1990 and 2000

	Black	White	All Races
1980			
Beneficiaries			
total	3,576,014	31,431,133	35,584,955
retired workers	1,533,904	17,780,617	19,562,085
disabled workers	432,449	2,376,823	2,858,680
wives	229,177	3,147,297	3,436,099
husbands	3,719	36,728	41,328
children	645,162	3,501,249	4,606,517
widowed mothers and fathers	115,235	428,822	562,316
widows (nondisabled)	288,931	3,935,175	4,262,607
widowers (nondisabled)	2,208	17,870	20,328
widows (disabled)	20,168	104,847	126,679
widowers (disabled)	139	747	901
parents	1,921	12,052	14,779
special age-72 beneficiary	2,986	88,098	91,808
wife of special age-72 beneficiary	15	808	828
Average monthly benefit			
total	$236.00	$308.60	$300.20
retired workers	281.60	346.90	341.40
disabled workers	325.30	379.70	370.70
wives	119.00	168.30	164.20
husbands	111.50	132.10	130.00
children	154.00	200.00	187.60
widowed mothers and fathers	196.60	261.70	246.20
widows (nondisabled)	244.80	316.90	311.00
widowers (nondisabled)	210.00	243.20	239.40
widows (disabled)	169.80	212.60	205.40
widowers (disabled)	131.50	148.10	145.70
parents	247.00	282.60	276.00
special age-72 beneficiary	104.90	104.90	104.90
wife of special age-72 beneficiary	52.60	52.60	52.60

continued on the next page

Table 8.01 continued

	Black	White	All Races
1990			
Beneficiaries			
total	3,707,980	34,846,200	39,814,330
retired workers	1,904,140	22,287,520	24,826,230
disabled workers	489,450	2,335,560	3,011,130
wives	187,660	3,046,270	3,329,830
husbands	4,170	28,610	36,570
children	544,780	1,745,840	3,193,070
widowed mothers and fathers	55,290	233,640	305,080
widows (nondisabled)	388,010	4,501,160	4,963,820
widowers (nondisabled)	4,200	28,380	33,790
widows (disabled)	19,060	77,510	100,150
widowers (disabled)	390	1,130	1,630
parents	800	4,190	5,840
special age-72 beneficiary	310	6,790	7,190
Average monthly benefit			
total	$443.10	$558.60	$544.50
retired workers	505.80	612.60	602.60
disabled workers	531.70	603.00	587.00
wives	226.20	306.80	300.10
husbands	175.60	189.30	183.90
children	na	na	na
widowed mothers and fathers	350.80	432.70	409.00
widows (nondisabled)	442.40	569.10	557.70
widowers (nondisabled)	384.00	417.40	411.00
widows (disabled)	341.40	404.40	389.50
widowers (disabled)	213.40	233.20	228.50
parents	425.50	506.10	491.00
special age-72 beneficiary	167.50	166.80	166.80

continued on the next page

Table 8.01 continued

	Black	White	All Races
2000			
Beneficiaries			
total	4,622,040	38,853,370	45,417,470
retired workers	2,282,550	25,401,010	28,505,990
disabled workers	868,070	3,701,770	5,035,840
wives	150,600	2,662,350	2,925,950
husbands	5,020	23,310	36,070
children	827,670	2,590,050	3,810,490
widowed mothers and fathers	34,090	141,800	201,270
widows (nondisabled)	406,230	4,152,820	4,661,540
widowers (nondisabled)	5,980	29,290	37,120
widows (disabled)	40,160	145,890	195,340
widowers (disabled)	1,310	3,190	4,790
parents	360	1,830	3,000
Average monthly benefit			
total	$635.70	$791.50	$767.40
retired workers	724.20	859.90	844.60
disabled workers	731.40	809.30	787.00
wives	330.30	429.30	419.20
husbands	240.40	239.40	232.10
children	357.80	434.50	406.30
widowed mothers and fathers	508.40	633.10	593.00
widows (nondisabled)	646.90	831.40	811.80
widowers (nondisabled)	585.80	614.90	606.30
widows (disabled)	465.90	542.70	523.00
widowers (disabled)	387.20	342.80	352.80
parents	643.50	735.50	701.00

SOURCE: U.S. Department of Health & Human Services, Social Security Administration, Social Security Bulletin, Annual Statistical Supplement, 1982, pp. 112-123, table 70; 1991, pp. 149-159, table 5.A1; 2001, pp. 159-169, table 5.A1. SSA 1 22/2-(year)

NOTES: 'All Races' includes other races not shown separately.

UNITS: Beneficiaries in number of beneficiaries, average monthly benefit in current dollars.

Table 8.02 Social Security Benefits and Beneficiaries, 2003

	Black	White	All Races
2003			
Beneficiaries			
total	4,836,700	39,644,330	47,053,140
retired workers	2,405,600	26,128,930	29,547,530
disabled workers	991,810	4,220,300	5,867,460
wives	137,360	2,468,390	2,733,950
husbands	4,880	24,430	39,680
children	842,050	2,618,820	3,966,480
widowed mothers and fathers	28,640	128,940	188,320
widows (nondisabled)	380,760	3,881,710	4,458,120
widowers (nondisabled)	6,030	28,230	41,780
widows (disabled)	37,730	139,530	201,390
widowers (disabled)	1,350	3,860	6,240
parents	240	1,190	2,190
Average monthly benefit			
total	$705.40	$868.70	$840.60
retired workers	802.60	939.40	922.10
disabled workers	800.20	890.40	861.70
wives	362.60	465.40	453.10
husbands	271.20	261.40	254.30
children	386.40	475.60	444.80
widowed mothers and fathers	565.90	706.50	659.70
widows (nondisabled)	710.10	911.60	890.10
widowers (nondisabled)	683.00	709.60	701.10
widows (disabled)	502.20	583.30	567.40
widowers (disabled)	429.60	381.80	397.90
parents	827.50	830.40	803.10

SOURCE: U.S. Department of Health & Human Services, Social Security Administration, Social Security Bulletin, Annual Statistical Supplement, 2004, pp. 5.1 – 5.15, table 5.A1. SSA 1 22/2 (year)

NOTES: 'All Races' includes other races not shown separately.

UNITS: Beneficiaries in number of beneficiaries, average monthly benefit in current dollars.

Table 8.03 Selected Characteristics of Farms and Farm Operators, 2002

	Black farms	All farms
Characteristics of farms		
Farms and land in farms		
farms (number)	29,090	2,128,982
land in farms (acres)	3,355,791	938,279,056
harvested cropland (acres)	na	302,697,252
Farms by size		
1-9 acres	2,626	179,346
10-49 acres	10,607	563,772
50-179 acres	11,398	658,705
180-499 acres	3,557	388,617
500 acres or more	902	338,542
Owned and rented land in farms		
owned land in farms		
farms	26,488	1,979,140
acres	2,196,264	584,963,623
rented or leased land in farms		
farms	9,896	700,846
acres	1,159,527	353,315,433
2002 Market value of agricultural products sold, (in thousands of dollars)		
total	$506,881	$200,646,355
average per farm	17,425	94,245
crops (including nursery and greenhouse crops)	233,710	95,151,954
livestock, poultry and their products	273,171	105,494,401
Farms by value of sales		
less than $1,000	8,635	430,953
$1,000-$2,499	6,359	307,368
$2,500-$4,999	4,539	243,026
$5,000-$9,999	3,947	246,624
$10,000-$24,999	2,953	272,333
$25,000-$49,999	1,225	163,521
$50,000 or more	1,432	465,157

continued on the next page

Table 8.03 continued

	Black farms	All farms
Farms by North American Industry Classification System		
oilseed and grain farming (1111)	2,767	37,540,988
vegetable and melon farming (11112)	1,377	13,145,448
fruit and tree nut farming (1113)	703	13,489,154
greenhouse, nursery, and floriculture production (1114)	288	15,065,589
other crop farming (1119)	4,854	14,548,102
tobacco farming (11191)	925	1,506,953
cotton farming (11192)	408	3,789,565
sugarcane farming, hay farming, and all other crop farming (11193, 11194, 11199)	3,521	8,315,743
beef cattle ranching and farming (112111)	15,000	19,755,572
cattle feedlots (112112)	474	22,895,343
dairy cattle and milk production (11212)	231	22,737,525
hog and pig farming (1122)	1,179	12,337,959
poultry and egg production (1123)	405	24,410,930
sheep and goat farming (1124)	288	445,366
animal aquaculture and other animal production (1125, 1129)	1,524	4,274,380
Operator characteristics		
Total operators	36,370	2,128,982
Residence		
on farm operated	23,832	1,680,160
not on farm operated	12,538	448,822
Principal occupation		
farming	19,542	1,224,246
other	16,828	904,736
Days of work off farm		
none	17,392	962,200
any	18,978	1,166,782
1-49 days	2,344	122,248
50-99 days	1,447	66,306
100-199 days	2,527	145,880
200 days or more	12,660	832,348

continued on the next page

Table 8.03 continued

	Black farms	All farms
Characteristics of the farm operator - continued		
Years on present farm		
2 years or less	1,690	74,754
3 or 4 years	2,976	143,599
5 to 9 years	7,217	374,756
10 years or more	24,487	1,535,873
average years on present farm	na	20.7
Age		
under 25 years old	523	16,962
25-34 years old	1,233	106,097
35-44 years old	4,263	366,306
45-54 years old	9,123	572,664
55-64 years old	9,201	509,123
65 years old and over	12,027	557,830
average age	57.8	55.3
Sex		
male	29,631	1,891,163
female	6,739	237,819
Principal operator is a hired manager		
farms	1,046	55,372
acres	204,697	103,135,293

SOURCE: U.S. Bureau of the Census, 2002 Census of Agriculture, Vol. 1 Geographic Area Series, Part 51, U.S. Summary and State Data; p. 8, table 2; p. 16, table 9; p. 52, table 50; pp. 214-226, table 61; pp. 48-29, table 47; pp. 54-55, table 52. C 3 31/4 002/v. 1/ pt 51

NOTES: 'All farms' includes farms owned/operated by persons of all races.

UNITS: Farms, farms by size, farms by organization, farms by value of sales, farms by Standard Industrial Classification, in number of farms; land in farms and harvested crop lands in acres; market value of agricultural products sold in thousands of dollars. Characteristics of farm operators in number of farm operators.

Table 8.04 Black Owned Firms, by Major Industry Group, 1992 and 1997

	all firms		firms with paid employees			
	firms	sales & receipts	firms	sales & receipts	employees	annual payroll
1992						
All industries	620,912	$32,197,361	64,478	$22,589,676	345,193	$4,806,624
agricultural services, forestry and fishing	9,820	265,089	1,491	159,119	3,904	45,547
mining	490	65,621	51	46,000	293	6,454
construction	43,381	2,651,356	8,798	1,962,727	28,545	447,362
manufacturing	10,469	1,319,193	1,958	1,155,011	12,977	251,322
transportation and public utilities	49,095	2,498,102	4,072	1,305,091	20,308	308,376
wholesale trade	7,550	2,944,321	1,510	2,745,412	8,649	203,544
retail trade	86,840	6,967,644	12,096	5,591,522	82,931	760,051
finance, insurance, and real estate	40,924	3,777,171	3,194	2,771,537	17,606	380,056
services	332,981	11,057,136	30,081	6,773,932	169,248	2,393,563
industries not classified	39,363	651,727	1,226	79,325	731	10,350

continued on the next page

Table 8.04 continued

	all firms		firms with paid employees			
	firms	sales & receipts	firms	sales & receipts	employees	annual payroll
1997						
All industries	823,499	$71,214,662	93,235	$56,377,860	718,341	$14,322,312
agricultural services forestry and fishing	12,464	417,169	1,356	259,649	5,457	77,198
mining	231	21,551	16	12,867	186	5,319
construction	56,508	7,712,059	12,973	6,587,348	70,928	1,510,252
manufacturing	10,447	3,682,510	1,931	3,463,861	26,624	652,787
transportation and public utilities	71,586	6,376,645	6,184	4,252,240	47,289	909,470
wholesale trade	8,120	5,818,734	2,139	5,573,907	13,746	471,320
retail trade	87,568	13,803,266	14,074	12,244,399	125,480	1,497,111
finance, insurance, and real estate	37,934	3,088,582	4,820	2,189,556	18,379	498,318
services	437,646	25,925,092	43,529	19,503,488	388,398	8,212,775
industries not classified	101,128	4,369,056	6,347	2,290,545	21,853	487,761

SOURCE: U.S. Bureau of the Census, 1992 Economic Censuses MB92-1 Survey of Minority-Owned Business Enterprises: Black, pp. 9-10, table 1. C3 258-92-2, 1997 Economic Censuses Survey of Minority-Owned Business Enterprises: Black, pp. 17-18, table 1. EC97CS-3

NOTES: Data from the 1992 and 1997 Economic Censuses.

UNITS: Firms in number of firms; sales and receipts in thousands of dollars; employees in number of employees; annual payroll in thousands of dollars

Table 8.05 Black Owned Firms, by State, 1997

	all firms		firms with paid employees			
	firms	sales & receipts	firms	sales & receipts	employees	annual payroll
United States	823,499	$71,214,662	93,235	$56,377,860	718,341	$14,322,312
Alabama	19,077	1,008,966	2,266	728,041	13,232	231,869
Alaska	876	55,713	117	44,394	704	13,094
Arizona	3,582	314,497	503	252,736	5,704	92,407
Arkansas	6,721	386,958	761	264,831	2,464	40,975
California	79,110	6,395,311	7,377	4,552,255	56,252	1,081,299
Colorado	4,926	512,868	740	423,043	4,204	88,485
Connecticut	7,251	528,164	857	403,166,	4,761	135,296
Delaware	2,707	184,549	322	144,443	3,450	43,258
District of Columbia	10,909	1,334,651	1,232	na	na	na
Florida	59,732	4,092,155	6,424	2,925,260	31,035	556,186
Georgia	55,766	4,110,716	6,073	3,111,892	40,593	741,509
Hawaii	638	34,165	168	20,562	561	7,502
Idaho	164	17,535	16	14,220	231	7,321
Illinois	41,244	3,913,240	3,747	3,253,027	35,034	787,773
Indiana	11,107	1,192,143	1,440	1,035,570	10,775	199,604
Iowa	1,353	233,466	262	216,904	1,931	41,387
Kansas	3,396	593,636	524	547,688	5,834	174,203
Kentucky	5,629	658,535	611	588,703	7,717	121,353
Louisiana	25,782	1,917,295	3,050	1,451,135	27,441	464,477
Maine	257	28,088	36	23,600	346	6,871
Maryland	47,614	3,964,600	4,214	3,180,637	41,755	946,386
Massachusetts	11,834	1,013,134	1,239	804,314	8,267	188,731
Michigan	24,954	4,623,414	2,843	4,157,785	37,688	921,765
Minnesota	4,024	523,126	472	459,125	4,352	99,939
Mississippi	17,617	852,824	2,205	559,182	9,773	121,522
Missouri	13,678	1,261,398	2,142	1,060,253	14,503	252,769
Montana	62	na	15	na	na	na
Nebraska	1,565	129,219	238	110,006	1,874	29,722
Nevada	2,796	225,880	344	183,015	2,344	53,820
New Hampshire	326	32,351	54	26,200	506	11,137
New Jersey	26,500	2,160,441	3,236	1,580,808	16,862	375,877
New Mexico	1,132	142,847	165	130,131	1,121	20,051

continued on the next page

Table 8.05 continued

	all firms		firms with paid employees			
	firms	sales & receipts	firms	sales & receipts	employees	annual payroll
New York	86,469	$5,067,265	7,822	$3,445,063	45,703	$1,005,200
North Carolina	39,901	2,299,285	5,441	1,701,399	33,914	441,415
North Dakota	99	na	8	na	na	na
Ohio	26,970	3,946,848	3,486	3,499,457	32,719	788,525
Oklahoma	5,309	333,094	618	259,565	4,847	77,957
Oregon	2,219	436,156	357	398,916	2,968	66,799
Pennsylvania	19,791	1,993,512	2,909	1,652,223	19,979	437,813
Rhode Island	1,269	124,434	181	104,097	1,935	26,805
South Carolina	23,216	1,408,925	3,148	1,030,411	17,713	234,660
South Dakota	150	17,294	22	na	na	na
Tennessee	20,196	1,644,529	2,730	1,276,080	17,583	334,204
Texas	60,427	6,857,330	6,684	5,695,691	70,904	1,469,459
Utah	440	23,005	35	16,831	327	5,480
Vermont	168	37,324	36	35,449	341	4,481
Virginia	33,539	3,408,165	4,956	2,878,899	46,971	905,842
Washington	5,553	504,109	893	411,968	8,321	125,629
West Virginia	1,148	87,649	129	76,923	1,018	14,203
Wisconsin	4,848	550,114	798	462,623	8,179	139,501
Wyoming	232	12,670	64	na	na	na

SOURCE: U.S. Bureau of the Census, 1997 Economic Censuses EC97C3-3 Survey of Minority-Owned Business Enterprises: Black, p. 19, table 2. C 3 258 97-3

NOTES: Data from the 1997 Economic Censuses.

UNITS: Firms in number of firms; sales and receipts in thousands of dollars; employees in number of employees; annual payroll in thousands of dollars.

Table 8.06 Summary of Results of the 2000 Consumer Expenditure Survey

	Black consumer units	White consumer units	All consumer units
Number of consumer units	13,230	96,137	109,367
income before taxes	$32,657	$46,260	$44,649
Average number in consumer unit:			
persons	2.7	2.5	2.5
children under 18 years old	.9	.6	.7
persons 65 and over	.2	.3	.3
earners	1.3	1.4	1.4
vehicles	1.3	2.0	1.9
percent homeowner	46%	68%	66%
Average annual expenditures			
Total	$28,152	$39,406	$38,045
food	4,095	5,304	5,158
food at home	2,691	3,066	3,021
- cereals and bakery products	393	462	453
- meats, poultry, fish, and eggs	909	780	795
- dairy products	245	336	325
- fruits and vegetables	454	530	521
- other food at home	691	959	927
food away from home	1,404	2,238	2,137
alcoholic beverages	211	394	372
housing	9,906	12,651	12,319
shelter	5,678	7,312	7,114
- owned dwellings	2,607	4,877	4,602
- rented dwellings	2,843	1,923	2,034
- other lodging	227	512	478
utilities, fuels and public services	2,571	2,478	2,489
household operations	468	714	684
housekeeping supplies	303	507	482
household furnishings and equipment	887	1,640	1,549
apparel and services	1,695	1,878	1,856

continued on the next page

Table 8.06 continued

	Black consumer units	White consumer units	All consumer units
transportation	$5,214	$7,721	$7,417
- vehicle purchases	2,285	3,574	3,418
- gasoline and motor oil	956	1,337	1,291
- other vehicle expenses	1,705	2,361	2,281
- public transportation	268	448	427
health care	1,107	2,198	2,066
entertainment	1,014	1,980	1,863
personal care products and services	627	555	564
reading	72	157	146
education	383	666	632
tobacco products and smoking supplies	243	329	319
miscellaneous	572	804	776
cash contributions	700	1,260	1,192
personal insurance and pensions	2,313	3,510	3,365
- life and other personal insurance	358	404	399
- pensions and Social Security	1,955	3,105	2,966

SOURCE: U.S. Department of Labor, Bureau of Labor Statistics, Consumer Expenditure Survey, 2000, table 7, accessed 4 March 2003. <ftp://ftp bls gov/pub/special requests/ce/standard/2000/tenracar txt>

NOTES: 'All consumer units' includes consumer units of all races.

UNITS: Number of consumer units in thousands; average numbers as shown; average annual expenditures by category, averages in current dollars.

Table 8.07 Summary of Results of the 2002 Consumer Expenditure Survey

	Black consumer units	White consumer units	All consumer units
Number of consumer units	13,554	98,553	112,108
income before taxes	$35,944	$51,177	$49,430
Average number in consumer unit:			
persons	2.7	2.5	2.5
children under 18 years old	.9	.6	.7
persons 65 and over	.2	.3	.3
earners	1.3	1.	1.4
vehicles	1.3	2.1	2.0
percent homeowner	48%	69%	66%
Average annual expenditures			
Total	$30,136	$42,135	$40,677
food	4,186	5,542	5,375
food at home	2,669	3,159	3,099
- cereals and bakery products	390	459	450
- meats, poultry, fish, and eggs	862	789	798
- dairy products	232	342	328
- fruits and vegetables	460	565	552
- other food at home	725	1,004	970
food away from home	1,517	2,383	2,276
alcoholic beverages	190	402	376
housing	10,756	13,633	13,283
shelter	6,279	8,043	7,829
- owned dwellings	3,223	5,432	5,165
- rented dwellings	2,852	2,065	2,160
- other lodging	204	546	505
utilities, fuels and public services	2,768	2,673	2,684
household operations	509	733	706
housekeeping supplies	313	578	545
household furnishings and equipment	887	1,606	1,518
apparel and services	1,704	1,756	1,749

continued on the next page

Table 8.07 continued

	Black consumer units	White consumer units	All consumer units
transportation	$5,447	$8,077	$7,759
- vehicle purchases	2,420	3,836	3,665
- gasoline and motor oil	925	1,278	1,235
- other vehicle expenses	1,875	2,553	2,471
- public transportation	228	411	389
health care	1,339	2,490	2,350
entertainment	1,124	2,211	2,079
personal care products and services	488	531	526
reading	67	148	139
education	463	792	752
tobacco products and smoking supplies	210	336	320
miscellaneous	606	818	792
cash contributions	917	1,327	1,277
personal insurance and pensions	2,640	4,072	3,899
- life and other personal insurance	312	419	406
- pensions and Social Security	2,328	3,653	3,493

SOURCE: U.S. Department of Labor, Bureau of Labor Statistics, Consumer Expenditure Survey, 2002, table 7, issued February 2004.

NOTES: 'All consumer units' includes consumer units of all races.

UNITS: Number of consumer units in thousands; average numbers as shown; average annual expenditures by category, averages in current dollars.

Table 8.08 Occupied Housing Units, by Tenure, 1980 - 2003

	Black householder	White householder	Householders of all races
1980			
All households	8,382	68,810	80,390
owner occupied			
number	3,724	46,671	51,795
percent	44.4%	67.8%	64.4%
renter occupied	4,657	22,139	28,595
1999			
All households	12,936	83,624	102,803
owner occupied			
number	6,013	60,041	68,796
percent	46.5%	71.8%	66.9%
renter occupied	6,923	23,583	34,007
2001			
All households	13,292	85,292	106,261
owner occupied			
number	6,318	62,465	72,265
percent	47.5%	73.2%	68.0%
renter occupied	6,974	22,826	33,996
2003			
All households	13,005	87,512	105,867
owner occupied			
number	6,192	63,141	72,254
percent	47.6%	72.2%	68.2%
renter occupied	6,813	24,370	33,614

SOURCE: U.S. Bureau of the Census, Statistical Abstract of the United States, 1999; p. 730, table 1214; 2001; p. 606, table 955; 2002; p. 599, table 938; 2003; p. 621, table 962; 2004; p. 611, table 950. C 3 134 (year)

NOTES: 'All Races' includes other races not shown separately.

UNITS: Number of housing units; percent as a percent of total as shown.

Table 8.09 Housing Affordability, Families, 1995

	Black	White	All Races
Percent that cannot afford a median priced home in their region using conventional, fixed rate, 30 year financing			
All families	80.5%	47.4%	52.2%
married couples	62.8	39.9	42.2
male householder (no wife present)	89.6	69.2	73.2
female householder (no husband present)	94.0	79.4	84.5
Percent that cannot afford a median priced home in their region using FHA, fixed rate, 30 year financing			
All families	79.5%	46.1%	51.0%
married couples	60.5	38.3	40.6
male householder (no wife present)	87.1	69.6	73.2
female householder (no husband present)	94.4	79.4	84.6

continued on the next page

Table 8.09 continued

	Black	White	All Races
Percent that cannot afford a modestly priced home in their region using conventional, fixed rate, 30 year financing			
All families	72.5%	39.6%	44.4%
married couples	52.4	32.2	34.2
male householder (no wife present)	79.5	59.6	64.1
female householder (no husband present)	88.2	72.0	77.7
Percent that cannot afford a modestly priced home in their region using FHA, fixed rate, 30 year financing			
All families	70.9%	37.2%	42.1%
married couples	49.3	29.3	31.4
male householder (no wife present)	81.4	58.2	62.8
female householder (no husband present)	87.5	71.3	77.0

SOURCE: U.S. Bureau of the Census, Current Housing Reports: Who Can Afford to Buy A House in 1995?, table 2-2; table 3-2. C 3 215 H121/99-1

NOTES: 'All Races' includes families of all races.

UNITS: Percent as a percent of families as shown.

Table 8.10 General Mobility, 1999-2000 and 2002-2003

	Black	White	All Races
1999-2000			
Total	34,948	221,703	270,219
non-movers	28,226	187,810	226,831
moved to			
same county	4,078	18,811	24,399
different county, same state	1,208	7,135	8,814
different state, same region	807	2,992	4,062
different division, same region	111	1,076	1,261
different region	346	2,633	3,105
abroad	172	1,247	1,746
2002-2003			
Total	35,333	228,198	282,556
non-movers	28,981	197,953	242,463
moved to			
same county	4,120	17,418	23,468
different county, same state	1,002	6,111	7,728
different state, same region	605	2,873	3,752
different division, same region	147	931	1,181
different region	336	2,135	2,695
abroad	142	777	1,269

SOURCE: U.S. Bureau of the Census, Current Population Survey, Geographic Mobility: March 1999 to March 2000, pp. 1-6, table 2; Geographic Mobility: March 2002 to March 2003, table 2.

NOTES: 'All Races' includes other races not shown separately. Mobility data from March 1999 to March 2000, and from March 2002 to March 2003.

UNITS: Number of persons one year old and over in thousands.

Glossary

ACUTE CONDITION see **CONDITION (HEALTH).**

AGE ADJUSTMENT

Age adjustment, using the direct method, is the application of the age specific rates in a population of interest to a standardized age distribution in order to eliminate the differences in observed rates that result from age differences in population composition. This adjustment is usually done when comparing two or more populations at one point in time, or one population at two or more points in time.

AGGRAVATED ASSAULT see **CRIME**.

ARSON see **CRIME**.

AVERAGE see **MEAN; MEDIAN**.

BED (HOSPITAL; NURSING HOME)

Any bed that is staffed for use by inpatients is counted as a bed in a facility.

BED-DISABILITY DAY see **DISABILITY DAY**.

BIRTH see **LIVE BIRTH**.

BURGLARY see **CRIME**.

CAUSE OF DEATH

For the purpose of national mortality statistics, every death is attributed to one underlying condition, based on information reported on the death certificate and utilizing the international rules (International Classifications of Disease) for selecting the underlying cause of death from reported conditions. Selected causes of death are shown on tables.

CHRONIC CONDITION see **CONDITION (HEALTH)**.

CIVILIAN LABOR FORCE

All persons (excluding members of the Armed Forces) who are either employed or unemployed. (The experienced civilian labor force is a subgroup of the civilian labor force, composed of all persons, employed and unemployed, that have worked before.)

Employed persons are those persons 16 years old and over who were either a) "at work"- those who did any work at all as paid employees, or in their own business or profession, or on their own farm, or worked 15 or more hours as unpaid workers on a family farm or in a family business; or b) "with a job but not at work"- those who did not work during the reference period but had jobs or businesses from which they were temporarily absent due to illness, bad weather, industrial dispute, vacation, or other personal reasons. Excluded from the employed are persons whose only activity consisted of work around the house or volunteer work for religious, charitable, and similar organizations.

Employed persons are classified as either **full-time workers**, those who worked 35 hours or more per week; or **part-time workers**, those who worked less than 35 hours per week.

Unemployed persons are those who were neither "at work" nor "with a job, but not at work" and who were a) looking for work, and b) available to accept a job. Also included as unemployed are persons who are waiting to be called back to a job from which they have been laid off. The unemployed are divided into four groups according to reason for unemployment:

--**job losers** (including those who have been laid off)

--**job leavers** who have left their job voluntarily

--**reentrants**, persons who have worked before and are reentering the labor force

--**new entrants** to the labor force looking for work

CIVILIAN NONINSTITUTIONAL POPULATION see **POPULATION**.

CIVILIAN POPULATION see **POPULATION**.

COLLEGE

A postsecondary school which offers a general or liberal arts education, usually leading to an associate, bachelor's, master's, doctor's, or first professional degree. Junior colleges and community colleges are included. See also **Institution of Higher Education; University.**

COMMUNITY HOSPITAL

All non-federal short term hospitals, excluding hospital units of institutions, whose services are available to the public. **Short term hospitals** are those where the average length of stay is less than 30 days.

CONDITION (HEALTH)

A health condition is a departure from a state of physical or mental well-being. Based on duration, there are two categories of conditions: acute and chronic.

An **acute condition** is one that has lasted less than three months, and has involved either a physician visit (medical attention) or restricted activity.

A **chronic condition** is any condition lasting three months or more, or is one classified as chronic regardless of the time of onset. See also **Health Limitation of Activity.**

CONSOLIDATED METROPOLITAN STATISTICAL AREA (CMSA)

A geographic area concept introduced in June, 1984, which, in combination with Metropolitan Statistical Area (MSA), and Primary Metropolitan Statistical Area (PMSA), replace the Standard Metropolitan Statistical Area (SMSA) concept. CMSAs are designated in accordance with criteria established by the federal Office of Management and Budget (OMB). In general CMSAs are MSAs with a population of one million or more, and which have component PMSAs. See also **Metropolitan Statistical Area.**

CONSUMER EXPENDITURE SURVEY

A survey of current consumer expenditures reflecting the buying habits of American consumers. Begun in 1979 and conducted jointly by the U.S. Bureau of Labor Statistics and the U.S. Bureau of the Census, the survey consists of two parts: an interview panel survey in which the expenditures of consumer units are obtained in five interviews conducted every three months, and a diary or recordkeeping survey completed by the participating households for two consecutive one-week periods. See also **Consumer Unit.**

The Consumer Expenditure Survey, which collects data on expenditures, should not be confused with the Consumer Price Index, which measures the average change in prices of consumer goods and services.

CONSUMER UNIT

An entity used as the basis of the Consumer Expenditure Survey. A consumer unit comprises either

--all the members of a particular household who are related by blood, marriage, adoption, or other legal arrangements; or

--a person living alone or sharing a household with others, or living as a roomer in a private home or lodging house or in a permanent living quarters in a hotel or motel, but who is financially independent; or

--two or more persons living together who pool their income to make joint expenditure decisions.

A consumer unit may or may not be a household.

CRIME

A crime is an action which is prohibited by law. Their are two major statistical programs which measure crime in the United States. The first is the Uniform Crime Reporting (UCR) program, administered by the FBI. The Bureau receives monthly and annual reports from most police agencies around the country (covering approximately 97% of the population). These reports contain information on eight major types of crime (called collectively, serious crime), which are known to police. Serious crime consists of four violent crimes (murder and non-negligent manslaughter, which includes willful felonious homicides and is based on police investigations rather than determinations of a medical examiner; forcible rape, which includes attempted rape; robbery, which includes stealing or taking anything of value by force or violence, or by threat of force or violence, and includes attempted robbery; and aggravated assault which includes intent to kill), and four property crimes (burglary, which includes any unlawful entry to commit a felony or theft and includes attempted burglary and burglary followed by larceny; larceny, which includes theft of property or articles of value without use of force, violence, or fraud, and excludes embezzlement, con games, forgery, etc.; motor vehicle theft, which includes all cases where vehicles are driven away and abandoned, but excludes vehicles taken for temporary use and returned by the taker; and arson, which includes any willful or malicious burning or attempt to burn, with or without the intent to defraud, of a dwelling house, public building, motor vehicle, aircraft, or personal property of another.)

The second approach to the measurement of crime is through the National Crime Survey (NCS) administered by the Bureau of Justice Statistics. The survey is based on a representative sample of approximately 49,000 households, inhabited by about 102,000 persons age 12 and over. Although the categories of crime are similar to those used by the

FBI in the UCR, the NCS is based on reports of victimization directly by victims, as opposed to crimes reported to police as in the UCR. As might be imagined, not all crimes are reported or known to police, therefore NCS estimates of crime tend to be significantly higher than UCR figures. The NCS also differs from the UCR in that only crimes whose victims can be interviewed are included (hence there are no homicide statistics), and only victims who are 12 years old or older are counted. The two central concepts in the NCS are victimization, which is the specific criminal act as it affects a single victim, and a criminal incident, which is a specific criminal act involving one or more victims. Thus in regard to personal crime, there are more victimizations, than incidents.

DEATH see **CAUSE OF DEATH; INFANT MORTALITY**.

DISABILITY

The presence of a physical, mental, or other health condition which has lasted six or more months and which limits or prevents a particular type of activity. See also **Work Disability.**

DISABILITY DAY

A day on which a person's usual activity is reduced because of illness or injury. There are four types of disability days (which are not mutually exclusive). They are

--a **restricted-activity day**, a day on which a person cuts down on his or her usual activities because of illness or an injury.

--a **bed-disability day,** a day on which a person stays in bed more than half of the daylight hours (or normal waking hours) because of a specific illness or injury. All hospital days are bed-disability days. Bed disability days may also be work-loss days or school loss days.

--a **work-loss day**, a day on which a person did not work at his or her job or business for at least half of his or her normal workday because of a specific illness or injury. Work loss days are determined only for employed persons.

--a **school-loss day**, a day on which a child did not attend school for at least half of his or her normal schoolday because of a specific illness or injury. School-loss days are determined only for children 6 to 16 years of age.

DISPOSABLE INCOME see **INCOME.**

EMPLOYED PERSONS see **CIVILIAN LABOR FORCE**.

EMPLOYMENT STATUS see **LABOR FORCE STATUS**.

ENROLLMENT

The total number of students registered in a given school unit at a given time, generally in the fall of the year. See also **Full-Time Enrollment; Part-Time Enrollment.**

EVER MARRIED PERSONS see MARITAL STATUS.

EXPERIENCED CIVILIAN LABOR FORCE

That portion of the Civilian Labor Force, both employed and unemployed, that have worked before. Excludes new entrants to the Civilian Labor Force. See also **Civilian Labor Force.**

EXPERIENCED WORKER see **EXPERIENCED CIVILIAN LABOR FORCE**.

FAMILY

A type (subgroup) of household in which there are two or more persons living together (including the householder) who are related by birth, marriage, or adoption. All such related persons in one housing unit are considered as members of one family. (For example, if the son or daughter of the family householder and that son's or daughter's spouse and/or children are members of the household, they are all counted as part of the householder's family.) However, non-family members who are not related to the householder (such as a roomer or boarder and his or her spouse, or a resident employee and his or her spouse who are living in), are not counted as family members but as unrelated individuals living in a family household. Thus for Census purposes, a housing unit can contain only one household, and a household can contain only one family. See also **Family Type; Household; Householder; Unrelated Individual.**

FAMILY INCOME see **INCOME**.

FAMILY TYPE

Families are classified by type according to the sex of the householder and the presence of a spouse and children. The three main types of households are: **Married Couples,** in which a husband and wife live together (with or without other persons in the household); **Male Householder, No Wife Present,** in which a male householder lives together with other members of his family but without a wife; and **Female Householder, No Husband Present,** in which a female householder lives together with other members of her family but without a husband. See also **Family; Family Household; Household.**

FARM

As defined by the Bureau of the Census (and adopted by the Department of Agriculture), a farm is any place from which $1,000 or more of agricultural products were sold, or would have been sold during a given year. Control of the farm may be exercised through ownership or management, or through a lease, rental or cropping arrangement. In the case of landowners who have one or more tenants or renters, the land operated by each is counted as a separate farm. This definition has been in effect since 1974.

FARMLAND

All land under the control of a farm operator, including land not actually under cultivation or not used for pasture or grazing. Rent free land is included as part of a farm only if the operator has sole use of it. Land used for pasture or grazing on a per head basis that is neither owned nor leased by the farm operator is not included except for grazing lands controlled by grazing associations leased on a per acre basis.

FARM INCOME

Gross farm income comprises cash receipts from farm marketings of crops and livestock, federal government payments made directly to farmers for farm-related activities, rental value of farm homes, value of farm products consumed in farm homes, and other farm-related income such as machine hire and custom work.

FULL-TIME ENROLLMENT (HIGHER EDUCATION)

The number of students enrolled in higher education courses with a total credit load equal to at least 75% of the normal full-time course load.

FULL-TIME WORKERS see **CIVILIAN LABOR FORCE**.

HEALTH LIMITATION OF ACTIVITY

A characteristic of persons with chronic conditions. Each person identified as having a chronic condition is classified as to the extent to which his or her activities are limited by the condition as follows:

--persons unable to carry on a major activity (that is the principal activity of a person of his or her age-sex group: for persons 1-5 years of age, it refers to ordinary play with other children; for persons 6-16 years of age, it refers to school attendance; for persons 17 years of age and over, it usually refers to a job, housework, or school attendance.)

--persons limited in the amount or kind of major activity performed.

--persons not limited in major activity, but otherwise limited.

--persons not limited in activity.

See also **Condition (Health).**

HEALTH MAINTENANCE ORGANIZATION (HMO)

A prepaid health plan delivering comprehensive care to members through designated providers, having a fixed monthly payment for health care services, and requiring members to be in the plan for a specified period of time (usually one year). HMOs are distinguished by the relationship of the providers to the plan. HMO model types are: **Group** -- an HMO that delivers health services through a physician group controlled by the HMO, or an HMO that contracts with one or more independent group practices to provide health services; **Individual Practice Association (IPA)** -- an HMO that contracts directly with physicians in independent practice, and/or contracts with one or more associations of physicians in independent practice, and/or contracts with one or more multispecialty group practices (but the plan is predominantly organized around solo-single specialty practices).

HIGHER EDUCATION see **INSTITUTION OF HIGHER EDUCATION**.

HISPANIC ORIGIN

An aspect of a person's ancestry. The Bureau of the Census in many of its survey asks persons if they are of Hispanic origin. There are four main subcategories of Hispanic origin: Mexican, Puerto Rican, Cuban, and other Hispanic. Hispanic origin is not a racial classification. Persons may be of any race and of Hispanic origin. Hispanic origin is used interchangeably with Spanish and Spanish origin.

HOME OWNERSHIP see **TENURE**.

HOSPITAL see **COMMUNITY HOSPITAL**.

HOSPITAL DAY

A hospital day is a night spent in a hospital by a person admitted as an inpatient.

HOUSEHOLD

The person or persons occupying a housing unit. There are two main types of households: family households, which consist of two or more persons related by birth, marriage, or adoption living together (see also **Family; Family Type**); and non-family households, which consist of a person living alone, or together with unrelated individuals (see Unrelated Individuals). See also **Householder.**

HOUSEHOLD INCOME see **INCOME**.

HOUSEHOLD TYPE see **HOUSEHOLD**.

HOUSEHOLDER

The person in whose name a housing unit is rented or owned.

HOUSING UNIT

A house, apartment, mobile home or trailer, group of rooms, or single room occupied as a separate living quarter, or, if vacant, intended for occupancy as a separate living quarter. Separate living quarters are those in which the occupants live and eat separately from any other persons in the building and which have direct access from the outside of the building or through a common hall.

Both occupied and vacant housing units are counted in many surveys; however, recreational vehicles, boats, caves, tents, railroad cars, and the like are only included if they are occupied as someone's usual place of residence. Vacant mobile homes are included if they are intended for occupancy on the site where they stand. Vacant mobile homes on dealer's sales lots, at the factory, or in storage yards are excluded.

Most housing unit data is for year-round housing units which comprises all occupied housing units plus vacant housing units intended for year round use. Vacant units held for seasonal use or migratory labor are excluded. See also **Occupancy Status, Rooms, Specified Owner-Occupied Housing Units, Tenure, Value (Housing).**

HOUSING TENURE see **TENURE**.

INCIDENT see **CRIME**.

INCOME

The term income has different definitions depending on how it is modified and in what situation it is used. Like many government statistical terms, income can be viewed hierarchically.

Personal income is the current income received by persons from all sources, minus their personal contributions for social insurance. Persons include individuals (including owners of unincorporated firms), non-profit institutions serving individuals, private trust funds, and private non-insured welfare funds. Personal income includes transfers (payments not resulting from current production) from government and business such as Social Security benefits, public assistance, etc., but excludes transfers among persons. Also included are certain non-monetary types of income, chiefly estimated net rental value to owner-occupants of their homes, the value of services furnished without payment by financial intermediaries, and food and fuel produced and consumed on farms.

Disposable personal income is personal income less personal tax and non-tax payments. It is income available to persons for spending and saving. Personal tax and non-tax payments are tax payments (net of refunds) by persons (excluding contributions for social insurance) that are not chargeable to business expenses, and certain personal payments to general government that are treated like taxes. Personal taxes include income, estate and gift, personal property, and motor vehicle licenses. Non-tax payments include passport fees, fines and penalties, donations, tuition and fees paid to schools and hospitals mainly operated by the government.

Money income is a smaller less inclusive category than personal income. Money income is the sum of the amounts received from wages and salaries, self-employment income (including losses), Social Security, Supplemental Security Income, public assistance, interest, dividends, rents, royalties, estate or trust income, veterans payments, unemployment and workers' compensation payments, private and government retirement and disability pensions, alimony, child support, and any other source of money income which was regularly received. Capital gains or losses and lump-sum or one-time payments, such as life insurance settlements, are excluded. Also excluded are non-cash benefits such as food stamps, health benefits, housing subsidies, rent-free housing, and the goods produced and consumed on farms. Money income is reported for households and various household types as well as for unrelated individuals. (In regard to family money income it should be noted that only the amount received by all family members 15 years old and over is counted, and excludes income received by household members not related to the householder.) It is reported in aggregate, median, mean, and per capita amounts. Money income is also used for determining the poverty status of families and unrelated individuals.

INFANT MORTALITY

The deaths of live-born children who do not reach their first birthday. Infant mortality is usually expressed as a rate per 1,000 live births.

INPATIENT DAYS (HOSPITALS)

The number of adult and pediatric days of care rendered during a given period. See also Hospital Day.

INSTITUTION OF HIGHER EDUCATION

An institution which offers programs of study beyond the secondary school level terminating in an associate, baccalaureate, or higher degree. See also **College; University.**

JAIL

A facility, usually operated by a local law enforcement agency, holding persons detained pending adjudication and/or persons committed after adjudication to a sentence of one year or less.

LABOR FORCE STATUS

A term which refers to whether or not a person is in the labor force, and, if in the labor force, whether he or she is employed or unemployed, a full-time worker or a part-time worker, etc. Persons are in the labor force if they are in the civilian labor force or in the Armed Forces.

The civilian labor force consists of both employed and unemployed persons, full-time and part-time workers. Generally, persons outside the labor force consist of full-time homemakers, students who do not work, retired persons, and inmates of institutions. "Discouraged workers," those who do not have a job and have not been seeking one, are also considered to be not in the labor force. See also **Civilian Labor Force.**

LARCENY see **CRIME**.

LIMITATION OF ACTIVITY see **HEALTH LIMITATION OF ACTIVITY**.

LIVE BIRTH

The live birth of an infant, defined as the complete expulsion or extraction from its mother of a product of conception, irrespective of the duration of the pregnancy, which, after such separation, breathes or shows any evidence of life such as heartbeat, umbilical cord pulsation, or definite movement of voluntary muscles, whether or not the umbilical cord has been cut or the placenta is attached. Each such birth is considered live born.

MARITAL STATUS

All persons 15 years of age and older are classified by the Bureau of the Census according to marital status. The Bureau defines two broad categories of marital status: **Single** - all those persons who have never been married (including persons whose marriage has been annulled), and **Ever married** - which is composed of the now married, the widowed, and the divorced. **Now married** persons are those who are legally married (as well as some persons who have common law marriages, along with some unmarried couples who live together and report their marital status as married), and whose marriage has not ended by widowhood or divorce. The now married are sometimes further subdivided: married, spouse present; separated; married, spouse absent; married, spouse absent, other. **Married, spouse present** covers married couples living together. **Separated** includes those persons legally separated or otherwise absent from their spouse because of marital discord (such as persons who have been deserted or who have parted because they no longer want to live together but who have not obtained a divorce). Separated includes persons with a limited divorce. **Married, spouse absent** covers those households where the both the husband and the wife were not counted as members of the same household, (or where both husband and wife lived together in group quarters). **Married, spouse absent, other**, includes those married persons whose spouse was not counted as a member of the same household, besides those who are separated. Included are persons whose spouse was employed and living away from home, absent in the armed forces, or was an inmate of an institution. **Widowed** includes widows and widowers who have not remarried. **Divorced** includes persons who are legally divorced and have not remarried.

MARRIED COUPLES see **FAMILY TYPE.**

MARRIED PERSONS see **MARITAL STATUS.**

MEAN

The arithmetic average of a set of values. It is derived by dividing the sum of a group of numerical items by the total number of items. Mean income (of a population), for example, is defined as the value obtained by dividing the total or aggregate income by the population. Thus, the mean income for families is obtained by dividing the aggregate of all income reported by persons in families by the total number of families. See also **Median.**

MEDIAN

In general, a value that divides the total range of values into two equal parts. For example, to say that the median money income of families in the United States in 1985 was $27,735 indicates that half of all families had incomes larger than that value, and half had less. See also **Mean.**

MEDICAID

A federally funded but state administered and operated program which provides medical benefits to certain low income persons in need of medical care. The program, authorized in 1965 by Title XIX of the Social Security Act, categorically covers participants in the Aid to Families with Dependent Children (AFDC) program, as well as some participants in the Supplemental Security Income (SSI) program, along with those other people deemed medically needy in each participating state. Each state determines the benefits covered, rates of payment to providers, and methods of administering the program.

MEDICARE

A federally funded nationwide health insurance program providing health insurance protection to people 65 years of age and over, people eligible for social security disability payments for more than two years, and people with end-state renal disease, regardless of income. The program was enacted July 30, 1965, as title XVIII, Health Insurance for the Aged, of the Social Security Act, and became effective on July 1, 1966. It consists of two separate but coordinated programs: hospital insurance (Part A), and supplementary medical insurance (Part B).

METROPOLITAN AREA see **CONSOLIDATED METROPOLITAN STATISTICAL AREA; METROPOLITAN STATISTICAL AREA; PRIMARY METROPOLITAN STATISTICAL AREA; STANDARD CONSOLIDATED STATISTICAL AREA; STANDARD METROPOLITAN STATISTICAL AREA**

METROPOLITAN STATISTICAL AREA (MSA)

A geographic concept introduced in June, 1984, to replace the Standard Metropolitan Statistical Area (SMSA). In general, an MSA is a geographic area consisting of a large population nucleus, together with adjacent communities that have a high degree of economic and social integration with that nucleus. MSAs are designated in accordance with a detailed 16 section criteria established by the federal Office of Management and Budget (OMB). In general, MSAs are a county based concept which must include a city that, with contiguous, densely settled territory, constitutes a Census Bureau defined urbanized area having at least 50,000 population. (However, if an MSA's largest city has less than 50,000 population, the MSA as a whole must have a total population of at least 100,000). Adjacent MSAs are consolidated into a single MSA if certain conditions relating to commuting to work, size, and geographic proximity are met. See also **Consolidated Metropolitan Statistical Area; New England County Metropolitan Area; Primary Metropolitan Statistical Area.**

NEW ENGLAND COUNTY METROPOLITAN AREA (NECMA)

A geographic concept developed for the New England states (Massachusetts, Connecticut, Rhode Island, Maine, New Hampshire, Vermont) to present data that is only available on a county-level basis . Unlike the rest of the country, Metropolitan Statistical Areas (MSAs) in the New England states are officially defined in terms of cities and towns instead of counties. As a result New England MSA data may not be directly comparable to MSA data in the rest of the country. NECMAs are county-based geographic areas (which follow the same general guidelines of MSAs in other parts of the country) and thus provide a basis of comparison with other states. NECMAs do not replace the MSAs in New England, but supplement them.

MOBILE HOME see **HOUSING UNIT.**

MONEY INCOME see **INCOME.**

MURDER see **CRIME.**

NATIONAL CRIME SURVEY

A twice yearly survey of 49,000 households comprising over 102,000 inhabitants 12 years of age and older. Administered by the Bureau of Justice Statistics, the survey measures criminal victimization by surveying victims directly. It differs from the FBI Uniform Crime Report (UCR) which is based on crimes reported to police. See also **Crime.**

NURSING HOME

A facility with three or more beds providing adults with nursing care and/or personal care (such as help with bathing, eating, using toilet facilities, or dressing) and/or supervision over such activities as money management, walking, and shopping.

OCCUPANCY STATUS (HOUSING)

The classification of all housing units as either occupied or vacant. **Occupied housing units** are those that have one or more persons living in them as their usual residence, and include units whose usual occupants are temporarily absent (e.g., on vacation). **Vacant housing units** are those that have no one living in them as their usual residence. Also classified as vacant are housing units that are temporarily occupied solely by persons who have a usual residence elsewhere, newly constructed units completed to the point where all exterior windows and doors are installed and final usable floors are in place, and vacant mobile homes or trailers intended to be occupied on the site on which they stand.

OCCUPATION

The kind of work a person does at a job or business. Occupation is reported for a given survey period, (most frequently the period covered by the survey, the reference period, is the week including March 12). If the person was not at work during the reference period, occupation usually refers to the person's most recent job or business. Persons working at more than one job are asked to identify the job at which he or she works the most hours, which is then counted as his or her occupation.

Occupations are classified according to the Standard Occupational Classification system (SOC), a system promulgated by the federal Office of Management and Budget.

OWNER OCCUPIED HOUSING UNIT see **TENURE**.

PART-TIME ENROLLMENT (HIGHER EDUCATION)

The number of students enrolled in higher education courses with a total credit load of less than 75% of the normal full-time credit load.

PART-TIME WORKERS see **CIVILIAN LABOR FORCE**.

PERSONAL INCOME see **INCOME**.

POPULATION

The number of inhabitants of an area. The total population of the United States is the sum of all persons living within the United States, plus all members of the Armed Forces living in foreign countries, Puerto Rico, Guam, and the U.S. Virgin Islands. Other Americans living abroad (e.g., civilian federal employees and dependents of members of the Armed Forces or other federal employees are not included).

The **resident population of the United States**, is the population living within the geographic United States. This includes members of the Armed Forces stationed in the United States and their families as well as foreigners working or studying here. It excludes foreign military, naval, and diplomatic personnel and their families located here and residing in embassies or similar quarters, as well as Americans living abroad.

Resident population is often the denominator when calculating birth and death rates, incidence of disease, and other rates.

The **civilian population** is the resident population excluding members of the Armed Forces. However, families of members of the Armed Forces are included.

The **civilian non-institutional population** is the civilian population not residing in institutions. Institutions include, correctional institutions; detention homes and training schools for juvenile delinquents; homes for the aged and dependent (e.g., nursing homes and convalescent homes); homes for dependent and neglected children; homes and schools for the mentally and physically handicapped; homes for unwed mothers; psychiatric, tuberculosis, and chronic disease hospitals; and residential treatment centers.

POVERTY STATUS

Although the term poverty connotes a complex set of economic, social, and psychological conditions, the standard statistical definition provides for only estimates of economic poverty. These are based on the receipt of money income before taxes and exclude the value of government payments and transfers such as food stamps or Medicare; private transfers, such as health insurance premiums paid by employers; gifts; the depletion of assets; and borrowed money. Thus the term poverty as used by government agencies, classifies persons and families in relation to being above or below a specified income level, or poverty threshold. Those below this threshold are said to be in poverty, or more accurately, as below the poverty level. Poverty thresholds vary by size of family, number of children, and age of householder and are updated annually. Poverty status is also determined for unrelated individuals living in households, but not for those living in group quarters nor for persons in the Armed Forces. The poverty threshold is revised each year according to formula based on the Consumer Price Index.

PRIMARY METROPOLITAN STATISTICAL AREA (PMSA)

This geographic concept, introduced in June, 1984, combines with Metropolitan Statistical Area (MSA) and Consolidated Metropolitan Statistical Areas (CMSA), to replace the Standard Metropolitan Statistical Area (SMSA) concept. PMSAs are designated according to criteria established by the federal Office of Management and Budget. In general PMSAs are those counties with populations of at least 100,000 (60% must be urban), in which less than 50% of its resident workers commute to jobs outside the county. PMSAs are parts of Consolidated Metropolitan Statistical Areas (CMSAs).

PRISON

A confinement facility having custodial authority over adults sentenced to confinement for a period of more than one year. Prisons are usually run by State or federal authorities.

PRIVATE SCHOOL see **SCHOOL.**

PROPERTY CRIME see **CRIME.**

PUBLIC SCHOOL see **SCHOOL.**

RACE

The Bureau of the Census in many of its surveys (most notably in the decennial censuses of population) asks all persons to identify themselves according to race. The concept of race as used by the Bureau reflects the self-identification of the respondents. It is not meant to denote any clear cut scientific or biological definition.

Although it is often reported with racial categories, **Hispanic origin**, or Spanish origin, is not a racial category. Persons may be of any race and of Hispanic origin. Those who describe themselves as Hispanic (or Mexican, Cuban, Chicano, etc.) in response to a question about race, are included by the Bureau in the racial classification, "other." See also **Hispanic Origin.**

RAPE see **CRIME**.

REFERENCE PERSON

Most frequently, the person who responds to a government survey. Most surveys done by the federal government are based on households and begin by asking the initial respondent the name of the person in whose name the housing unit is owned or rented (this person is designated as the householder). Usually the householder is the reference person. Other household members are defined in relation to the householder.

REGION

The Bureau of the Census has divided the United States into four regions. This division is the primary geographic subdivision of the nation for statistical reporting purposes. As a result, almost all federal agencies, along with many private data collectors, have adopted the regional subdivision and use it for presenting statistical data. The four regions are the **Northeast** (Maine, New Hampshire, Vermont, Massachusetts, Rhode Island, Connecticut, New York, New Jersey, Pennsylvania); the **Midwest** (Ohio, Indiana, Illinois, Michigan, Wisconsin, Minnesota, Iowa, Missouri, North Dakota, South Dakota, Kansas, Nebraska); the **South** (Delaware, Maryland, District of Columbia, Virginia, West Virginia, North Carolina, South Carolina, Georgia, Florida, Kentucky, Tennessee, Alabama, Mississippi, Arkansas, Louisiana, Oklahoma, Texas); and the **West** (Montana, Idaho, Colorado, Wyoming, New Mexico, Arizona, Utah, Nevada, Washington, Oregon, California, Alaska, Hawaii). In this book, all regional data conform to this definition.

REGULAR SCHOOL see **SCHOOL.**

RENTER OCCUPIED HOUSING UNIT see **TENURE.**

RESIDENT POPULATION see **POPULATION.**

RESTRICTED-ACTIVITY DAY see **DISABILITY DAY.**

ROBBERY see **CRIME.**

ROOMS (HOUSING)

The number of whole rooms intended for living purposes in both occupied and vacant housing units. These rooms include living rooms, dining rooms, kitchens, bedrooms, finished recreation rooms, enclosed porches suitable for year-round use, and lodger's rooms. Excluded are strip or Pullman kitchens, bathrooms, open porches, balconies, foyers, halls, half-rooms, utility rooms, unfinished attics or basements, or other space used for storage. A partially divided room, such as a dinette next to a kitchen or living room, is a separate room only if there is a partition from floor to ceiling, but not if the partition consists solely of shelves or cabinets.

RURAL see **URBAN/RURAL POPULATION**.

SCHOOL

Elementary and secondary schools are divisions of the school system consisting of students in one or more grade groups or other identifiable groups, organized as one unit with one or more teachers giving instruction of a defined type, and housed in a school plant of one or more buildings. More than one school may be housed in one school plant as is the case where elementary and secondary programs are housed in the same building.

Regular schools generally are those which advance a person toward a diploma or degree. They include public and private nursery schools, kindergartens, graded schools, colleges, universities, and professional schools.

Public schools are controlled and supported by local, state, or federal government agencies.

Private schools are controlled and supported mainly by religious organizations, private persons, or private organizations.

SCHOOL ENROLLMENT see **ENROLLMENT**.

SCHOOL-LOSS DAY see **DISABILITY DAY**.

SELF-EMPLOYMENT INCOME

A type of money income which comprises net income (gross receipts minus operating expenses) received by persons from an unincorporated business, profession, and/or from the operation of a farm as a farm owner, tenant, or sharecropper. See also **Money Income.**

SEPARATED PERSONS see **MARITAL STATUS**.

SERIOUS CRIME see **CRIME**.

SINGLE PERSON HOUSEHOLDS see **HOUSEHOLD**.

SINGLE PERSONS see **MARITAL STATUS**.

SPECIFIED OWNER-OCCUPIED HOUSING UNITS

Specified owner-occupied units are single family houses on less than ten acres, which have no commercial enterprise or medical practice on the property. Excluded are owner-occupied condominium housing units, mobile homes, trailers, boats, tents, or vans occupied as a usual residence as well as owner-occupied non-condominium units in multi-family buildings. See also **Housing Unit.**

STANDARD CONSOLIDATED STATISTICAL AREA (SCSA)

A large concentration of metropolitan population composed of two or more contiguous Standard Metropolitan Statistical Areas (SMSAs) which together meet certain criteria of population size, urban character, social and economic integration, and/or contiguity of urbanized areas. Each SCSA must have a population of one million or more. The SCSA concept was replaced with the new metropolitan area classifications in June, 1984. See Consolidated Metropolitan Statistical Area; Metropolitan Statistical Area; Primary Metropolitan Statistical Area.

STANDARD METROPOLITAN STATISTICAL AREA (SMSA)

A geographic area concept used until 1984. In general, an SMSA is a large population nucleus and nearby communities which have a high degree of economic and social integration within that nucleus. Each SMSA consists of one or more entire counties (or county equivalents) that meet certain criteria of population, commuting ties, and metropolitan character. In New England, towns and cities rather than counties are the basic units and count as county equivalents. An SMSA includes a city and, generally, the entire surrounding urbanized area and the remainder of the county or counties in which the urbanized area is located. An SMSA also includes those additional outlying counties which meet specified criteria relating to metropolitan character and level of commuting ties.

The SMSA concept was developed in 1949 and has been refined for each succeeding decennial census since 1950. In June, 1984, SMSAs were superseded by three new metropolitan area concepts: Metropolitan Statistical Areas (MSAs), Consolidated Metropolitan Statistical Areas (CMSAs), and Primary Metropolitan Statistical Areas (PMSAs).

TAXES

Compulsory contributions exacted by a government for public purposes (except employee and employer assessments for retirement and social insurance purposes, which are classified as insurance trust revenue). All tax revenue is classified as general revenue and comprises amounts received (including interest and penalties, but excluding protested amounts and refunds) from all taxes imposed by a government.

TENURE

A concept relating to housing units. All occupied housing units are classified as being either owner-occupied or renter occupied. A housing unit is owner-occupied if the owner or co-owner lives in the unit even if the unit is mortgaged or not fully paid for. All other housing units are considered to be renter occupied, regardless of whether or not cash rent is paid for them by a member of the household. See also **Housing Unit.**

UNEMPLOYED PERSONS see **CIVILIAN LABOR FORCE.**

UNEMPLOYMENT see **CIVILIAN LABOR FORCE.**

UNIFORM CRIME REPORTING (UCR) PROGRAM

A program administered by the FBI which collects reports from most police agencies in the nation (covering approximately 95% of the population) on serious crimes known to police (violent crime and property crime), arrests, police officers and related items. The Bureau issues monthly and annual summary reports based on the program. See also **Crime.**

UNIVERSITY

An institution of higher education consisting of a liberal arts college, a diverse graduate program, and usually two or more professional schools or faculties and empowered to confer degrees in various fields of study. See also **Higher Education.**

UNRELATED INDIVIDUAL

An unrelated individual is generally a person living in a household, and is either: 1) a householder living alone or only with persons who are not related to him or her by blood, marriage, or adoption, or; 2) a roomer, boarder, partner, roommate, or resident employee unrelated to the householder. Certain persons living in group quarters (who are not inmates of institutions) are also counted as unrelated individuals.

URBAN/RURAL POPULATION

Urban and rural are type of area concepts rather than specific areas outlined on maps. The urban population comprises all persons living in urbanized areas and in places of 2,500 or more inhabitants outside urbanized areas. The rural population consists of everyone else. Therefore, a rural classification need not imply a farm or sparsely settled areas, since a small city or town is rural when it is outside an urbanized area and has fewer than 2,500 inhabitants. The terms urban and rural are independent of metropolitan and non-metropolitan; both urban and rural areas occur inside and outside metropolitan areas. See also **Urbanized Area.**

URBANIZED AREA

A population concentration of at least 50,000 inhabitants, generally consisting of a central city and the surrounding, closely settled, contiguous territory (suburbs). The urbanized area criteria define a boundary based on a population density of at least 1,000 persons per square mile, but also include some less densely settled areas, such as industrial parks and railroad yards, if they are within areas of dense urban development. The density level of 1,000 persons per square mile corresponds approximately to the contiguously built-up area around a city or cities. The urban fringe is that part of the urbanized area outside of a central city or cities.

Typically, an entire urbanized area is included within an Standard Metropolitan Statistical Area (SMSA) or Metropolitan Statistical Area (MSA). The SMSA (or MSA) is usually much larger in terms of area and includes territory where the population density is less than 1,000. Occasionally more than one urbanized area is located within an SMSA (MSA). In some cases a small part of an urbanized area may extend beyond an SMSA (MSA) boundary, or possibly into an adjacent SMSA (MSA). Urbanized areas sometimes cross state boundaries as well.

VACANCY STATUS see **OCCUPANCY STATUS**.

VALUE (HOUSING UNITS)

In surveys done by the Bureau of the Census, the value of owner-occupied housing units is the respondent's estimate of the current dollar worth of the property; for vacant units, the value is the price asked for the property. A property is defined as the house and the land on which it stands. Respondents are asked by the Bureau to estimate the value of the house and land even if they own only the house, or own the house jointly. Statistics for value are only gathered by the Bureau for owner-occupied condominium units and for specified owner-occupied units (single family houses on less than ten acres, and with no business on the property).

VICTIMIZATION see **CRIME**.

VIOLENT CRIME see **CRIME**.

VOTING AGE POPULATION

All persons over the age of 18 (the voting age for federal elections) in a given geographic area comprise the voting age population. The voting age population does include a small number of persons who, although of voting age, are not eligible to vote (e.g. resident aliens, inmates of institutions, etc.). The voting age population is estimated in even numbered years by the Bureau of the Census.

WAGES AND SALARIES

Wages and salaries are a type (subgroup) of money income and include civilian wages and salaries, Armed Forces pay and allowances, piece-rate payments, commissions, tips, National Guard or Reserve pay (received for training periods), and cash bonuses before deductions for taxes, pensions, union dues, etc. See also **Money Income.**

WIDOWED PERSONS see **MARITAL STATUS**.

WORK DISABILITY

A health condition which limits the kind or amount of work a person can do, or prevents working at a job. A person is limited in the kind of work he or she can do if the person has a health condition which restricts his or her choice of jobs. A person is limited in amount of work if he or she is not able to work at a full-time (35 hours or more per week) job or business. See also **Condition (Health).**

WORK-LOSS DAY see **DISABILITY DAY**.

Index